Diffusion of Korean Popular Culture in Western Countries

Diffusion of Korean Popular Culture in Western Countries

First edition published by Seoul National University Press in 2021

Seoul National University Press
1 Gwanak-ro, Gwanak-gu, Seoul 08826, Republic of Korea
Tel: +82-2-880-5252
Fax: +82-2-889-0785
Homepage: http://www.snupress.com
Facebook: @snupress1947
Instagram: @snupress
E-mail: snubook@snu.ac.kr

ISBN 978-89-521-2963-5 (93330)

DIFFUSION OF KOREAN POPULAR CULTURE IN WESTERN COUNTRIES

Edited by
Do Kyun David Kim

SNUPRESS
Seoul National University Press

Contents

Preface

Polycultural Approach to the Diffusion of Korean Popular Culture in Western Countries

Editor **Do Kyun David Kim**, University of Louisiana at Lafayette

Why and how could Korean popular culture (K-culture) diffuse across Western countries and generate K-culture fandom? This book explores the popularity of Korean popular culture products, such as Korean pop music (K-pop), television dramas (K-dramas), films (K-films), cosmetics (K-beauty), and food, particularly in Western countries. Presenting *authentic* Westerners' views on why they like and consume Korean popular culture products, all chapters of this book provide theoretically and empirically supported analyses regarding the popularity of K-pop music, K-dramas, and K-films.

K-pop is no longer a strange term among the public in Western countries. The Korean boy group, BTS, was ranked #1 in Billboard Charts twice in 2019. In the same year, the Korean film, *Parasite*, directed by Bong Joon Ho received the highest honors in several major international film festivals including the Palme d'Or, the top prize at the Cannes Film Festival and, in the next year, four Oscars including the Best Picture of the year. Korean cosmetics are being displayed in a special booth called "K-beauty" in the nationwide pharmacy and cosmetics store Walgreen's in the U.S. Likewise, one of the world's largest bookstore chains, Barnes & Noble, also has special BTS and/or K-pop booths. As part of a major cultural trend, numerous Westerners are now consuming Korean cultural products at unprecedented rates.

Contemporary pop culture products are heavily influenced by technology and monetary investment as such technological and economic infrastructures enable the pop culture to produce sophisticated products, target mass audiences, and facilitate a far-reaching process of dissemination. Especially, advancements in media (and communication) technology have bolstered pop culture producers' desires to spread their products to as many people as possible in the public sphere. With their advanced media technologies and accumulated capital, western countries that experienced industrial revolutions earlier than other parts of the world have been able to develop present forms of pop culture products. As a result, Western popular culture products (e.g., pop songs, blockbuster movies, and diverse television shows) have enjoyed global popularity, especially since media technology began developing in other countries, enabling them to become ready markets for Western pop culture products played through record players, radio, television, theater systems and many other media devices.

South Korea has been known as a rapidly industrialized country since the country initiated a series of nationwide economic development projects in the 1960s, focusing on technology and international trade as the main industries to compete with other countries. South Korea's prolific advancement of media and communication technology has significantly contributed to building strong infrastructures for the diffusion of K-culture throughout the world and raising globally competitive companies that manufacture media and communication devices, such as Samsung and LG that occupy a large portion of global telecommunication and media device markets.

In addition, South Korea has countless pop culture contents that have been developed over more than five thousand years of national history. The history of popular culture is as old as the history of humans; for example, ancient cave art dates back to the Ice Age (Clottes, n.d.). Although it is debatable, the longer a country's history, the more likely it is to have sophisticated cultural heritages and contents. In fact, the history of Korean popular culture began with the Korean myth of Dangun, the legendary founder of Gojoseon, the first Korean kingdom, in 2333 BC.

> *A long time ago, Hwanin, the God of the Heavens, noticed that his son Hwanung was nurturing interest in the human world under the heavens, and as Hwanin gazed down at the area around Mt. Taebaek, he saw it was an ideal place to found a kingdom, and sent down Hwanung to rule the land, giving him the Three Seals of Heaven (Cheonbuin). Hwanung led a group of three thousand and descended on the summit of Mt. Taebaek, where he*

> *began overseeing some three hundred and sixty affairs of the human world, including grains, life, disease, punishment, and good and evil, with the Wind God, Rainfall God and Cloud God under his command. At this time, a bear and a tiger that lived in the same cave prayed and prayed to Hwanung for their wish to become human. Hwaung gave them divine mugwort and twenty garlic bulbs, explaining, "If you live on this and avoid sunlight for one hundred days, you shall acquire the appearance of humans." The bear turned into a woman after twenty-one days of observing the taboos, but the tiger failed to abide by them, thereby failing to acquire a human body. Everyday Ungnyeo (Bear Woman) prayed under Sindansu (Divine Altar Tree) to conceive a child, but there was no one for her to marry, so Hwanung turned into a man and married Ungnyeo, giving birth to a son who was given the name Dangun Wanggeom. Dangun set up a capital at Pyeongyang Fortress and named his kingdom Joseon.* (An excerpt from National Folk Museum of Korea, n.d.)

This myth was circulated and enjoyed among Koreans and descended through generations until now. From this historic perspective, the long history of Korea can be viewed as a long-lasting or, perhaps, everlasting foundation and energy of current K-culture diffusion to the world.

The global popularity of K-culture differs from the domestic popularity within South Korea because the global popularity depends mostly on how people in other countries view the Korean cultural products that have stemmed from different traditions and modes of entertainment. Related to this, intercultural studies often employ two contrary perspectives to elucidate how a group of people consider different cultures: the globalist and tribalist perspectives (Barber, 1995). Individuals with the globalist perspective tend to have cosmopolitan lifestyles and supranational identifications, while those of the tribalist perspective differentiate their culture(s) from others, often with a false nostalgia for an alleged "pure" society that may no longer exist. To some extent, tribalists are more likely to perceive differences in the frame of hierarchy and eschew embracing of other cultures as seen in reactionary anti-immigrant movements in many countries (Morris, Chiu, & Liu, 2015). With this theoretical framework of globalist and tribalist perspectives in response to intercultural contact, the diffusion of K-culture in Western countries, regardless of whether the intercultural contact is by interpersonal communication or exposure to media content, demonstrates an increasing trend of the globalist perspective in the new millennium. Through this globalist perspective, this book advocates and posits polyculturalism as the overarching theoretical scope to analyze the diffusion of K-culture throughout Western countries.

Polyculturalism is a theoretical framework for understanding how different cultures are mutually influenced by one another and continuously change in response to dynamic interactions and communication among diverse people within different cultures (Bernardo, Rosenthal, & Levy, 2013). Based on this framework, individuals' relationships to cultures are not *categorical*, but *partial* and *plural* (Morris, Chiu, & Liu, 2015). Some views of recognizing different cultures in society are based on the notion of "categorical" that separates different cultures by their distinctive traits or categories. As opposed to this categorical perspective, polyculturalism emphasizes dynamic interactions among different cultures, suggesting an individual's engagement even with her or his primary culture is partial as s/he simultaneously engages with certain elements of other cultures. Because of this interactive nature, polyculturalism provides cultural researchers with a communicative perspective in analyzing and elucidating global diffusion of contemporary popular culture as seen in the diffusion of K-culture in Western countries.

Policulturalism seeks the roots of individuals' cultural differences from their personal propensities and preferences that guide them in the process of choosing a culture from many others in their social surroundings. As many cultures coexist in society, cultures chosen for adoption by an individual depend on the individual's preferences and active choices, as opposed to imposing a particular culture on individuals by an external agency, such as a government or an ethnic group. Therefore, an individual can be a conduit of the dissemination of culture to others in her/his communication networks. Moreover, an individual's reaction to a different or foreign culture can trigger macro-level cultural shifts when it is exposed and imitated by others (Boyd & Richerson, 2004). This demonstrates the process of cultural diffusion. In the theory of diffusion of innovations, an informal opinion leader can accelerate the diffusion process as the opinion leader's choice, behavior, and attitude are observed and mimicked by followers who would communicate with others and immediately or later replicate the opinion leader's decisions (Rogers, 2003).

Although an individual can subjectively adopt a culture with her/his own will and preference in a polycultural environment, a necessary condition that makes a polycultural environment truly polycultural is whether or not the pool of cultures in a society is truly polycultural and allows easy access to the pool of diverse cultures. If the pool has a high and thick threshold that other cultures have difficulty stepping into, an individual's cultural choices become very limited. Hence, lowering the cultural threshold in society is a critical task in the diffusion of an exogenous culture. How can a society lower its cultural threshold, so other cultures can be infused from outside and added to the pool of cultures? Here comes communication.

People communicate interpersonally and use communication media or tools to communicate with others. As mentioned above, communication and media technologies that help produce and present a high quality of sound and video have greatly contributed to the diffusion of K-culture. In addition, the advancement of Internet technology has accelerated the dissemination of K-culture products throughout the world. Overall, the diffusion of K-culture in Western countries was made possible through the combined influence of both communication/media technology and polycultural individuals' communication with others in their communication networks.

Some expected the trends of K-culture would not last long. However, its influence has continuously grown in more and more countries throughout the world. This continuation of K-culture popularity insinuates the implicit and explicit social change caused by a mix of cultures and new generations who have wider openness to other cultures. Intellectually, the cultural ideology of *melting pot* that was mainly pursued by the U.S. government to blend different cultures and create a new and sole national identity had revealed its critical limitation; the model was not able to reflect many unblended uniquenesses of different cultures in society. Later, *multiculturalism* recognized the inescapable reality of coexistence of different cultures with a somewhat negative connotation of *tolerance* fostered as a necessary condition of a harmonious society. However, it also faced other limitations that could not elucidate an individual's partial identity even with her/his prime culture, which still reinforced the categorical perspective, as explained above, in understanding cultures among individuals and within society. In order to overcome these limitations of past cultural perspectives that tried to explain and understand the global diffusion of K-culture, this book is based on the paradigm of polyculturalism and presents original research that aimed at solving the puzzle of how K-culture, particularly K-pop songs, K-dramas, and K-films diffuse throughout Western countries. Uniquely, most chapters of this book were written by scholars who were born or raised in Western countries to provide readers with more authentic analyses from the Western point of view. Finally, this book will give readers not only knowledge about the diffusion of K-culture in Western countries, but also a polycultural means of understanding the trend of cultural change within society and motivation to embrace other cultures in order to enrich people's lives with diverse pop culture products.

References

Barber, B. R. (1995). *Jihad vs. McWorld: How globalism and tribalism are reshaping the world.* New York, NY: Crown.

Bernardo, A. B., Rosenthal, L., & Levy, S. R. (2013). Polyculturalism and attitudes towards people from other countries. *International Journal of Intercultural Relations, 37*(3), 335-344.

Boyd, R., & Richerson, P. J. (2004). Culture, adaptation, and innateness. In P. Carruthers, S. Laurence, & S. Stich (Eds.), *The innate mind: Culture and cognition* (pp. 23-38). New York, NY: Oxford University Press.

Clottes, J. (n.d.). Cave art. *Encyclopedia Britannica.* Chicago, IL: Encyclopedia Britannica.

Morris, M. W., Chiu, C. Y., & Liu, Z. (2015). Polycultural psychology. *Annual Review of Psychology, 66*, 631-659.

National Folk Museum of Korea (n.d.). Myth of Dangun. *Encyclopedia of Korean Folk Culture.* Retrieved from http://folkency.nfm.go.kr/en/topic/detail/5336

Rogers, E. M. (2003). *Diffusion of innovations (5th ed.).* New York, NY: Free Press.

DIFFUSION OF KOREAN POPULAR CULTURE IN WESTERN COUNTRIES

CHAPTER 1

LOVE MYSELF: The BTS Campaign that Brings Hope to Teens

Nancy Wiencek, Rider University &
Aimee Wiencek, Case Western Reserve University

The diffusion of BTS and its brand of Korean pop culture has been unprecedented in Western countries. Despite singing primarily in the Korean language, the group built their reputation on bringing a socially conscious message to young people. The band's passionate and diverse fandom, affectionately called ARMY, fueled the band's success in topping Billboard's music charts and setting social media records. But it was BTS' LOVE MYSELF campaign, launched in 2017, that crowned the band's meteoric rise to superstardom.

The LOVE MYSELF campaign centered on the BTS' message of self-love and the importance of bringing compassion, hope, and love to fans around the world. In addition to BTS' own initiatives to promote the message, the band partnered with UNICEF to #ENDviolence against children and young people. The centerpieces of the joint campaign included a speech by BTS at the United Nations General Assembly and a visually compelling campaign music video. The BTS ARMY, already a driving force behind the band's success, catapulted the campaign's success raising millions for UNICEF and generating countless volunteer initiatives around the globe. The pivotal youth empowerment initiative in partnership with the United Nations landed BTS on *TIME* magazine's October 22, 2018, cover and the magazine's list of the "Next Generation of Leaders."

The Diffusion of K-Pop into Western Countries

To understand the success of BTS in general and their LOVE MYSELF campaign in particular, it is important to begin by exploring the rise of K-pop as well as its slow and unlikely diffusion into Western countries. It is widely recognized that the K-pop revolution began with Seo Taiji and Boys when, in 1992, the group performed on a live TV talent show that was broadcast to millions of South Korean homes (BBC, 2019). While the impact of this performance was immense, the performance was limited to Asia. Even with the excitement for and popularity of performers like Rain and Wonder Girls, K-pop groups had difficulty gaining attention in the United States. Korean media content producers were pressured to find "more effective ways to reach out and captivate audiences from different cultural backgrounds" (Chung & Lee, 2011, p. 448).

It was with an unlikely rapper by the name of Psy and his song "Gangnam Style" that K-pop finally found international success (Shin & Lee, 2017). According to Bernie Cho, President of DFSB Kollective, a Seoul-based creative agency, and former manager of MTV Korea's Creative & Content Department, "[Psy] completely shattered the mould and the myth in terms of what it takes to get to number one, not only in the US market but worldwide. Psy was not a Korean version of a big pop star. Psy was Korea's version of Psy, and it turns out that's what the world wanted" (BBC, 2019, para. 10).

Although Psy and his "Gangnam Style" did not look or sound like the K-pop norm, it started an avalanche that launched the Korean Wave or *Hallyu* across western cultures (St. Michel, 2017). As Kim and Kim (2011) explain, *Hallyu* is about "constructing a cross-national identity of ready consumers of popular culture" (p. 10). To document this wave, one can look at the rise of KCON, the world's largest fan celebration of Korean culture and music. The flagship event was launched in Los Angeles in 2012, but at that time it only drew a few hundred fans. Since then, KCON has expanded across the globe drawing more than one million fans at its events in New York, Tokyo, Bangkok, Abu Dhabi, as well as cities in France and Mexico. According to *RollingStone*, "The event's popularity coincides with the worldwide explosion of K-pop, which has swelled in the past five years from a niche genre to a $5 billion global industry" (Wang, 2018, para. 2).

BTS' Rise to Superstardom

BTS is a South Korean idol boyband that was formed by Bang Si-hyuk, founder and co-CEO of Big Hit Entertainment, and consists of seven members: RM, Suga, J-Hope, Jimin, Jungkook, V, and Jin. The band's name, BTS, or the Bangtan Boys, is an acronym for the band's Korean name, Bangtan Sonyeondan, which translates to Bulletproof Boy Scouts. According to Wickman (2018), the name "was chosen to represent the main goal of the group: to protect and to talk about the problems and worries of people in their teens and twenties," a theme that would later resonate with the band's fandom (para. 7).

Officially debuting in 2013 with their song "No More Dream" from their *2 Cool 4 Skool* album, BTS was not initially met with overwhelming enthusiasm. *Seoulbeats*, a platform for ongoing discussion and dissection of the world of *Hallyu*, reviewed the band's breakout music video finding that, while the band met its advertised hip-hop image, the boys did not "bring anything special to the table…For a song about rebellion and dreaming outside of the box, this [music video] is incredibly produced and contrived" (Lindsay, 2013, para. 3). Similarly, the band was not an immediate success in the West. BTS' first free appearance in 2014 at a small club in Los Angeles attracted an audience of only about 400 fans (Dorof, 2018). Yet just one year later, things began to change. Despite facing possible ridicule for leaving the Korean hip-hop scene, the band's rappers RM, Suga, and J-Hope felt that they could shift the idol rapper perception while simultaneously continuing "to use their words as weapons for change" (Solano, 2019, para. 2).

From the band's first series *Skool* (2013-2014) to the second series *The Most Beautiful Moment in Life* (2015-2016), and their following albums *Wings* (2016) and *You Never Walk Alone* (2017), the band's music and style continued to evolve. However, according to Big Hit Entertainment's Bang, the band has "never suddenly switched gears or changed pace" (Bruner, 2019, para. 8). Bang gave the band members the freedom to explore their vision while providing the resources of Bit Hit's in-house production team and studio. The result was that the band maintained a vulnerable authenticity that was embraced by their growing fanbase. Fans connected with the songs, many of which the band members wrote themselves. The songs shed light on BTS' own anxieties and personal struggles with social issues that they, too, were facing as teenagers and young adults.

While BTS continued to attract a loyal fanbase, it was their *Love Yourself* (2017-2018) series and subsequent tour that made history. According to Wang (2018), BTS' takeover of the West was finally cemented on October 6, 2018, when BTS became the first K-pop group to play a U.S. stadium. Up to this point, K-pop bands had only found minor success in the U.S. However, after selling out New York's Citifield in a matter of minutes, this was the success that BTS had sought. The success and experience was overwhelming for the members of the band. As reported in *The Guardian*, Jimin broke down at the end of the Citifield concert and was quoted as saying, "On this tour we played some very large venues, and it makes us see that people really love us. Being inundated by all these emotions, it kind of got to me" (Glasby, 2018, para. 2).

The band's visibility continued to rise as they began making the rounds on American television. BTS was the first South Korean musical guest to perform on *Saturday Night Live*, the band members and Jimmy Fallon tackled the "*Fortnite* Dance Challenge" on *The Tonight Show*, fans watched the band channel The Beatles on *The Late Show with Stephen Colbert*, and BTS entertained viewers with carpool karaoke on *The Late Late Show with James Corden*. Fans like Lenika Cruz, who writes for *The Atlantic*, described her experience as she watched the band for the first time on April 13, 2019, on NBC's *Saturday Night Live*: "It might not be your thing but something about BTS intrigues you anyway, like their synchronicity, their good looks, or the fact that they dance hard while singing and rapping live. Or how when the song ends, the guys stretch their hands toward the crowd, beaming and bowing as cheers drown out their thank-yous" (Cruz, 2019, para. 3).

As the BTS fandom grew, their fans successfully catapulted the band to the first ever group since The Beatles to earn three No. 1 albums on the Billboard 200 chart in less than year. In a light-hearted tribute to The Fab Four, BTS members "turned back time and inserted themselves into the infancy of Beatlemania, moptops and all" with their performance of "Boy With Luv" on *The Late Show with Stephen Colbert* in the Ed Sullivan Theater, the same theater that The Beatles made history 50 years earlier (Brandle, 2019, paras. 1-3). BTS-mania gripped the theater while fans continue to relive the performance that has now garnered over 10 million views on YouTube.

Embracing both the Korean and English Language

According to Shin, "No one expected that songs in Korean-language lyrics would enjoy popularity on a global scale, and this is also true for Koreans" (Shin & Lee, 2017, p. xi). It seemed to the music industry that, in order for K-pop groups to find success with Western audiences, the bands would need to transcend the obvious obstacle of performing their songs in the Korean language. To begin to overcome this seeming deficit, K-pop entertainment agencies purposefully chose group names like BTS or BlackPink. These names consisted of unique abbreviations or English words that could be easily understood by international audiences (Zhou, 2019). In addition, English titles were given to K-pop songs and key English phrases were embedded in the songs themselves. For example, in BTS' song "FAKE LOVE," the band members sing in English, "I am so sick of this fake love." Similarly in "Euphoria," the refrain, which is sung in English, is, "Take my hand now, you are the cause of my euphoria." But BTS' Suga says, "Even if there is a language barrier, once the music starts, people react pretty much the same wherever we go. It feels like the music really brings us together" (Bruner, 2018, para. 8).

Another factor in the success to bridging the language barrier between Korean and Western audiences is the role that fan translators have played in the globalization of K-pop. Some estimate that there may be more than 89 million non-Korean volunteer translators dedicated to translating everything from their favorite song to other parts of the cultural phenomenon including reviews of K-beauty and K-food (Marking, 2019). For the translators interested in music, whose accounts tend to be artist-specific, they not only translate, complete, or correct English translations online for K-pop fans, but they also see it as an opportunity to help groups that follow to succeed (Dodson, 2019). In an interview with Kristine Ortiz, a community manager at the company that owns *Soompi*, one of the biggest online K-pop communities, Ortiz states: "In Korea, it's already a part of the culture, and they speak the same language...In the U.S., it's a process of self-discovery and that makes it really exciting for fans. Users find one song and they start digging on their own. There's a level of motivation and socializing you don't see with American artists" (Wang, 2018, para. 8).

Despite the fact that singing in the Korean language was thought to pose a challenge for K-pop groups that sought to break into Western countries, BTS has no plans to fully sing in English. In an interview with *Entertainment Weekly*, BTS' RM stated that, "We don't want to change our identity or our genuineness to get the number one. Like if we sing suddenly in full English, and change all these other things, then that's not BTS. We'll do everything, we'll try. But if we couldn't get number one or number five, that's okay" (Greenblatt, 2019, para. 24). Nevertheless, collaborations with Western artists like Halsey, The Chainsmokers, Steve Aoki, and Lauv, have helped bring both visibility and success to the band by introducing Western popular music fans to K-pop.

The Power of the BTS ARMY

In trying to pinpoint what has made BTS a success, it is impossible to overlook the power of the band's ARMY, a loyal fanbase, which, according to music data analytics company Next Big Sound, may be the most quantifiably active fandom in history (Blake, 2018). Myungji Chae, a dedicated ARMY fan and translator @btsarmy_salon, believes that the main factor to BTS' success is their genuine personality, quality content, and sincere music. She says, "As a translator, I cannot create something that isn't [from] the original context. BTS [is] successful because they are simply really good at what they do" (Kelley, 2017, para. 9).

According to many in BTS' ARMY, which stands for the Adorable Representative M.C. for Youth, their loyalty stems from what they have learned about the band members and their vision via the band's online postings. Through honest confessional-type messages, band members have conveyed a rare authenticity in which fans believe that what they see on camera is who the individual band members actually are in real life (Dorof, 2018). One BTS ARMY member explains:

> *Even though we started liking BTS because of their music, it isn't the reason we call ourselves ARMY. We listen to loads of music but don't feel personally invested in the artists' health and well-being and success... The members are very close to each other and their personalities—or at least the sides of their personalities we saw on Bangtan Bombs, V Lives, interviews, performances, and social media—got us hooked...They talk about loneliness, how they struggle with expectations, the need to succeed and staying true to themselves. All of this lends itself to its relatability. Fans might not be travelling the world, winning awards and performing concerts but to see their struggles and what they do to overcome it helps fans connect with them in a way which few stars do* (Daily Vox Team, 2018a, para. 8).

BTS' ARMY launched its own U.S. website (usbtsarmy.com) in 2014 with a stated mission, "To inspire, celebrate and spread BTS' message of love and acceptance to ARMYs and any others who cross our path." Fans use the website to share news about the band including their upcoming schedule, discographies, interviews, campaigns, awards, and merchandise; information regarding ARMY etiquette, an ARMY dictionary, ARMY concert survival guides, and an official club membership; as well as tutorials ranging from learning BTS fan chants to pairing your BTS light stick with your concert seat. Estimates of ARMY's numbers vary, but Brandwatch, a leading social intelligence company, provides a conservative estimate of at least 48 million fans based on the number of unique authors mentioning the band between 2013-2019 (Reid, 2020). The BTS fandom is also diverse. While ticket purchasers are more likely to be female, the band's fans are ethnically diverse and yet, according to a report by Vivid Seats, only about 39% are estimated to be in the 18 to 24 age range, with a growing following particularly within the 25 to 35 age range and beyond (Yann, 2019).

BTS fans are both committed and passionate about doing whatever is possible to contribute to the band's success. Herman (2018) notes that, "Not only do BTS' fans support the group in digital spaces and financially through typical means, such as buying albums and concert tickets, but their dedication has led to immense charitable efforts, marketing and ad-buying campaigns, and a multitude of other activities, including translating the band's content, based around their passion for the group" (para. 19). For example, on BTS' fifth anniversary, ARMY wanted to do something special for the band so they bought an electronic billboard in New York's Times Square that featured footage of the group's music videos, as well as individual portraits of the members. In another case, one dedicated member shared with *CNN* that she not only ran a fan-based website, but also devoted hours to chatting with fellow fans online, planned a hashtag for singer Jin's upcoming birthday, and mobilized fans to help get BTS a GRAMMY, which they have yet to be awarded (Seo & Hollingsworth, 2019). To the members in BTS, the fans are a major reason behind their success and, as a result, they thank their ARMY at every concert and after each award.

BTS Fandom and Social Media Engagement

From their earliest days as a trainee idol band, BTS has worked to create a social media presence. Band members have shared vlogs on their BANGTANTV YouTube channel, experimented with Vine and Musical.ly (now TikTok), and actively contributed to Korea's global V Live video platform, thus allowing BTS to always maintain "a direct and unscripted line to their fans" (Dorof, 2018, para. 11). According to Williams (2020), the band's social presence "bridges the gap between mainstream celebrity and everyday people" as the band members "share personal stories, moments, achievements, and passions that are deeply relatable to their fans" (para. 12). BTS fans see the band's members on a more personal level, more like friends, and, as a result, develop a loyal connection with the members. It is that kind of intimacy, say Seo and Hollingsworth (2019), that has inevitably added to the band's popularity.

Jung (2017) explains that "Social media channels such as YouTube, Twitter, and Facebook now play a central role in this changing music landscape and the new mode of global cultural flows," noting that this socially-distributed form of pop content is driven largely by a tech savvy, youth-oriented consumer group (p. 47). The role that ARMY fans play in maintaining their webpage or as volunteering to be fan translators, are just two examples of this form of social distribution. But BTS' fan engagement is much more than this, as its ARMY has dedicated itself well-beyond most other pop fandoms. For example, on Twitter, the band has 24.4 million followers on its Korean language page @BTS_twt and another 19.3 million on its official English language page @

bts_bighit. And while the number of followers on BTS' Twitter pages are fewer than other popular artists like Taylor Swift, it is the band's active fandom who create millions more mentions per week (Vultaggio, 2019).

To gain a further perspective on BTS' social media presence, Brandwatch examined social data between the years 2013-2019, and tracked an astounding 2.2 billion mentions of BTS across all social media platforms, with 17% of social traffic coming from the U.S. surpassing their home nation that tracks at only 13% (Reid, 2020). Fans in Western countries devote themselves to creating and trending new hashtags, which not only gets the views of other fans, but also people who may have never have heard of the band before the social media post. In 2019 alone, BTS fans kept the band relevant through their likes and shares fueling 10 of the top 101 viral brand moments, which included: Target's pre-order announcement for BTS' new album drop, Pantene's picture of the band members and post "May the Best Hair Win" at the BBMAs, MTV's news tweet in which Detective Pikachu dances to BTS, and Dior's announcement that it will create outfits for the band (Brandwatch, 2019).

Big Hit Entertainment recognizes ARMY's loyalty and pervasiveness on social media, stating in an interview: "ARMY played a crucial role in spreading BTS music across the world. Whenever BTS releases a new album or drops new content, they instantly pick it up, translate it into different languages and help spread them everywhere. ARMY globalized BTS" (Brown, 2019, para. 10). This unrelenting and aggressive strategy helped BTS to successfully beat Justin Bieber, Selena Gomez, Ariana Grande, and Shawn Mendes for the top social artist title at the Billboard Music Awards in both 2017 and 2018. In addition, the band's fandom to engage on social media has earned BTS two more records—the first being in 2018 for the most viewed music video online in 24-hours by a K-pop group for "DNA," and then in 2019 for the most Twitter engagements, a record previously held by Harry Styles from boyband One Direction. In 2020, BTS claimed additional records because of their fans including the "Boy With Luv" featuring Halsey, including most viewed YouTube video in 24 hours. The BTS fandom has also been recognized with their own awards. In 2018, the BTS ARMY won for Fiercest Fans at the Radio Disney Music Awards and, in both 2018 and 2019, they won for Best Fan Army at the iHeartRadio Music Awards.

The LOVE MYSELF Campaign

From the very start, BTS has focused on the pain felt by today's younger generations by addressing themes such as societal displacement, prejudice, depression, and anxiety, topics that are rarely discussed, and are even more rarely heard, in pop music (Williams, 2020). Through the LOVE MYSELF campaign, launched November 1, 2017, the members of BTS, now all in their 20s, sought to raise their voices to support young people in this world with a stated mission to "Love myself, then make the world a better place for all with that love" (Big Hit Entertainment, n.d.) Prior to unveiling the LOVE MYSELF website, BTS' members shared selfies on their official Twitter account using the hashtag #LoveMyself to give the fans a heads-up of the announcement and encourage the fans to show self-love by posting their photos. BTS' socially conscious message of compassion, hope, and love resonated with fans around the world, with fan traffic crashing the website upon the campaign's unveil. Within one year, the hashtag #BTSLoveMyself was shared 6.7 million times.

As part of its launch, the band sought a partner that would empathize with and pursue their message. BTS found that partner with the Korean Committee for UNICEF and, as a result, a joint global campaign was launched to raise money and promote their mission to #ENDviolence, with its primary aim being to protect children and teens from violence and encouraging preventive measures. In working with UNICEF, the band members became the first artists in Korea to raise funds for a socially-based global campaign that included donating a portion of their income from album sales and all profits from the sale of goods.

The campaign emerged in unison with their *Love Yourself* series, the first album of which was released in 2017 just prior to the launch of the campaign. This latest series, like their past work, is a part of an extended story, which is "arranged into sections based on a traditional Asian storytelling format: 起 (beginning), 承 (development), 轉 (twist), and 結 (conclusion)" (Wickman, 2018, para. 15). The series' three albums begins with "Her," which focuses on falling in love; then "Tear," where one must face an unavoidable breakup; and finally, "Answer," in which there is an epiphany about self-love. As with previous albums and songs, the *Love Yourself* series, along with the launch of the campaign, had volunteer ARMY translators working to interpret song lyrics as well as transcribe interviews and social media posts for their fervent fanbase. The success of overcoming the Korean language barrier, with this and previous albums, "speaks to an unprecedented kind of global currency—one where pop music moves without barriers or borders, even as geopolitics seem to retreat further behind hard lines and high walls" (Greenblatt, 2019, para. 3).

The campaign expanded to Japan in 2018 when BTS formed a partnership with UNICEF JAPAN and excited fans were invited to visit the first ever UNICEF booths at Yokohama Arena and Osaka-jo Hall. Later that year, BTS' launch of its "Love Yourself World Tour" at the Seoul Olympic Stadium attracted more than 32,000 of the band's ARMY to UNICEF KOREA's special LOVE MYSELF for #ENDviolence booth, making it the highest official record for a single UNICEF event. Following the two-day concert in Seoul, BTS continued their world tour across 16 major cities in North America, Europe and Japan, continuing to break records for the campaign.

On September 24, 2018, BTS took their encouraging message to the 73rd United Nations "Youth 2030" event in New York to launch Generation Unlimited, a UNICEF global initiative that aims to ensure that all young people are in school, training, or employment by 2030. As BTS' only fluent English speaker in the group, RM, stated: "We started to hear remarkable stories from our fans all over the world, how our message helped them overcome their hardships in life and start loving themselves. These stories constantly remind us of our responsibility" (UNICEF, 2018, para. 18). The BTS ARMY made the speech go viral as the hashtag #BTSxUnitedNations trended worldwide on Twitter for several hours.

On the same day as their United Nations speech, BTS and Big Hit Entertainment signed an official partnership agreement with UNICEF USA for the LOVE MYSELF campaign. UNICEF USA celebrated the agreement by creating a microsite specifically for the LOVE MYSELF campaign so that fans could donate directly to the official website or donate $10 by sending the text message "BTSLM" to the number provided by UNICEF. On October 6, 2018, BTS and Big Hit Entertainment signed yet another partnership agreement with UNICEF UK, making the UK the fourth partner following South Korea, Japan, and the United States. BTS had raised over $2 million for the

#ENDviolence campaign as of 2019, with funds coming in through both direct donations and a portion of the sales from BTS' *Love Yourself* series (Zhou, 2019).

Through the use of social media, the LOVE MYSELF campaign ignited the BTS ARMY as fans were inspired to engage in volunteer work, make donations, and hold fundraisers in the band members' name. Just a few of the projects documented in a round-up article by Daily Vox Team's Ebrahim and Moosa (2020), included:

- BTS ARMY South Africa sponsored a reforestation project, as well as inspired young girls with self-defense classes and self-esteem workshops;
- BTS ARMY Peru organized a food, clothes, and gifts drive for children with special needs;
- Purple Ribbon ARMY Texas (a reference "I purple you," to a phrase coined by BTS member V, meaning "I trust and love you for a long time") raised money in honor of BTS members' birthdays which included the Fort Worth Botanical Gardens (RM), The Safe Alliance (Jimin), and 1Up on Cancer and the AbleGamers Charity (Jungkook).
- BTS ARMY India sponsored nationwide volunteering programs with NGO Teach for India to teach people about ending violence and the importance of loving themselves.

The success of the campaign has been attributed to the ability of BTS to connect with its fans, particularly during a time when young people feel the pressure to fit in exacerbated by a pervasive internet culture. In summarizing her reaction to the campaign, one fan states: "BTS spreads the message of self-love in all it's [sic] radical glory. Their message says to listeners that we are enough, that it's safe to be who we really are. When you love yourself, you help others to love themselves, too. And that's a revolution" (Daily Vox Team, 2018b, para.15).

The Global Campaign Video

As part of BTS' two-year LOVE MYSELF global campaign, the band released a campaign video with UNICEF on the International Day of

Friendship, July 30, 2019. The short 2:29 minute video is set to BTS' 2018 single, "Answer: Love Myself, " and features teens of all ethnic backgrounds that could be from anywhere in the world. The video shows images of isolated and bullied teens as the initially despondent BTS band members observe what is happening from a bleak reflecting pool. But as the band finds light, so do the teens in the video—each experiencing an inner light that warms their hearts or a friendly hand bringing them hope. The band's use of storytelling in the video, a technique they have incorporated into all of their album series, is rooted in their own experiences and provides a vulnerable authenticity that their fans not only relate to, but is produced in a way that has been described as an art form that is "spectacularly visual, auditory, and spiritual" (Briones, 2019, para. 4). The video ends with the words "Choose respect. Choose Support. Choose Kindness."

According to UNICEF, of the approximate 150 million students worldwide, half of all students 13 to 15 years of age report having experienced peer-to-peer violence, bullying, and fear in and around schools. In a tweet from BTS on the release of the video, the members say: "Our LOVE MYSELF campaign is all about encouraging every young person to find the love from within themselves & spreading that love to others. We want everyone to take part in ending violence by sharing love and kindness." Fans responded by sharing their own experiences with bullying, anxiety, and the difficulty in loving oneself, as well as an unending stream of positive messages about how BTS had inspired fans to learn how to "love myself." Within six months of its release, the video had garnered more than 14.5 million views.

The video had a profound impact with BTS' teenage fandom. As noted by Merrill (2017), "'Love Myself' is directly addressed to victims. Children and victims of trauma of any age can constructively remind themselves of this simple truth; saying 'Love Myself' to themselves is something they can do, or try to do...With this campaign BTS and their devoted fans worldwide address real pain and suffering by mobilizing the joy of music to improve lives of those who need help the most" (paras. 2-3). With the end of the video there comes a directive to fans:

1. Brighten someone's day with a kind note—online or IRL [In Real Life]
2. Share the note using #ENDviolence

As part of the joint campaign with BTS, UNICEF promoted the directives by creating an #ENDviolence webpage. In addressing the first directive, visitors to the page were encouraged to "Take Action" online by tagging a friend with a positive message using the hashtag #ENDViolence, by direct messaging (DM) someone with a kind message, or by sharing the BTS video. Visitors were also encouraged to "Take Action" offline by writing a note to a friend telling them why they are great, to write a positive message and leave it on a mirror, or leave an anonymous letter for someone that needs it. The second directive was executed with the creation of the #ENDViolence Youth Manifesto, drafted by a group of more than 100 young people in December 2018. The Manifesto, presented at the Education World Forum in London the following January, is a set of recommendations detailing what the students felt they needed to be protected in and around school (Ferguson, 2019).

At midnight on June 13, 2018, on BTS' fifth debut anniversary, a special video was uploaded to the official UNICEF Twitter page. It was a thank you message from UNICEF Executive Director Henrietta H. Fore to BTS and the BTS ARMY around the world. "Thank you BTS and the BTS ARMY...The LOVE MYSELF campaign is proof that young people around the world can come together and make a difference. From your music to your messages to your donations, you've shown the power of kindness. We here at UNICEF purple you!"

Conclusion

BTS catapulted to K-pop superstardom because of the vulnerable authenticity that was embraced by their fan base known as ARMY. This dedicated group of global fans tirelessly translates the group's lyrics, interviews, and online posts, and uses social media to engage fans well-beyond any other pop fandom. As a result of the support and passion of ARMY, BTS' LOVE MYSELF campaign has brought hope to countless teens who have reported experiencing peer-to-peer violence, bullying, and fear in and around schools.

To leverage the LOVE MYSELF campaign, BTS partnered with UNICEF to bring their message of self-love to a global stage. The band was invited to speak to the UN General Assembly in 2018 to help launch UNICEF's global initiative Generation Unlimited. Band member RM delivered the address reinforcing the campaign's central message: "No matter who you are, where you're from, your skin color, your gender identity, just speak yourself." A campaign video, set to the band's "Answer: Love Myself" single, was released on the International Day of Friendship in 2019. The video, which featured teens of every ethnic background, sought to encourage young people to not only find love from within themselves, but also to spread love to others. The band's message spread quickly across social media.

The success of the LOVE MYSELF campaign has contributed to BTS' continued meteoric rise in Western countries. BTS credits their ARMY for spreading the powerful message of self-love, as well as their enthusiasm for and active involvement in the campaign. As a result, the members of BTS were recognized by *TIME* magazine as the "Next Generation Leaders" in 2018, and ranked among the magazine's list of the 100 most influential people in the world in 2019.

Recommended Readings

Chung, W., & Lee, T. D. (2011). Hallyu as a strategic marketing key in the Korean media content industry. In D. K. Kim & M. Kim, *Hallyu: Influence of Korean popular culture in Asia and beyond* (pp. 431-460). Seoul, Korea: Seoul National University Press.

Jenkins, H., Ford, S., & Green, J. (2018). *Spreadable media: Creating value and meaning in a networked culture*. New York, NY: NYU Press.

Jung, S. (2017). Emerging social distribution: The case of K-pop circulation in the global pop market. In H. Shin & S. Lee, *Made in Korea: Studies in popular music* (pp. 47-48). New York, NY: Routledge.

Kim, D. K., & Kim, M. (2011). *Hallyu: Influence of Korean popular culture in Asia and beyond*. Seoul, Korea: Seoul National University Press.

Shin, H. & Lee, S. (2017). *Made in Korea: Studies in popular music*. New York, NY: Routledge.

Additional Sources

Big Hit Labels. (2019, July 29). *BTS (방탄소년단) LOVE MYSELF global campaign video*. Retrieved from https://www.youtube.com/watch?v=Eo_mo5vA7tw

LOVE MYSELF. *From USA to UK, the global expansion of the 'LOVE MYSELF' campaign*. Retrieved from https://www.love-myself.org/post-eng/us_uk_eng/

UNICEF. (2018, September 24). *BTS speech at the United Nations* [Video]. YouTube. Retrieved from https://www.youtube.com/watch?v=oTe4f-bBEKg

UNICEF USA. *How to donate to the LOVE MYSELF campaign*. Retrieved from https://donate.unicefusa.org/page/contribute/donate-to-the-love-myself-campaign

References

BBC. (2019, May 29). Where did it begin? How did K-pop conquer the world? *BBC Music*. Retrieved from http://www.bbc.com/culture/story/20190529-how-did-k-pop-conquer-the-world

Big Hit Entertainment. (n.d.). Love Myself campaign website. Retrieved from https://www.love-myself.org/eng/campaign-list/

Blake, E. (2018, April 4). The strength of K-pop fandom, by the numbers. *Forbes*. Retrieved from https://www.forbes.com/sites/emilyblake1/2018/04/04/k-pop-numbers/#60bae7cc48ab

Brandle, L. (2019, May 16). BTS pay homage to the Beatles with 'Boy with Luv' performance on 'Colbert': Watch. *Billboard*. Retrieved from https://www.billboard.com/articles/news/bts/8511677/bts-homage-beatles-boy-with-luv-colbert

Brandwatch. (2019). 101 Times brands went viral in 2019. *Brandwatch*. Retrieved from https://www.brandwatch.com/reports/101-times-brands-went-viral-in-2019/view/

Briones, I. (2019, May 5). The art of storytelling: Innovation by BTS. *Medium*. Retrieved from https://medium.com/@iya.briones/the-art-of-storytelling-innovation-by-bts-c7200594f0dd

Brown, E. R. (2019, September 20). Love yourself, love your fans: The BTS ARMY takes over. *Pollstar*. Retrieved from https://www.pollstar.com/News/love-yourself-love-your-fans-the-bts-army-takes-over-141102

Bruner, R. (2018, October 10). The next generation leaders: How BTS is taking over the world. *TIME*. Retrieved from https://time.com/collection-post/5414052/bts-next-generation-leaders/

Bruner, R. (2019, October 8). The mastermind behind BTS opens up about making a K-pop juggernaut. *TIME*. Retrieved from https://time.com/5681494/bts-bang-si-hyuk-interview/

Chung, W., & Lee, T. D. (2011). Hallyu as a strategic marketing key in the Korean media content industry. In D. K. Kim & M. Kim, *Hallyu: Influence of Korean popular culture in Asia and beyond* (pp. 431-460). Seoul, Korea: Seoul National University Press.

Cruz, L. (2019, July 18). I wasn't a fan of BTS. And then I was. *The Atlantic*. Retrieved from https://www.theatlantic.com/entertainment/archive/2019/07/bts-paved-the-way-army-fandom/592543/

Daily Vox Team. (2018a, June 13). What it means to be part of BTS ARMY. *The Daily Vox*. Retrieved from https://www.thedailyvox.co.za/what-it-means-to-be-part-of-bts-army-fatima-moosa-shaazia-ebrahim/

Daily Vox Team. (2018b, August 10). True love is loving yourself, BTS tells fans. *The Daily Vox*. Retrieved from https://www.thedailyvox.co.za/true-love-is-loving-yourself-bts-tells-fans-shaazia-ebrahim-fatima-moosa/

Daily Vox Team. (2020, October 2). How BTS ARMY worldwide has shared the love myself campaign. *The Daily Vox*. Retrieved from https://www.thedailyvox.co.za/bts-army-shared-love-myself-campaign-fatima-moosa-shaazia-ebrahim/

Dodson, P. C. (2019, July 4). As BTS's reach expands, an army of dedicated K-pop translators grow. *The New York Times*. Retrieved from https://www.nytimes.com/2019/07/04/arts/music/bts-kpop-translators.html

Dorof, J. (2018, June 12). A deeper look at why BTS has thrived in America. *Vulture, New York Magazine*. Retrieved from https://www.vulture.com/2018/06/

a-deeper-look-at-why-bts-has-thrived-in-america.html

Ferguson, S. (2019, January 18). Young people speak out: End violence in schools now. *Forbes*. Retrieved from https://www.forbes.com/sites/unicefusa/2019/01/18/young-people-speak-out-end-violence-in-schools-now/#7114a6482309

Glasby, T. (2018, October 11). How BTS became the world's biggest boy band. *The Guardian*. Retrieved from https://www.theguardian.com/music/2018/oct/11/how-bts-became-the-worlds-biggest-boyband

Greenblatt, L. (2019, March 28). The greatest showmen: An exclusive look inside the world of BTS. Entertainment exclusive. *Entertainment Weekly*. Retrieved from https://ew.com/music/2019/03/28/bts-exclusive-cover-story/

Herman, T. (2018, May 31). 7 factors that helped propel BTS to No. 1 on the Billboard 200. *Forbes*. Retrieved from https://www.forbes.com/sites/tamarherman/2018/05/31/7-factors-that-helped-propel-bts-to-no-1-on-the-billboard-200/#7076c42712a4

Jung, S. (2017). Emerging social distribution: The case of K-pop circulation in the global pop market. In H. Shin & S. Lee, *Made in Korea: Studies in popular music* (pp. 47-48). New York, NY: Routledge.

Kelley, C. (2017, December 21). Meet the BTS fan translators (partially!) responsible for the globalization of K-pop. *Billboard*. Retrieved from https://www.billboard.com/articles/columns/k-town/8078464/bts-fan-translators-k-pop-interview

Kim, D. K., & Kim, M. (2011). *Hallyu: Influence of Korean popular culture in Asia and beyond*. Seoul, Korea: Seoul National University Press.

Lindsay. (2013, June 14). Bangtan Boys MV "No More Dream" lacks reality. *Seoulbeats*. Retrieved from https://seoulbeats.com/2013/06/bangtan-boys-mv-no-more-dream-lacks-reality/

Marking, M. (2019, April 10). A few minutes to 10 hours daily: The world of K-pop fan translation. *Slator*. Retrieved from https://slator.com/demand-drivers/a-few-minutes-to-10-hours-daily-the-world-of-k-pop-fan-translation/

Merrill, P. (2017, November 1). BTS, UNICEF join forces against violence with Love Myself campaign, *Grammy Awards News*. Retrieved from https://www.grammy.com/grammys/news/bts-unicef-join-forces-against-violence-love-myself-campaign

Reid, L. (2020, January 8). 10 mind-blowing BTS facts and statistics. *Brandwatch*. Retrieved from https://www.brandwatch.com/blog/bts-facts-and-statistics/

Seo, Y., & Hollingsworth, J. (2019, October 20). BTS' army of admirers: Inside one of the world's most powerful fandoms. *CNN*. Retrieved from https://www.cnn.com/2019/10/12/asia/bts-fandom-army-intl-hnk/index.html

Shin, H., & Lee, S. (2017). *Made in Korea: Studies in popular music*. New York, NY: Routledge.

Solano, S. (2019, September 12). How RM has shifted the idol rapper perception of K-pop as BTS' leader. *Status*. Retrieved from https://statusmagonline.com/how-rm-has-shifted-the-idol-rapper-perception-of-k-pop-as-bts-leader/

St. Michel, P. (2017, July 13). PSY's 'Gangnam Style' changed pop music, whether you like it or not. *Pitchfork.com*. Retrieved from https://pitchfork.com/thepitch/psys-gangnam-style-changed-pop-music-whether-you-like-it-or-not/

UNICEF. (2018, September 24). We have learned to love ourselves, so now I urge you to 'speak yourself.' Remarks by BTS' Kim Nam Jun (RM) at the launch of Generation Unlimited, at the UN General Assembly. Retrieved from https://www.unicef.org/press-releases/we-have-learned-love-ourselves-so-now-i-urge-you-speak-yourself

Vultaggio, M. (2019, November 19). BTS has an unrivaled Twitter fan base. *Statista*. Retrieved from https://www.statista.com/chart/19998/bts-has-an-unrivaled-twitter-fan-base/

Wang, A. (2018, August 21). How K-pop conquered the West. *RollingStone*. Retrieved from https://www.rollingstone.com/music/music-features/bts-kpop-albums-bands-global-takeover-707139/

Wickman, G. (2018, October 17). Love Yourself: The message behind BTS's record breaking album series. *Bangtan Journal*. Retrieved from https://medium.com/bangtan-journal/love-yourself-the-message-behind-btss-record-breaking-album-series-229119e81902

Williams, L. (2020, February 13). How BTS became the internet's biggest obsession. *Kotaku*. Retrieved from https://www.kotaku.com.au/2020/02/bts-bangtan-boys-kpop-internet-obsession/

Yann. (2019, March 3). BTS lists a more diverse ticket-buying fanbase age range this year, According to vivid seats. *HELLOKPOP*. Retrieved from https://www.hellokpop.com/kpop/bts-more-diverse-ticket-buyers-new-tour/

Zhou, Z. (2019, January 15). The global influence of K-pop: Korean musical explosion breaks records and cultural barriers. *The Queen's University Journal*. Retrieved from https://www.queensjournal.ca/story/2019-01-14/pop-culture/the-global-influence-of-k-pop/

CHAPTER 2

K-Pop as a Case of Inter-Group Similarity and Acceptance in Cross-Cultural Communication

Carolyn A. Lin, University of Connecticut, **Suji Park**, Woosong University & **Xiaowen Xu**, Butler University

When the Korean singer, PSY, whose *Gangnam Style* music video exceeded one billion views on YouTube in 2013, it was a landmark event in digital media history. At the time of this writing, this video has garnered just under 3.5 billion views and it is ranked as the seventh most watched video (George, 2019). PSY's music is part of a larger music scene originated in South Korea. The Korean Wave, which refers to the widespread popularity of Korean popular culture across East and Southeast Asia, began in the late 1990s (Cho, 2011; Chuang & Lee, 2013). Subsequently, the Korean Wave expanded from television dramas to popular music, movies, animation and games in the late 2000's, in addition to large international fan clubs for Korean celebrities (Jung, 2017). When BTS, a K-pop boy band topped the U.S. Billboard Top 200 Chart in May of 2018, the popularity of K-pop appears to have gained some momentum in the U.S. (Liu, 2017). Hence, the question of interest is what has propelled K-pop since its start in 2007—to the biggest stage of western pop music in 2018—i.e., the American pop music scene? It would appear that several key factors might have helped contribute to the popularity of K-pop in the late 2010's, which reflects in part a form of successful soft-power diplomacy (Suntikul, 2019). These factors, as elaborated below, appear to coincide with the development of communication technology, the Asian economic growth, and the globalization of consumer market in the 21st century (Huang & Wang, 2011).

Key Factors for K-Pop Diffusion

As a disruptive form of digital communication, YouTube has liberated video sharing between Internet users. YouTube first introduced K-pop to the American audience and has continued to fuel the awareness and interest of K-pop videos (Jin, 2016). The arrival of other social media platforms such as Twitter and Instagram allows for instantaneous sharing of news, opinions, images and videos about K-pop across large legions of followers (Jin, 2016). In 2018, 85% of American teens (ages 13-17) were "often" YouTube users; their regular ("often") usage of other social media platforms indicates the following: Instagram at 72%, Snapchat at 69%, Facebook at 51%, and Twitter at 32% (Anderson & Jiang, 2018). In terms of the "often" motivations for social media use among teens, the breakdown shows 57% for passing time, 37% for connecting with others, and 30% for learning new things (Schaeffer, 2019). These statistics paint a picture of how teenagers have used the social media platforms and their smartphones to post, share and exchange information about content that satisfies their needs for stimulation and social interaction. K-pop could thus be seen as a social media phenomenon for American teens to explore and share as a novel, interesting and fun pop culture topic (Ahn, Oh, & Kim, 2013).

Smartphone ownership is nearly universal among the younger generations in the U.S. According to a national study, 95% of adolescents aged 13-17 (Anderson & Jiang, 2019) and 96% of young adults aged 18-29 (Pew Research Center, 2019) owned a smartphone. As such, the popularity of Samsung and LG's smartphones, along with their other electronic products and Korean automobile brands (e.g., Hyundai), could all have played a significant role in boosting the image of South Korea as a modern, trendy and technology-savvy country (Kinsey & Chung, 2013). When 25% of the smartphones sold in the U.S. are of the Samsung brand and another 12% bear an LG label (Counterpoint, 2019), it would appear that numerous American consumers are likely using Korean-made electronic devices to access K-pop entertainment.

In addition, the immigration share from East and South Asia (27%) outpaced that from Mexico (25%) in 2017; this Asian immigration growth has been highly consistent since 2010 (Radford, 2019). This immigration trend, combined with a number of popular American television series featuring prominent Korean American actors (e.g.,

Sandra Oh in *Grey's Anatomy*, Steven Yeun in The *Walking Dead* and Daniel Dae Kim in *Lost*), could have also contributed to greater acceptance of Korean entertainers in popular media. Moreover, the Korean government has also been behind the strategic promotion of K-pop and Korean cuisine (Gain, 2015). Online retailer search services such as *Yelp* reported that Korean food is now in high demand in the U.S. (Theden, 2019). Korean food is also the trendy cuisine that is gaining a strong following in the UK (Chaudhary, 2019). Hence, as people became more acquainted with Korean products, pop culture, immigrants and cuisine, a fringe benefit of this cultural familiarity could be perceived normalcy of such commercial and cultural presence in American society.

Inter-Group Similarity (IGS) and Inter-Group Acceptance (IGA)

K-pop exemplifies a fusion of *Eastern tradition* and *Western modernity* into an East-meets-West hybrid. K-pop music videos have a reputation for slick and synchronized dance and "colorful, sophisticated, and extravagant visual effects" (Park, 2013b, p. 8). As suggested by Jung (2017), "K-pop distinctly appeals to Americans by exemplifying a world of pop culture as a total package: catchy tunes, good singing, attractive appearance, mesmerizing performances, well-thought-out merchandise, and most of all, Humbleness" (p. 231). This prompts the American audiences/fans—non-white and white—finding Korean popular culture "comfortably appealing," instead of exoticization (Jung, 2017, p, 234). Comparing American pop and K-pop videos, a content analysis reported that while male performs from both cultures display masculine fashion and feminine styles (via wearing excessive accessories and long hair), female performers exhibit stereotyped gender norms and sexual images by exposing their body and conforming to Western beauty standard (Jin & Ryoo, 2014). By implication, K-pop is not "strange" to American pop music fans because it sounds and looks Western, except that the young and attractive performers who dance in expertly choreographed and staged production sing in Korean only.

Inter-Group Similarity

Individuals form their social identity partially as an expression of their self-concept based on their group membership; they tend to perceive their group identity as being superior to that of other groups, according to social identity theory (Tajfel & Turner, 1979). The perception of similarity between personal identities is necessary for individuals to form a group identity, according to the similarity-attraction hypothesis (Byrne & Griffitt, 1973). Perceived similarity also helps reduce interaction anxiety within the group (Selfhout et al., 2009). Likewise, self-revealing group attributes (e.g., interests, opinions, beliefs and values) could help decrease cross-group interaction anxiety and increase interest in sustaining a cross-group relationship, where perceived similarity is peripheral to the objectives of between-group interaction (West et al., 2014).

With the theoretical framework elaborated above, it is reasonable to assume that perceived similarity in the cross-group interaction related to K-pop and American pop music would be facilitated via the perceived intergroup similarity in the cross-cultural fan base. In particular, K-pop offers a sound familiar to American pop music fans. If one compares K-pop to American pop music, it is clear that K-pop has been greatly influenced by the latter, as the dancing and singing styles do not differ from modern Western music (Hogarth, 2013). For instance, K-pop bands emulate popular American teen idols such as Justin Bieber, Backstreet Boys and Boyz II Men (Wood, 2019) in their sound and dance styles. As empirical research is lacking on the role of music in cross-cultural communication, a relevant study conducted in the field of musicology suggests that Western audiences enjoy culturally similar Western music more than culturally dissimilar music (i.e., Indian music) in experiencing a more positive mood and social connectedness with a stranger (Stupacher & Wood, 2018). In essence, familiarity with the sound and performance style of the music could bring connectedness to the culture affiliated with that music and even unknown individuals present in the environment. As K-pop offers a Western sound and dance style, American music fans could perceive a culturally "inter-group similarity" between K-pop and Western pop music, while recognizing K-pop performers as foreigners who appreciate, share and embody American pop music culture.

Inter-Group Acceptance

If K-pop is regarded as a cultural form that shares a culturally "inter-group similarity" among American pop music fans, then it is likely that a form of "inter-group acceptance" could evolve over time. As indicated by social identity theory, individuals automatically gravitate toward those who share similar social identifiers,—such as age, gender and skin color—through a categorization process that contrasts an in-group with an out-group (Brewer, 1988; Fiske & Neuberg, 1990). From the perspective of psychological distance (Trope, Liberman, & Wakslak, 2007), perceived social distance between individuals could depend on their degree of acceptance toward each other's ethnic identity (Bogardus, 1925) and perceived comfort level when interacting with each other interpersonally (Birrell, 1989). The concepts of social identity and social distance have yet to be applied to examine individual responses toward "imported" popular culture products such as K-pop. Relevant research conducted in the marketing communication context found that perceived familiarity with a brand and a known online retailer could elicit a shorter psychological distance than their unfamiliar and unknown counterparts (Edwards, Lee, & Ferle, 2009). Another study found that while White participants' perceived social distance toward Asian and African Americans was small but remained larger than that toward other Whites, such perceived distance had no significant effect on purchase intention after exposure to non-White product spokespersons (Lin & Xu, 2017).

By further elucidating the constructs of social identity and social distance via the Common Ingroup Identity Model (Dovidio et al., 2001), it appears that individuals could recategorize out-group members in an inter-group membership by devaluing between-group dissimilarities and develop positive attitudes/behavior toward these reclassified proxy "in-group" members. Again, as empirical research still needs to apply this model to study cross-cultural communication, relevant work in third-person effects indicates that perceived distance between self and other is strongly associated with a perceived sense of community and shared commonalities among community members (Perloff, 1993; Eveland et al., 1999). By implication, when individuals downplay the dissimilarities between an in-group and an out-group identity, then social distance could decrease, and an out-group could be reclassified with an accepted inter-group membership.

Based on the technology, economic, demographic and social cognitive factors discussed above, this chapter will analyze the composition and appeal of K-pop as a popular culture phenomenon. It will describe the different K-pop content elements that enable them to engender the anticipated inter-group similarity and inter-group acceptance, when American music fans interact with this Korean cultural product. As the current chapter reports the findings of a content analysis study, audience perceptions of inter-group similarity and inter-group acceptance were not directly evaluated. Instead, this content analysis study measured concepts that are relevant to elicit such cognitive and affective responses via the presentation of cultural images, gender roles, gender expressions and visual appeals. A set of research questions that explores the substance of the K-pop content elements are proposed here to guide our analysis as follows: 1) What are the cultural images projected by the performers? 2) What are the gender roles portrayed by the performers? 3) What are the gender-expressions presented by the performers; and 4) what are the visual appeals via dance and fashion styles as choreographed for the performers?

Methods

An image frame analysis was conducted via a content analysis. The sample for the frame analysis was selected from the most popular “Korean pop music” search results on YouTube and from the «K-pop hot top-100» list on Billboard from the past five years. The music groups and their music videos were chosen to represent the most distinct K-pop images that embody the appeal of K-pop music. These music videos include 25 male and 17 female groups, totaling 80 videos.

Coding Scheme

A codebook was constructed to operationally define each of the concepts tested in the four research questions as shown above. Measurement items were developed for coding gender-specific items unique for either male or female performers as well as gender-neutral items applicable to both male and female performers. All measurement items were coded on a three-point scale—fully (coded as "3"), somewhat (coded as "2") and not at all (coded as "1")—unless otherwise described. The unit of analysis for the coding scheme is each video featuring either a male group or a female group.

Cultural images were coded for two different dimensions (Jung, 2011). First, *cultural stereotypes for males* describe the indication of "nerdy, asexual, or meek" characteristics for male performers. Second, *cultural stereotypes for female* indicate the presentation of "dainty, exotic or fragile" attributes for female performers. *Gender roles* were operationalized to reflect how traditional gender-specific portrayals were displayed (Wallis, 2011). This concept measures the indication of "domineering, subservient, sex object, aggressive" demeanors for male and female performers. *Gender expressions* refer to how traditional gender-specific representation is embodied in dance by each gender (Jung, 2011; Park, 2013a). This variable demonstrates the degree of "boyish, girlish, masculine and feminine" exhibitions for male and female performers.

Visual Appeals involve two different aspects of performance for both male and female groups (Aubrey & Frisby, 2011; Frisby & Aubrey, 2012; Turner, 2011). First, *dance style* describes whether the dance movements communicate "sexy, cute, provocative or boisterous" images for each gender. Second, *fashion style* records whether the performers' attire is revealing. *Clothing fit* is described by "tight" (coded as "3"), "adequate" (coded as "2") or "loose fit" (coded as "1') of the wardrobe. Second, *midriff exposedness* is measured by "mostly" (coded as "3"), "partly" (coded as "2") or "not exposed" (coded as "1") of the middle section of the body. *Chest exposedness* is recorded to show whether the chest area is "mostly" (coded as "3"), "partly" (coded as "2") or "not exposed" (coded as "1")." For male performers, *upper-leg exposedness* is indicated by the extent to which the length of their outfit as "cover the butt" (coded as "3"), "above the knee" (coded as "2") or "about knee length or longer" (coded as "1"). For female performers, *upper-leg exposedness* was coded by the length of the shorts or skirts they wore via three categories: "cover the buttocks" (coded as "3"), "above the knee" (coded as "2"), or "knee length or longer" (coded as "1").

Coding Procedure

A codebook was developed and utilized as the instructional manual for coding training. Two research assistants were trained to comprehend and discuss the different features of sample videos together. After the training session, the two research assistants each viewed and coded the same 10 videos (or 12.5% of the sample) from the male and female groups separately. These 10 videos were randomly and separately selected from the male and female groups. Coding results were compared to compute the initial intercoder reliability; the initial reliability levels average around .29-.96, as computed with Kappa's formula. The research assistants then went through a second training session to resolve their differential interpretations of the coding scheme. Following that, the research assistants each coded the entire sample of male and female group videos. The final intercoder reliabilities of all coding items range from .41 to 1.0.

Results

Of the 80 videos that feature male and female groups, several concepts in the coding scheme were not applicable to systematically identify, classify and code the content of the videos. This is because some of the videos contain images or behaviors that don't reflect a coherent storyline, thematically connected scenes or clear visual presentation components to meet the operational definitions of selected concepts in the coding scheme. Due to the fact that a strong skewness level is present in the frequency distribution of most coded items, a Kappa's alpha at .65 was utilized as the cut-off for acceptable intercoder reliability. This decision was made based on the rule, which determines that it is difficult to generate a significant Kappa value (in effect size or p-value) when the distribution is skewed (Eubanks, 2017).

Cultural Images

The first research question explores the cultural images of K-pop videos. Results showed that K-pop male groups did not display culturally stereotyped images in their music videos, after excluding the "asexual"

Table 1. Descriptive Statistics for Cultural Images

	Male		
	Not at all	Somewhat	Very
Nerdy	100%	0%	0%
M(SD)	1.00(0)		
Md	1.00		
N	21		
Meek	85%	15%	0%
M(SD)	1.15 (0.37)		
Md	1.00		
N	20		

concept that did not yield any cases to match the coding scheme. For male performers, the following concepts were coded—nerdy, asexual and meek—the concept of "asexual" did not yield any cases via the coding scheme. Specifically, None of the male performers were identified to have a nerdy image (M = 1.00, SD = 0; K = .77). In addition, while 85% of the male performers were not portrayed as meek in their music videos, 15% of them were identified as 'somewhat meek' (M = 1.15, SD = .37; K = .72). For female performers, the following concepts were coded: dainty, exotic and fragile. Similar to their male counterparts, female performers also did not appear in culturally stereotyped images, as none of these concepts were identified in our study findings.

Gender Roles

The second research question inquires what the gender-role displays in K-pop videos are. Four concepts were coded for this variable: domineering, subservient, sex object and aggressive. Findings indicated that K-pop performers did not demonstrate traditional gender roles, after excluding the concepts of "domineering" and "subservient" which did not yield any cases through the coding procedure. For male performers, 85% of them were not displayed as a sex object, but the rest of the 15% were (M = 1.30, SD = .73; K = .67). While 50% of

Table 2. Descriptive Statistics for Gender Roles

	Male (n = 20)		
	Not at all	Somewhat	Very
Sex Object	85%	0%	15%
M(SD)	1.30(0.73)		
Md	1.00		
Aggressive	50%	20%	30%
M(SD)	1.80(0.89)		
Md	1.50		

the male performers did not show any aggressive behavior in their videos, 20% were coded as "somewhat aggressive" and 30% were recorded as being "very aggressive" (M = 1.80, SD = .89; K = .70). As for female performers, the acceptable Kappa values achieved for the same coding items in the male performer cases did not materialize here. In particular, sex object and aggressive behavior had lower than acceptable Kappa values.

Gender Expressions

The third research question investigates the gender expressions exhibited by the performers. This variable was coded for four concepts: boyish, girlish, masculine and feminine. No cases were identified for either the "boyish" or the "girlish" concept through the coding procedure, respectively. Of the male music videos, 84.4% of male music videos did not demonstrate feminine dance movements, whereas 15.6% showed moderately feminine dance styles (M = 1.16, SD = .37; K = .70). Approximately 60% of male performers demonstrated overly masculine dance performance and 40% performed moderately masculine choreography (M = 2.59, SD = .50; K = .70). Among female music videos, most of the female performers showed feminine choreography in their music videos (77.8%) and 22.2% showed moderately feminine performance (M = 2.78, SD = .42; K = 1.00). On the other hand, 92% of female performers did not include masculine dance styles in their music videos and 8% showed moderately masculine performance (M = 1.08, SD = .28; K = .69).

Table 3. Descriptive Statistics for Gender Expressions

	Male (n = 32)			Female (n = 36)		
	Not at all	Somewhat	Very	Not at all	Somewhat	Very
Feminine	84.4%	15.6%	0%	0%	22.2%	77.8%
M(SD)	1.16(0.37)			2.78(0.42)		
Md	1.00			3.00		
Masculine	0%	40.6%	59.4%	91.7%	8.3%	0%
M(SD)	2.59(0.50)			1.08(0.28)		
Md	3.00			1.00		

Visual Appeals

The fourth research question queries what the choreographed visual appeals of K-pop videos are. Two sets of items were used to measure two variables—dance style and fashion style—to address this question. For the variable of dance style, the following concepts were coded: sexy, cute, provocative or boisterous; the concept of "cute" was not present through the coding procedure. The variable of fashion style was coded for the following concepts—midriff, chest and upper-legs exposure of the performers—to detect whether the clothing style is revealing.

Dance style. Among the videos from the male groups, 85% of male performers did not engage in a sexy performance, 12% showed moderately sexy dance and 3% performed overly sexy movements ($M = 1.18$, $SD = .47$; $K = .83$). Most of the male performers (94%) did not have any choreograph that qualifies as a provocative dance style and only 6% performed moderately provocative movements ($M = 1.06$, $SD = .25$; $K = .79$). Similarly, 25% of male performers illustrated boisterous dance movements, whereas 55% did not and another 20% showed somewhat boisterous choreography ($M = 1.70$, $SD = .87$; $K = .70$).

By contrast, 47% of female performers demonstrated overly sexy choreography and 28% showed moderately sexy dance style ($M = 2.22$, $SD = .83$; $K = .77$). Female performers also demonstrated provocative performance quite frequently, with 39% showing overly provocative choreography and 20% exhibiting moderately provocative movements ($M = 1.97$, $SD = .91$; $K = .83$). The coding results for the concepts of boisterous have lower than acceptable Kappa values for female

Table 4a. Descriptive Statistics for Visual Appeals via Dance Style

	Male			Female		
	Not at all	Somewhat	Very	Not at all	Somewhat	Very
Sexy	84.8%	12.1%	3%	25%	27.8%	47.2%
M(SD)	1.18(0.47)			2.22(0.83)		
Md	1.00			2.00		
N	33			36		
Provocative	93.8%	6.2%	0%	41.7%	19.4%	38.9%
M(SD)	1.06(0.25)			1.97(0.91)		
Md	1.00			2.00		
N	32			36		
Boisterous	55%	20%	25%			
M(SD)	1.70(0.87)					
Md	1.00					
N	20					

performers and are not reported here.

Fashion style. Among male performers, 82% of them wore adequately fitting clothes, about 10% wore loose-fitting clothes and another 7.7 % were in somewhat tight-fitting clothes (M = 1.97, SD = .26; K = .71). Very few male performers exposed their bodies, with 93% fully covered their midriff and the rest of them slightly exposed their midriff (M = 1.08, SD = .27; K = .85). Similarly, in terms of chest exposedness, 83% fully covered their chest and the rest of them either partly or slightly exposed their chest (M = 1.14, SD = .32; K = .92). The concept of *upper-leg exposedness* did not yield an acceptable Kappa value.

For female performers, results of clothing fit indicated that 35% of them wore tight-fitting clothes, 27.5% had somewhat tight-fitting, 35% of them were outfitted with adequate-fitting clothes and another 2.5% showed up in loose-fitting clothes. (M = 2.48, SD = .45; K = .72). With regard to midriff exposedness, 40% of the female performers fully covered their midriff, 8% mostly exposed their midriff and the rest of them partly covered their midriff (M = 1.59, SD = .61; K = .95). In terms of how revealing the chest area was, 63% fully covered their chest and the rest of them partly covered their chest (M = 1.24,

Table 4b. Descriptive Statistics for Visual Appeals via Male Fashion Style

	Male				
	Loose Fit (1)	1.5[a]	Adequate Fit (2)	2.5[b]	Tight Fit (3)
Clothing Fit	2.6%	7.7%	82%	7.7%	0%
M(SD)	1.97(0.26)				
Md	2.00				
N	39				
	Not Exposed (1)	1.5[a]	Partly Exposed (2)	2.5[b]	Mostly Exposed (3)
Midriff Exposedness	92.5%	0%	7.5%	0%	0%
M(SD)	1.08(0.27)				
Md	1.00				
N	40				
Chest Exposedness	82.5%	7.5%	10%	0%	0%
M(SD)	1.14(0.32)				
Md	1.00				
N	40				

Notes.

a. The category of "1.5" on the 3-point scale means a state between 1 and 2, for example for "Clothing Fit," it means that the clothing is "Tighter" than it is "Loose."

b. The category of "2.5" on the 3-point scale means a state between 2 and 3, for example for "Clothing Fit," it means that the clothing is "Tighter" than it is "Adequately Fit."

SD = .34; K = .90). Female performers exhibited a strong preference for shorts, with 87% wearing shorts that covered their buttocks and another 13% were in shorts that stayed above their knees (M = 2.87, SD = .34; K = .80). While just less than half of the female performers were dressed in miniskirts (46%), about 9% had on skirts that went below their knees (M = 2.51, SD = .55; K = .69).

Discussion

Past research has suggested that music videos play a crucial role in conveying cultural stereotypes and gender roles (Andsager & Roe, 1999; Ward, Hansbrough, & Walker, 2005). The current study demonstrates both male and female K-pop performers did not exhibit an image that

Table 4c. Descriptive Statistics for Visual Appeals via Female Fashion Style

	Female (n = 40)				
	Loose Fit (1)	1.5[a]	Adequate Fit (2)	2.5[b]	Tight Fit (3)
Clothing Fit	0%	2.5%	35%	27.5%	35%
M(SD)	2.48(0.45)				
Md	2.50				
	Fully Covered (1)	1.5[a]	Partly Covered (2)	2.5[b]	Mostly Exposed (3)
Midriff Exposedness	40%	20%	30%	2.5%	7.5%
M(SD)	1.59(0.61)				
Md	1.50				
Chest Exposedness	62.5%	27.5%	10%	0%	0%
M(SD)	1.24(0.34)				
Md	1.00				
	Knee or Longer (1)	1.5[a]	Above the Knee (2)	2.5[b]	Cover the Buttocks (3)
Shorts Length	0%	0%	12.9%	0%	87.1%
M(SD)	2.87(0.34)				
Md	3.00				
Skirt Length	2.9%	5.7%	22.9%	22.9%	45.7%
M(SD)	2.51(0.55)				
Md	2.50				

Notes.

a. The category of "1.5" on the 3-point scale means a state between 1 and 2, for example for "Clothing Fit," it means that the clothing is "Tighter" than it is "Loose."

b. The category of "2.5" on the 3-point scale means a state between 2 and 3, for example for "Clothing Fit," it means that the clothing is "Tighter" than it is "Adequately Fit."

embodies cultural stereotypes, traditional gender roles or conventional gender expressions. These findings both contradict and confirm past studies conducted across humanities and social sciences disciplines, which utilized different methodologies—including critical cultural analysis, media content analysis (of television programs and films) and survey research—to investigate audience perceptions of and/or attitudes toward Asians/Asian Americans.

Specifically, male K-pop performers were presented as pop stars who didn't exhibit any stereotypical images about Asian males such as nerdy or meek. These findings then contradict studies that reported the opposite results. For instance, Zhang's (2010) study revealed that people were less likely to initiate a friendship with Asian Americans than Blacks and Whites, due to their perceptions of Asian Americans as nerds; the study also showed that perceptions of Asians were in line with the media portrayals of Asian Americans. Likewise, a study comparing two focus groups (conducted in 2002 and 2011) concluded that the common stereotypes of Asian American men branded them as nerdy, socially awkward but technologically skilled (Sun et al., 2015). By contrast, other research found that Asian/Asian American men were portrayed as being intelligent, tech-savvy and hard-working—through the characters that they played in popular television series—such as Archie Johnson in the *CSI* or Hiro Nakamura in *Heroes* (Wong et al., 2012; Wu, 2010).

By the same token, the K-pop music videos analyzed in the current study did not show Asian women in a culturally stereotyped image. Our findings revealed that female K-pop performers presented themselves with a strong and independent identity which echoes a "female empowerment" image. These findings again are inconsistent with past literature, which suggests Asian/Asian American women are stereotypically perceived to be submissive, helpless, and dependent (Sun et al., 2015; Wu, 2010). On the opposite end of the spectrum, Asian women have also been portrayed as the "dragon lady" in entertainment media—a remnant from the old Hollywood films—with character traits such as strong, sneaky, seductive, and untrustworthy (Wu, 2010). The female K-pop performers did not appear to show any "dragon lady" traits, as they sing and dance to entertain their fans. This absence of Asian stereotypes found both for male and female singers indicates that K-pop singers are portrayed in a culturally-similar way to their Western counterparts, which may contribute to the perceived intergroup similarity and acceptance of K-pop by Western audiences.

Turning to gender role images, K-pop performers did not demonstrate any traditional gender roles in their music videos. Specifically, the scenes or storylines didn't describe any dominant or subservient behavior that could be clearly identified for either gender, neither did they present the performers as an obvious sex object regardless of their gender. The only exception showed that male performers did exhibit some aggressive gestures in their dance routine; these aggressive gestures tended to be more related to an athletically physical dance style rather than any hint of physical aggression. These results hence don't support previous findings that reported otherwise (e.g., Andsager & Roe, 1999; Arnett, 2002). However, the current study did find that half of the male performers acted in either somewhat or very aggressive manner in their videos. These findings thus are consistent with past studies that found typical images of males in Western music videos as being aggressive (Arnett, 2002; Ward, Hansbrough, & Walker, 2005).

With regard to gender expressions, K-pop performers did not display any overly boyish or girlish attributes that could be systematically and reliably categorized. These findings contrast with those that have described male and female K-pop performers as presenting themselves in a boyish or girlish manner, respectively (Jung, 2011; Park, 2013a). The present study did find that of all male performers, more than half of and about 40% presented a masculine and somewhat masculine image in their dance movements, respectively; none of them showed any feminine attributes through their choreography. Among female performers, a large majority and just less than a quarter did exhibit feminine and somewhat feminine dance movements, in that order; none of them danced in an obvious masculine style. These findings thus suggest that K-pop performers did not try to demonstrate any gender-bending expressions in the way that they danced. They also did not exhibit any overtly strong masculine or feminine dance moves that reflect the traditional gender stereotypes about Asian males and females. Findings also confirm past research that Asian women are seen as more feminine and less masculine than their counterparts in other racial groups (e.g., Wilkins, Chan, & Kaiser, 2011).

Looking at the visual appeals, the dance choreography appeared to generally fall along the gender line without portraying traditional gender-stereotyped images, even when the scenes or storylines in their music videos seemed to portray them as more "androgynous" characters. Specifically, most male performers did not appear to dance or act in a sexy, cute, provocative or boisterous manner. The performances of female performers nonetheless indicated a different style. While about three-quarters of them danced in sexy (under 50%) or somewhat sexy (under 30%) choreography, respectively, just under 60% of them did so with provocative (under 40%) or somewhat provocative (under 20%) dance movements. Even so, the choreography for female performers did not establish a "boisterous" dance style, as validated by the intercoder reliability reported above.

As for the performers' fashion, which is typically part of the choreographed production to construct a performer's looks and persona, it reflected a modest instead of a revealing style of dressing for the male groups. In particular, results indicate that an overwhelming majority of male performers did not wear tight-fitting clothes, expose their bodies, show their midriff or bare their chest. On the other hand, the female performers' fashion appears to be more revealing than their male counterparts, especially with their exposed upper legs. This was evidenced by the results which illustrated that about one-third of them were tight-fitting clothes, less than one-tenth had their midriffs fully exposed and just over one-third partially exposed their chest area. Moreover, an overwhelming majority of them did wear short shorts and just under half dressed in miniskirts.

The current study's findings of K-pop performers' attire are similar to the results reported by a study from Kwon (2004), which suggest that while female performers tend to expose their body, male performers favor masculine fashion but with many accessories—to present a bit of feminine touch—or to blur the conventional gender appearances. Comparing the results from this study to another content analysis study (King, Laake, & Bernard, 2006), it would appear that K-pop female performers' fashion is more modest and less revealing relative to that of the Western female pop stars who tend to wear very skimpy clothing that exposes a lot of their body. Specifically, King, Laake, & Bernard (2006) analyzed music videos aired on MTV, MTV2, BET, and GAC and reported that sexy female attire was shown 13 times more than sexy male attire in the music videos analyzed.

In sum, as indicated by previous literature, comparatively speaking, K-pop music has been heavily influenced by American pop music in its artistic expression, visual commonalities and even beauty standard (e.g., Kwon, 2004). Combined with the social media and smartphone culture among young music fans as well as the increased Asian immigration to the U.S., K-pop seems to have arrived just at the right moment to be the "opening act" for Asian pop culture to enter the mainstream in the West,—following the success of *Anime*—which also has a devoted fan base in the West as an animation art form (e.g., Lu, 2009). This K-pop "opening act" appears to have established not only a path for transnational cross-cultural communication, but also a means for Western pop music fans to appreciate the perceived inter-group similarities between East and West through the entertaining content of K-pop videos. Such perceived inter-group similarities could help contribute to inter-group acceptance to facilitate Western pop music fans' embrace of K-pop music. Acceptance of K-pop music is hence indicative of acceptance of the Eastern culture that K-pop represents and the East Asian identity that it embodies.

Conclusion and Implications

It is safe to say that K-pop music videos have broken the stereotypical beliefs about Asians and Asian culture to allow Western pop music fans to accept Asian pop stars who perform Western-style music with an Eastern twist. In essence, K-pop videos portray the performers—who represent the image of young Asian men and women in media—as young, attractive and vivacious stars who are dressed in high fashion to perform popular tunes and eye-catching dance choreography. These young performers are presented to the Western audience without the expectation or baggage of cultural stereotypes, traditional gender roles and conventional gender expressions. They embody the youth culture in the social media era, which has helped shape and promote what a contemporary, savvy and cool pop star should look and sound like, regardless of their racial identity.

This sense of perceived commonalities in the youth, social media and popular culture may thus be an important starting point for research that intends to further explore the influence of perceived social identity and social distance on inter-group similarity and acceptance in other domains of social importance. These domains could include, for instance, finding inter-group similarity and acceptance between diverse racial and ethnic groups through media narratives in popular music, television programs and film. Promoting media stories that aim at helping individuals with different political ideologies, cultural beliefs and religious faiths to find commonalities and acceptance to reduce social conflicts could be achieved different forms of popular art—

including music (e.g., Allsup & Shieh, 2012). If one considers how pop songs, including John Lennon's *Imagine*, have been utilized as a vehicle for bringing about social justice (Byard & Levy, 2013), then popular music leaders—including K-pop—could continue to take up that mantle to promote this long-standing pop culture tradition.

Recommended Readings

Han, B. (2017). Korean wave | K-pop in Latin America: Transcultural fandom and digital mediation. *International Journal of Communication, 11*, 2250-2269.

Jin, D. Y. (2018). An analysis of the Korean wave as transnational popular culture: North American youth engage through social media as TV becomes obsolete. *International Journal of Communication, 12*, 404-422.

Oh, I., & Park, G. S. (Eds.). (2013). The globalization of K-pop: Korea's place in the global music industry. *Korea Observer, 44*(3), 389-409.

Additional Sources

Kim, K. H., & Choe, Y. (Eds.). (2014). *The Korean popular culture reader*. Durham, NC: Duke University Press.

Kim, Y. (Ed.). (2013). *The Korean wave: Korean media go global*. London, UK: Routledge.

Kuwahara, Y. (Ed.). (2014). *The Korean wave: Korean popular culture in global context.* New York, NY: Palgrave Macmillan.

Yoon, T.-J., & Dal Jin, Y. (2017). *The Korean wave: Evolution, fandom, and transnationality*. New York, NY: Lexington Books.

References

Ahn, J., Oh, S., & Kim, H. (2013, July). Korean pop takes off! Social media strategy of Korean entertainment industry. *The 10th International Conference of Service Systems and Service Management.* Hong King, China.

Allsup, R. E., & Shieh, E. (2012). Social justice and music education: The call for a public pedagogy. *Music Educators Journal, 98*, 47-51.

Anderson, M., & Jiang, J. (2018). Teens, social media & technology 2018 [PDF file]. *Pew Research Center*. Retrieved from https://www.pewresearch.org/internet/2018/05/31/teens-social-media-technology-2018/

Andsager, J. L., & Roe, K. (1999). Country music video in country's year of the woman. *Journal of Communication, 49*, 69-82 .

Arnett, J. J. (2002). The sounds of sex: Sex in teens' music and music videos. In J. Brown, K. Walsh-Childers, & J. Steele (Eds.), *Sexual teens, sexual media* (pp. 253-264). Hillsdale, NJ: Lawrence Erlbaum.

Aubrey, J. S., & Frisby, C. M. (2011). Sexual objectification in music videos: A content analysis comparing gender and genre. *Mass Communication and Society, 14*(4), 475-501.

Birrell, S. (1989). Racial relations theories and sport: Suggestions for a more critical analysis. *Sociology of Sport Journal, 6*(3), 212-227.

Bogardus, E. S. (1925). Measuring social distance. *Journal of Applied Sociology, 9*, 299-308.

Brewer, M. B. (1988). A dual process model of impression formation. In T. K. Srull & R. S. Wyer Jr. (Eds.), *Advances in social cognition, Vol. 1. A dual process model of impression formation* (pp. 1-36). Hillsdale, NJ: Lawrence Erlbaum Associates, Inc.

Byard, D. C., & Levy, D. L. (2013). Exploring social justice through music. Association for Psychological Science. Retrieved from https://www.researchgate.net/publication/292606438

Byrne, D., & Griffitt, W. (1973). Interpersonal attraction. *Annual Review of Psychology, 24*(1), 317-336.

Chaudhary, V. (2019, April 21). Feast from the east-why Britain is surfing the Korean culture wave. *The Guardian*. Retrieved from https://www.theguardian.com/music/2019/apr/21/feast-from-east-britain-surfing-korean-culture-wave

Cho, Y. (2011). Desperately seeking East Asia amidst the popularity of South Korean pop culture in Asia. *Cultural Studies, 25*, 383-404.

Chuang, L. M., & Lee, H. E. (2013). Korean wave: Enjoyment factors of Korean dramas in the U.S. *International Journal of Intercultural Relations, 37*, 594-604.

Counterpoint. (2019, November 28). Smartphone market share: By quarter. *Counterpoint*. Retrieved from https://www.counterpointresearch.com/us-market-smartphone-share/

Dovidio, J. F., Gaertner, S. L., Niemann, Y. F., & Snider, K. (2001). Racial, ethnic, and cultural differences in responding to distinctiveness and discrimination on campus: Stigma and common group identity. *Journal of Social Issues, 57*(1), 167-188.

Edwards, S. M., Lee, J. K., & Ferle, C. L. (2009). Does place matter when shopping online? Perceptions of similarity and familiarity as indicators of psychological distance. *Journal of Interactive Advertising, 10*(1), 35-50.

Eubanks, D. (2017). (Re)Visualizing rater agreement: Beyond single-parameter measures. *Journal of Writing Analytics, 1*, 277-310.

Eveland Jr, W. P., Nathanson, A. I., Detenber, B. H., & McLeod, D. M. (1999). Rethinking the social distance corollary: Perceived likelihood of exposure and the third-person perception. *Communication Research, 26*(3), 275-302.

Fiske, S. T., & Neuberg, S. L. (1990). A continuum of impression formation, from category-based to individuating processes: Influences of information and motivation on attention and interpretation. *Advances in Experimental Social Psychology, 23*, 1-74.

Frisby, C. M., & Aubrey, J. S. (2012). Race and genre in the use of sexual objectification in female artists' music videos. *Howard Journal of Communications, 23*(1), 66-87.

Gain, C. (2015, March 22). Korea is pulling out all the stops to popularize its cuisine. *Public Radio International (PRI)*. Retrieved from https://www.pri.org/stories/2015-03-22/korea-pulling-out-all-stops-popularize-its-cuisine

George, A. (2019, December 27). These are the 10 most viewed YouTube videos of all time. *Digital Trends*. Retrieved from https://www.digitaltrends.com/web/most-viewed-youtube-videos/

Hogarth, H. K. (2013). The Korean wave: An Asian reaction to Western-dominated globalization. *Perspectives on Global Development and Technology, 12*, 135-151.

Huang, Y., & Wang, B. (2011, August). From the Asian miracle to an Asian century? Economic transformation in the 2000s and prospects for the 2010s. *RBA Annual*

Conference Volume. Reserve Bank of Australia, Australia.

Jin, D. (2016). Global penetration of Korea's smartphones in the social media era. *New Korean wave: Transnational cultural power in the age of social media*, 151-168.

Jin, D. Y., & Ryoo, W. (2014). Critical interpretation of hybrid K-pop: The global-local paradigm of English mixing in lyrics. *Popular Music and Society, 37*, 113-131.

Jung, H. (2017). Transnational media culture and soft power of the Korean wave in the United States. In D. Y. Jin & T.-J. Yoon (Eds.), *The Korean wave: Evolution, fandom, and transnationality*. Washington, DC: Lexington Books, 225-244.

Jung, S. (2011). K-pop, Indonesian fandom, and social media. *Transformative Works & Cultures, 8*. Retrieve from https://journal.transformativeworks.org/index.php/twc/article/view/289/219

King, K. A., Laake, R. A., & Bernard, A. L. (2006). Do the depictions of sexual attire and sexual behavior in music videos differ based on video network and character gender? *American Journal of Health Education, 37(*3), 146-153.

Kinsey, D. F., & Chung, M. (2013). National image of South Korea: Implications for public diplomacy. *The Journal of Public Diplomacy, 4*(1), 5-16.

Kwon, G. Y. (2004). The study of body expression and fashion appeared in music video in Korea and American. *Journal of the Korean Society of Clothing and Textile, 28*, 1231-1242.

Lin, C. A., & Xu, X. (2017). Effectiveness of online consumer reviews: The influence of valence, reviewer ethnicity, social distance and source trustworthiness. *Internet Research, 27*(2), 362-380.

Liu, M. (2017, May). Bigger than Bieber? K-pop group BTS beats US stars to win Billboard Music Award. *CNN Entertainment*. Retrieved from https://edition.cnn.com/2017/05/22/entertainment/k-pop-bts-billboard-music-awards/index.html

Lu, A. S. (2009). What race do they represent and does mine have anything to do with it? Perceived racial categories of anime characters. *Animation: An Interdisciplinary Journal, 4*(2), 169-189.

Park, G. (2013a). Manufacturing creativity: Production, performance, and dissemination of K-pop. *Korea Journal, 53*(4), 14-33.

Park, G. S. (2013b). From fragile cosmopolitanism to sustainable multicultural vigor. *Korea Journal, 53*(4), 5-13.

Perloff, R. M. (1993). Third-person effect research 1983-1992: A review and synthesis. *International Journal of Public Opinion Research, 5*(2), 167-184.

Pew Research Center. (2019, June 12). Mobile fact sheet. Retrieved from https://www.pewresearch.org/internet/fact-sheet/mobile/

Radford, J. (2019, June 17). Key findings about U.S. immigrants. Retrieved from https://www.pewresearch.org/fact-tank/2019/06/17/key-findings-about-u-s-immigrants/

Schaeffer, K. (2019, August 23). Most U.S. teens who use cellphones do it to pass time, connect with others, learn new things. Retrieved from https://www.pewresearch.org/fact-tank/2019/08/23/most-u-s-teens-who-use-cellphones-do-it-to-pass-time-connect-with-others-learn-new-things/

Selfhout, M., Denissen, J., Branje, S., & Meeus, W. (2009). In the eye of the beholder: Perceived, actual, and peer-rated similarity in personality, communication, and friendship intensity during the acquaintanceship process. *Journal of Personality and Social Psychology, 96*(6), 1152-1165.

Stupacher, J., & Wood, G. (2018). Effects of cultural background and musical preference on affective social entrainment with music. *Proceedings of Icmpc15/escom10*, 438-441.

Sun, C., Liberman, R., Butler, A., Lee, S. Y., & Webb, R. (2015). Shifting receptions: Asian American stereotypes and the exploration of comprehensive media literacy. *The Communication Review, 18*(4), 294-314.

Suntikul, W. (2019, March 1). BTS and the global spread of Korean soft power. *The Diplomat.* Retrieved from https://thediplomat.com/2019/03/bts-and-the-global-spread-of-korean-soft-power/

Tajfel, H., & Turner, J. C. (1979). An integrative theory of intergroup conflict. *The Social Psychology of Intergroup Relations, 33*(47), 74-88.

Theden, F. (2019, July 10). The rise of Korean food and ramen in America. Retrieved from https://blog.yelp.com/2019/07/the-rise-of-korean-food-and-ramen-in-america

Trope, Y., Liberman, N., & Wakslak, C. (2007). Construal levels and psychological distance: Effects on representation, prediction, evaluation, and behavior. *Journal of Consumer Psychology, 17*(2), 83-95.

Turner, J. S. (2011). Sex and the spectacle of music videos: An examination of the portrayal of race and sexuality in music videos. *Sex Roles, 64*(3-4), 173-191.

Wallis, C. (2011). Performing gender: A content analysis of gender display in music videos. *Sex Roles, 64*(3-4), 160-172.

Ward, L. M., Hansbrough, E., & Walker, E. (2005). Contributions of music video exposure to black adolescents' gender and sexual schemas. *Journal of Adolescent Research, 20*(2), 143-166.

West, T. V., Magee, J. C., Gordon, S. H., & Gullett, L. (2014). A little similarity goes a long way: The effects of peripheral but self-revealing similarities on improving and sustaining interracial relationships. *Journal of Personality and Social Psychology, 107*(1), 81-100.

Wilkins, C. L., Chan, J. F., & Kaiser, C. R. (2011). Racial stereotypes and interracial attraction: Phenotypic prototypicality and perceived attractiveness of Asians. *Cultural Diversity and Ethnic Minority Psychology, 17*(4), 427.

Wong, Y. J., Owen, J., Tran, K. K., Collins, D. L., & Higgins, C. E. (2012). Asian American male college students' perceptions of people's stereotypes about Asian American men. *Psychology of Men & Masculinity, 13*(1), 75-88.

Wood, M. (2019, March 22). Where is K-pop going in 2019? *Los Angeles Times*. Retrieved from https://www.latimes.com/entertainment/music/la-et-ms-spring-arts-preview-k-pop-bts-blackpink-20190322-story.html

Wu, Y. (2010). *Model minority stereotypes of Asian American women in American media: Perceptions and influences among women of diverse racial-ethnic backgrounds* (Doctoral dissertation). Kansas State University, Kansas.

Zhang, Q. (2010). Asian Americans beyond the model minority stereotype: The nerdy and the left out. *Journal of International and Intercultural Communication, 3*(1), 20-37.

Appendix 1. Coding Instructions

Coding Concept	Definition	Coding Scheme	Notes
Video clip ID	The number given in the music video sample file	Number	Ranges from 1 to 80
Group type	Gender of the singer group	Male Group (0) Female Group (1)	
Storyline	Whether there are story scenes other than simply dancing.	No (0) Yes (1)	It does not have to be a complete story. Presence of dramatic scenes will count as a storyline.
	Cultural Images (male)		
Nerdy	Displays characteristics that are socially inept and unattractive	(1) Not nerdy (2) Somewhat nerdy (3) Nerdy	
Asexual	Displays characteristics that reflect a lack of sex appeal or sexual desire	(1) Not asexual (2) Somewhat asexual (3) Asexual	
Meek	Displays traits that seem easily intimidated and mentally weak	(1) Not meek (2) Somewhat meek (3) Meek	
	Cultural Images (female)		
Dainty	Small, fragile and attractive; delicate, exquisite beauty	(1) Not dainty (2) Somewhat dainty (3) Dainty	
Exotic	Culturally different; not native to American culture, often seen as a sexual object	(1) Not exotic (2) Somewhat exotic (3) Exotic	
Fragile	Naturally delicate; easily broken or destroyed	(1) Not fragile (2) Somewhat fragile (3) Fragile	
	Gender Roles		
Domineering	Display of obvious physical act demonstrating domination and control over another	(1) Not domineering (2) Somewhat domineering (3) Domineering	

Subservient	Displays a demeanor or action that is unconditionally agreeable	(1) Not subservient (2) Somewhat subservient (3) Subservient	
A sex object	Displays characteristics that show the individual as an object of others' sexual desire	(1) Not a sex object (2) Somewhat a sex object (3) A sex object	
Aggressive	Displays a confrontational and assertive demeanor	(1) Not aggressive (2) Somewhat aggressive (3) Aggressive	
Gender Expression			
Boyish	Displays characteristics of a boy such as immature and exuberant qualities	(1) Not boyish (2) Somewhat boyish (3) Boyish	
Girlish	Displays characteristics of a girl such as innocence or childlike qualities	(1) Not girlish (2) Somewhat girlish (3) Girlish	
Masculine	Shows traits that are traditionally associated with men, especially strength and aggressiveness	(1) Not masculine (2) Moderately masculine (3) Overly masculine	
Feminine	Shows traits traditionally associated with women, such as nurturing and gentleness.	(1) Not feminine (2) Moderately feminine (3) Overly feminine	If you think their expression is opposite to feminine, choose (1); If there is nothing opposite to feminine, choose (3); Otherwise, choose (2).
Visual Appeals			
Sexy	Display sexually attractive or alluring traits	(1) Not sexy (2) Moderately sexy (3) Overly sexy	
Cute	Displays attractive traits in a pretty or endearing way	(1) Not cute (2) Moderately cute (3) Overly cute	

Provocative	Displays a demeanor that arouses sexual desire or interest deliberately	(1) Not provocative (2) Moderately provocative (3) Overly provocative	
Boisterous	Displays a demeanor of a lack of self-control or composure	(1) Not wild (2) Somewhat wild (3) Wild	
Fashion Style			Check all that apply to ALL group members
Clothing fit	Degree of fit between clothing and body shape	(1) Loose fit (2) Adequate fit (3) Tight fit	If you have no idea of the singer's body shape at all, choose (1); If you could tell the singer's body shape easily, choose (3).
Midriff exposure	The body part between the chest and the waist; belly	(1) Fully covered (2) Partly covered (3) Mostly exposed	If no skin is exposed or seen, choose (1); If clothing just covers the chest, choose (3).
Chest exposure	The front surface of a body between the neck and the abdomen	(1) Fully covered (2) Partly covered (3) Mostly exposed	For women: If only upper part of the chest is shown, choose (2); If other parts are shown, choose (3). For men: If topless or mostly topless, choose (3).
Upper-leg exposure (Shorts)	The length of shorts	(1) About knee length or longer (2) Above the knee (3) Cover the buttocks	
Upper-leg exposure (Skirt/dress)	The length of skirt or dress	(1) About knee length or longer (2) Above the knee (3) Cover the butt	Only for female groups

CHAPTER 3

Soft Masculinity in K-Pop and Fans in the United States

Hyeri Jung, Eastern University

This study unravels dynamic interactions between South Korean pop music (hereafter, K-pop) and its fans in the U.S. A handful of previous studies (Chua & Iwabuchi, 2008; Jung & Shim, 2014; Kim, 2009; Ryoo, 2009; Shim, 2006; Yang, 2012) looked at how individuals in different countries, primarily in Asia, engage with Korean popular culture, which has become a regional global phenomenon. However, very few investigations have explored it empirically with first-hand accounts in Western contexts, particularly the United States. This is mainly because the reverse cultural flow from the Asian sphere to the Western sphere has been relatively limited, at least until now, which led most Korean Wave[1] scholars to focus only on the analysis of intraregional cultural flows within the Asian/Pacific region. However, the increasing prominence of the Korean Wave, especially K-pop among the young digital generation in the United States, compels scholars to reexamine the phenomenon much further.

This study revisits relevant theoretical concepts and frameworks—soft power and gender representation—of K-pop in order to address the following inquiries: What motivates American fans to interact with K-pop? What are the cross-cultural similarities and differences they see in K-pop versus American pop music? How do they interpret K-pop? What aspects of soft power can be found in their reception of

[1] The term Korean Wave refers to the favorable reception of Korean popular culture outside of Korea.

K-pop? And what cultural, social, and political implications does K-pop yield in the U.S. context? This study employs soft power and gender representation as pieces of a broader theoretical argument. Recognizing their aggregate power can help us better understand the complex webs of K-pop as transnational media culture, albeit provisional. Some of the ways to do so is when we start to take fans' reception of transnational popular culture more seriously and closely interact with them through a trans-local ethnographic approach at the heart of globalization.

This study employs participant observation and qualitative interviews to analyze the rich corpus of data collected over a period of two years to examine the nature of transnational media and fans of K-pop in the U.S. This study does not attempt to provide generalizations about American fans' reception of Korean popular culture. Instead of providing generalizations about American fans' reception of K-pop, this study provides detailed analyses and possible conceptualizations of recurring patterns, a major strength of qualitative media ethnographic research.

Soft Power and K-Pop

The K-pop phenomenon has proven to be more than a pop cultural craze as it penetrates into the world politics and international relations (Chua & Iwabuchi, 2008; Kim, 2015). Soft power is a useful term to describe the K-pop phenomenon in the U.S.. More than a simple persuasion, soft power is the ability to entice, allure and attract others from outside of the country to think of the country favorably (Nye, 2004). Soft power has been challenged for not being a thorough theoretical concept for its illusive features (Brown, 2008; Fan, 2008; Frum & Perle, 2004; Murphy, 2010), and as just another form of imperialism (Schiller 1991). However, this approach oversimplifies the nature of multi-faceted soft power in the context of transnational popular culture.

The way K-pop creates soft power is distinct from the way historically powerful colonizers and imperialists, such as the United States, Britain, France, Germany or Japan, exert their soft power in global/international contexts. Within the Asian sphere, it is true that Japan's strong political, economic, and cultural power has influenced many Asian countries, which traces back to its colonial period.

However, the colonial past prevents Japanese popular culture from deeply penetrating into some parts of Asia (Hong, 2014; Ryoo, 2009). There is a lingering anti-colonial sentiment lurking in the memories of people in many Asian countries. However, K-pop appears to benefit from the sense of solidarity and sympathy more than resentment in which people have toward a country that shared a similar colonial past and continues to struggle in a current postcolonial situation.

For example, Korea's sentiment of *han* (deep sorrow) is seen to be a less problematic source of power and ideological threat than Japanese cultural odor, which may remind of Japanese brutality during the colonial era (Hong, 2014; Iwabuchi, 2002). Whereas the Japanese popular culture industry consciously made it culturally odorless in an effort to universalize products and underplay associations with Japanese imperial history (Iwabuchi, 2002), K-pop emphasizes hybridity of formats with localized content and appeal (Kim, 2009; Ryoo, 2009; Shim, 2006). K-pop and K-drama possess explicit cultural odor in terms of the agents who are associated with the country's bodily, racial and ethnic characteristics. In other words, the people in Korean audiovisual products represent physical features of a country of origin, as well as images of its nation, and these agents with Korean ethnicity physically appeal to international fans.

Geopolitically, other countries that have had a pan-Asian influence have been unpleasant political actors. China and Japan were imperial powers in the past and were perceived as colonialist across Asia (Hong, 2014). Unlike China and Japan, Korea has followed a different path by exerting power through its popular culture, not through coercive military and political hard power. Korea, which Chen (2000) calls a 'sub-Empire' in a globalized world, has a relatively smaller land size with limited natural resources. However, all these limitations and historical contexts work together to exert unique layers of soft power that differs from those of historical imperials. The K-pop craze was not intentionally created by the government for the political purposes as cultures always exist beyond politics. The development and proliferation of social media facilitated the spread of K-pop (Jin & Yoon, 2014), and its polished and aesthetically pleasing audiovisual content has attracted the U.S. fans.

Methods and Informants

There is an online social media site of local groups in Austin, Texas where people sharing similar interests gather together to improve themselves and their local communities. Within this site, there is a *Korean Interest Group* (a pseudonym, hereafter KIG), which is a non-profit and non-governmental organization founded in the 2010s. Most members in this group live in Texas and share a similar interest: Korean popular culture. There are about 400 members registered in KIG as of late 2010s. Among them, about 30 members regularly meet once or twice a week and participate in various activities related to Korean popular culture; learning Korean language, watching K-dramas, discussing and sharing information about Korean popular culture and Korean celebrities, cooking and eating Korean cuisine, attending K-pop concerts, practicing K-pop choreography, etc.

KIG is comprised of people with the U.S. nationality except a couple of native Koreans (including myself), and the group consists of multiple races and ethnicities: Caucasian American, African American, Hispanic American, Asian American and a few others. None of them previously knew each other before joining the group. Among the regular 30 members of the group, females outnumber males approximately by three to one. The ages range from teens to 50s with most participants clustered in the 20s and 30s. Some of them are self-claimed dedicated K-pop and/or K-drama *fans*, while others perceive themselves to be general *audiences* who have genuine interests in Korean popular cultures—such as Korean language, cuisine, films, etc.

Data was collected by close interaction between the author of this study and 9 key informants on a regular basis and conducted in-depth interviews periodically between 2015 and 2017. My 9 key informants are considered a large enough number because that is when recurring patterns emerged during the interview process. Qualitative interview scholars (Spradley, 1979; Weiss, 1994) consistently note that one has enough interviews when one begins to see consistent and recurring patterns. Based on our close rapport, it seemed appropriate to use a friendship model of interviewing (Tracy, 2013) for my interviews in which the interviewer and the interviewee treat each other as intimate friends rather than as objects. This study also employed an ethnographic interview technique, which is more informal, conversational, and

Table 1. Major Informants

Number	Pseudonym	Age	Gender	Nationality	Native Language	Race
1	Angie	Early 30s	Female	USA	English	Caucasian
2	Anya	Late 40s	Female	USA	English	Caucasian
3	Binzy	Late 30s	Female	USA	English	South Asian
4	Greyson	Late 20s	Male	USA	English	Caucasian
5	Iliana	Late 10s	Female	USA	English	South Asian
6	J.C.	Mid 20s	Female	USA	English	Black
7	Leoy	Late 20s	Female	USA	English	Caucasian
8	Miranda	Late 10s	Female	USA	English	Hispanic
9	Rosalie	Late 20s	Female	USA	English	Half-Black, Half-Asian

emergent.

The key informants come from diverse backgrounds, but the following criteria are what they have in common; they were all raised in the United States and lived in Texas for the most part of their lives, are not native Korean, speak English as their first language, and primarily identify themselves as American. My informants voluntarily took part in my research mainly because we had established close rapport with them by regularly attending KIG events and hanging out with them. All of my interactions and participant observations before, during, and after the actual interviews also provide data for this study. Although they have diverse experiential circumstances and histories, they share one common identity: Fans of the Korean popular culture and a stronger desire to build their cultural capital of Korean popular culture than general audiences.

My multiple layers of identities—one in which a native Korean who has lived in the U.S. trying to understand how Americans interact with Korean popular culture—and my participation in the field may have affected the reception and expression of my participants and primary informants. Ethnographers, as an instrument, not only participate in the field, but also in their data as they analyze it, and that is what I did. I moved in and out of my data, which enabled me to provide more than objective and positivist perspectives. I carried a "burden of authorship" (Ang, 1996) throughout all stages of my project. My ethnographic authorship is a form of cultural inscription that reveals the politics of our intellectual work. My ultimate responsibility as an ethnographer is to have an honest and transparent self-reflexivity in my identity and research process and to show sincere respect toward my informants.

Throughout my entire ethnographic journey, I tried to be honest and transparent when interacting with the KIG and my informants. From very early on when I joined KIG, I identified myself as a transnational researcher from a university and an acafan (an academic who is a fan of pop culture) of Korean popular culture. I was sometimes outspoken about my particular research interests in Korean Wave, K-pop, and fandom culture. The complicated webs of cultures are always multidirectional, not unilateral. The more I immersed myself in building relationships with my major informants and the more I built closer rapport with them, I felt that my participant observation is more than an ethnographic observation. But rather, a complete participation in ways that my interaction with them inevitably has affected the formation of their identities and their reception of Korean popular culture and vice versa, and hence, creating a "circuit of cultures" (Hall, 1980).

Gender Representation

Since the early 2010s, the contraflow popularity of K-pop in the U.S.—especially among the digital-native generation fueled by social media—demonstrates its much more hybridized form as 'spreadable media' (Jin & Yoon, 2014). Two of the key questions addressed the cross-cultural similarities and differences U.S. fans see in K-pop versus their pop music, and what motivates them to interact with Korean popular culture. U.S. fans perceive K-pop as similar to their own in terms of both being based on capitalist-driven, industrialized, and economic societies, but different in the cultural plane. There are distinct scents of Korean modernity that motivate these fans to interact with K-pop. One of them is gender representation.

A modern form of K-pop, with its rigorous training system,[2] which

[2] K-pop training system is known for being intensely competitive and rigorous. K-pop entertainment companies hold auditions regularly and select only a few trainees. For

can be traced back to the 1990s, now has its own distinguishable cultural aesthetics and traits that international fans can easily recognize, such as *kkonminam*[3] or soft masculinity (Jung, 2011), K-pop training system, cute culture (or *aegyo*[4]), certain styles of makeup and outfits, just to name a few. One of the theoretical concepts to explicate the transnational popularity and appeal of K-pop has been fluid gender representation: Multiple layers of masculinity among male celebrities (Jung, 2011). Despite a long history of patriarchy in most parts of the world, women and men have produced and maintained feminist movements in their everyday lives (Ang, 1996). One of the recent examples is fans' active and pleasurable reception of the *multi-versatile masculinity* found in K-pop male singers.

K-pop uses skillfully hybridized concepts that reflect various layers of masculinity. When talking about K-pop male groups and their masculinity, mainstream media and casual observers in the West often make mistakes by looking at them as a simple imitation of American male groups, such as the Backstreet Boys and 'N Sync (Anderson, 2014; Caramanica, 2011). They use binary logic to describe K-pop male singers as either cute or tough, pretty or handsome, feminine or masculine, or gay or straight. They often judge K-pop male singers as appearing too feminine and therefore appearing too homosexual, at least by interpretive standards in the U.S. Angie, a fan of Korean audiovisual content, shares her thought in a similar vein. She thinks that watching Korean audiovisual content has helped her break the stereotypes she had toward East Asian men, which were perpetuated by the U.S. mainstream media. In the U.S. mainstream media, the portrayals of non-whites are structured in ways that support its dominant ideological power structure—heterosexual, white, middle-class men (Dyer, 1997; Oh, 2015b).

> Angie: ...I did not tend to find Asian men super attractive...We don't have attractive Asian men in our media, and the ones we do have are

often more than five years, they undergo rigorous training processes in singing, dancing, learning foreign languages, mannerism, etc. Only 20-30 out of 1,000 trainees ever get to debut (Lie, 2012), and only a couple of groups out of the 20-30 become popular.

[3] *Kkonminam* refers to males who are flower-like pretty.

[4] *Aegyo* refers to cute and baby-like behaviors.

> typically nerdy and thin like a smart tech guy. I think that in American culture, it's structured in such a way that it benefits white men. White men can make Asian men not as attractive by being like 'Oh they are so feminine,' and that bears out in our media.

K-pop male singers do not manifest binary either/or masculinity, but a range of fluid multi-versatile masculinity that occurs simultaneously (Anderson, 2014; Jung, 2011; Oh, 2014, 2015a, 2015b). This fluid, versatile masculinity reflects not only feminine masculinity, but also cute masculinity, pretty masculinity, boyfriend-like masculinity, or *oppa*[5]-like masculinity. This strategically and skillfully hybridized multi-versatile masculinity can be seen in the K-pop male singers' musical production, choreography, music videos, fashion, makeup, photo shoots, ways of talking and acting, interactions with other male singers, or off-stage portrayals.

This multi-versatile masculinity of K-pop male singers is simultaneously hybrid, fluid, and transnational. The multi-versatile masculinity represents an important aspect of the popularity of K-pop as the U.S. fans identify it as part of the appeal of K-pop. Fans are attracted to and find pleasure in the multi-versatile ways K-pop male singers portray their masculinity; some focus on their talent and politeness while others focus on pretty or tough images of masculinity portrayed throughout their music, choreography, fashion, and behavior. Others link K-pop's masculinity to their exceptionally beautiful *kkonminam* images. Miranda in late 10s and Binzy in late 30s, both K-pop enthusiasts, shared their thoughts:

> Miranda: K-pop male idols wear makeup, and they always look like the most beautiful people in the world.

> Binzy: They [K-pop male idols] look so good. So much is going on with the makeup and hair, and I just love that. I didn't feel like they were too feminine.

Another recurring pattern found in the data is the notion of cute

---

[5] *Oppa* is a respectful Korean word used by females to call older males.

culture, also known as *aegyo*. Cuteness, as an appeal, invites others to engage in social behaviors including companionship, cooperative action, and communication (Dale, 2016). It can also turn into a decentered form of soft power (Botz-Bornstein, 2016). In the East Asian region, cute culture has an overarching mainstream presence far more than in other regions of the world. The cute culture in Korea is much more mainstream and widely embedded in various facets of media and society than in the U.S.. Greyson, a white male K-pop fan in his late 20s, shared his thoughts:

> Greyson: It [cute culture such as *aegyo* is very much part of the [Korean] culture that you don't even think about it. In Korean people, there's natural *aegyo*.

K-pop uses skillfully hybridized concepts that reflect various layers of masculinity. What distinctively differentiates in K-pop male singers from Western pop artists is that, unlike Western male musicians, men are not hesitant to dress up, do *aegyo*, or dance in extremely "feminine" and gender-bending ways while being extremely humble and modest. The favorable reception of *Kkonminam* (flower boy) masculinity of K-pop male singers in the U.S. is particularly interesting for its social consequences in the Western sphere. Interestingly though, it was not the Western societies, but East Asian societies that first commodified multiple masculinity, including soft masculinity, not just as a subculture but as part of the popular mainstream. Leoy, a white K-pop enthusiast in her late 20s, shared her thoughts on gender representation:

> Leoy: [More fluid gender representation in K-pop is what] I really appreciate about in Korean pop culture that's different from American pop. You take any American male group, they will not participate in half of the stuff the male group in Korea would do [such as] the *aegyo*, all of the Korean male pop groups that dress up in girl group outfits in performances like that. There are so few American artists I can think of doing that or it would be less tastefully done. In Korea, it's done because they know it makes the fans happy and they are just having a good time. In America, I feel like if somebody in pop culture, who is a male dressed up like a girl, it would be more teasing. It'd seem like they're making fun of females.

According to Jung (2010), the *kkonminam* phenomenon is a realization and renegotiated transcultural identity among diverse audiences as a communicative process.

The notion of soft masculinity is less prevalent and welcomed in the United States perhaps because of the U.S. heterosexual males' fear of their constructed ideal masculinity being emasculated by such alternatives or because of the different perceptions the U.S. society in general has toward cute culture (Dale, 2016). Multi-versatile masculinity well aligns with the reality of today's era passing from information age toward "a dream society of icons and aesthetic experience" (Dator & Seo, 2004). In this emerging era, hypermasculinity faces a considerable lack of legitimacy as delicate, sophisticated, and fluid soft masculinity increasingly gains prominence in everyday life. Therefore, many—mostly females—fans' fanatical craze for K-pop male singers is not something about which men should feel threatened or emasculated; rather, they should feel welcomed. What is disappearing is not masculinity per se but hypermasculinity as the only ideal masculinity. I see soft masculinity as liberating men rather than threatening or emasculating them. Greyson, a white male K-pop fan in his late 20s and J.C., a black female K-pop fan in her mid-20s, shared their thoughts:

> Greyson: There is something that I very much hate about American culture and it is the 'I have to be hypermasculine' thing. I feel like that's [men wearing makeup, dressing up, doing *aegyo*] very much more acceptable in Asian culture in general. I think it's great... So we, we meaning Western men, have had it beaten to our heads since birth that you have to be this stone booth of statue of no emotion. If you show an emotion, you are weak and saying stuff like 'Don't be like a girl.' Showing any sort of vulnerability is seen as weak. I've had a depression issue for a long time. It's a part of my personality. I was self-medicating watching K-dramas because a lot of it was an identity issue revolving around Western—you have to be a robot—type, you can't feel things as a man.

> J.C.: [Men crying] is not off putting at all because it shows there is emotion. That's definitely American thing—hypermasculinity, not showing emotions.

A distinctive difference between K-pop male singers and Western pop singers is that, unlike Western male musicians, men are not hesitant to dress up, do *aegyo*, dance in extremely *feminine* and gender-bending ways, and cry. Anya, a white K-pop enthusiast and music lover in her late 40s and a mother of two children, shared her thoughts:

> Anya: I think they [Korea media] allow both men and women to be more vulnerable in different ways... The men don't have to be macho masculine.

The soft masculinity has developed not because males have become feminized, but as a consequence of the deconstruction and the hybridization of female/male sexual identities (Kim, 2013). Female K-pop fans find ways to express, define, and enjoy their desire for their own measures of masculinity through K-pop male singers. Although soft masculinity is a context-bound perception and is only a partial picture of the whole ecology of transnational K-pop phenomenon, it nevertheless provides women an alternative and fluid way to choose what ideal masculinity means to them. J.C. and Binzy, both K-pop fans, shared their thoughts:

> J.C.: They look softer than the men we have here. Soft masculinity [the term I once used and explained to J.C.] was something you [referring to me] were exposed at an early age. But now that I've been into K-pop, I expand the idea of what attractiveness can be. I think now my idea of ideal masculinity has changed because before I'd have said 'tall dude, muscles, being huge and bulky.' But now it's changed. Now I think I don't have a single ideal masculinity. It can be fluid.

> Binzy: The way I talked about humbleness. That kind of act [soft behavior, not about the physique] would be interpreted as 'man up!'

The economic power of single women in their twenties and thirties who demonstrate a high propensity to consume entertainment and cultural products has drastically increased in some parts of the world since the late 1990s. Soft masculinity in K-pop male singers closely relates to the changing reality of a capitalist society as women are gaining more economic, social, political, and cultural power.

Soft masculinity in K-pop represents how capitalism can work with feminism, and how capitalism works through feminization of mass culture by taking women's pleasure of fantasy seriously. Fantasy is created within reality and reflected on reality. The U.S. fans' favorable reception of multi-versatile masculinity embodied by K-pop male performers is an actualization of one of the multifaceted political pleasures of women (and men to some extent). The ethnographic data I collected and analyzed for more than two years provides a pattern. I frequently noticed that the K-pop fans in the U.S. find pleasure in their interpretation and reception of K-pop male singers' fluid masculinity. Some members of KIG—mostly my major informants—and I would frequently ask one another which K-pop singers we find attractive, handsome, or pretty. We would compare and contrast our beauty standards and talk about our perceptions. Seen in this vein, "the politics of pleasure"—a main theme that started with romance reading and soap opera reception in the West (Ang, 1985; Radway, 1984)—provides another twist to the hegemonic notion of masculinity in the context of the US fans' reception of K-pop male singers and their multi-versatile masculinity.

Conclusion

According to Appadurai (1996), the collective experience of popular media culture creates solidarities of cultural taste among audiences from different countries and enables them to participate in a shared imagination regardless of nation-states. The transnational traits of multi-versatile masculinity embedded in K-pop male singers enable their images as media texts to easily travel beyond national boundaries, especially via social media. The notion of soft masculinity is becoming more global as international audiences familiarize themselves with it. The pan-East Asian identity of *kkonminam* has crossed national borders not only because they are aesthetically pleasing enough to attract international audiences, but also because its media text is increasingly and easily spreadable in the global "social mediascape" (Jenkins, Ford, & Green, 2013; Jin & Yoon, 2014).

Jung's (2011) theoretical concept of soft masculinity as a cultural form has gone beyond the transnational and has started to become a semi-global identity. There is less and less cultural discount found in K-pop as its characteristic of soft masculinity is becoming more transnational and global. The transcultural identity of *kkonminam* has been referred to as the pan-East Asian identity (Miller, 2006) for its popularity among non-Korean-Asian audiences. However, this unique transnational image of K-pop in East Asia are becoming more and more recognized beyond Asia. The *kkonminam* image of K-pop as a spreadable media text has clearly influenced the contemporary constructions of an ideal masculinity in East Asia and is starting to influence the West (Jung, 2010; 2011). The global K-pop phenomenon shows that global fans recognize, accept, and enjoy different images of masculinity exhibited by K-pop male singers. Women deconstruct the dominant hegemony of masculinity and defy what ideal masculinity—which was set by heterosexual white male power in patriarchal society—should be. Those who are tired of hypermasculinity prevalent in American pop culture get to decide and reconstruct what ideal masculinity means on their own terms, for example, by considering *kkonminam* or soft masculinity as another attractive masculinity instead of perceiving Asian men as too *feminine* to be sexually attractive.

The distinct scents of Korean modernity—cute culture and fluid gender representation—are some of the major motivations for the U.S. fans to interact with K-pop. One of the purposes for studying the reception of K-pop among fans in the U.S. is not to impose the idea of the great soft power of Korean-ness as a neo-colonial global cultural power, but to reexamine globalization that recognizes the dynamic formations of identity and hybridity at the local level while not dismissing the power hierarchy in international settings.

The spread of and exposure to foreign popular culture does not guarantee its popularity overseas. The transnational reception of popular culture is neither fully controllable nor predictable by media producers and policymakers because media texts are never self-sufficient structures of meanings themselves. In the midst of the K-pop phenomenon in the U.S., there are the often-neglected participatory fans as legions of craftspeople who enthusiastically and willingly consume, interpret, share, and reproduce the culture of the "Other," actualizing the Korean Wave.

Recommended Readings

Jin, D., & Yoon, T. (2017). *The Korean wave: Evolution, fandom, and transnationality*. Lanham, MD: Lexington Books.

Jung, H. (2018). Reversed ethnography in the reception of the Korean wave. *International Journal of Korean Studies, XXII*(2), 47-74.

Jung, S. (2011). *Korean masculinities and transcultural consumption: Yonsama, Rain, Oldboy and K-pop idols*. Hong Kong, China: Hong Kong University Press.

Kim, Y. (2013). *The Korean wave: Korean media go global*. London, UK: Routledge.

Korean pop. In Y. Kuwahara (Ed.), *The Korean wave: Korean popular culture in global context* (pp. 53-81). New York, NY: Palgrave Macmillan.

Oh, C. (2014). The politics of the dancing body: Racialized and gendered femininity in Korean pop. In Y. Kuwahara (Ed.), *The Korean wave: Korean popular culture in global context* (pp. 53-81). New York, NY: Palgrave Macmillan.

Additional Sources

Big Hit Labels. (2016, October 9). *BTS 'Blood Sweat & Tears' Official MV* [Video]. Youtube. https://www.youtube.com/watch?v=hmE9f-TEutc

Fantagio. (2016, February 22). *ASTRO-HIDE&SEEK M/V* [Video]. YouTube. https://www.youtube.com/watch?v=KEgSjGQEZnM

SMTOWN. (2013, July 31). *EXO 'GROWL' MV (Korean Ver.)* [Video]. YouTube. https://www.youtube.com/watch?v=I3dezFzsNss

References

Anderson, C. (2014). That's my man! Overlapping masculinities in Korean popular music. In Y. Kuwahara (Ed.), *The Korean wave: Korean popular culture in global context* (pp. 117-131). New York, NY: Palgrave Macmillan.

Ang, I. (1985). *Watching Dallas: Soap opera and the melodramatic imagination*. New York, NY: Methuen & Co.

Ang, I. (1996). *Living room wars: Rethinking audiences for a postmodern world*. New York, NY: Routledge.

Appadurai, A. (1996). *Modernity at large: Cultural dimensions of globalization*. Minneapolis, MN: University of Minnesota Press.

Botz-Bornstein, T. (2016). Kawaii, kenosis, Verwindung: A reading of kawaii through Vattimo's philosophy of 'weak thought.' *East Asian Journal of Popular Culture, 2*(1), 111-123.

Brown, J. (2008, January 30). Donald Rumsfeld's soft side. *The Guardian*. Retrieved from http://www.theguardian.com/commentisfree/2008/jan/30/rummyresurfacesannounced

Caramanica, J. (2011, October 24). Korean pop machine, running on innocence and hair gel. *The New York Times*. Retrieved from https://www.nytimes.com/2011/10/25/arts/music/shinee-and-south-korean-k-pop-groups-at-madison-square-garden-review.html

Chen, K. (2000). The imperialist eye. *Positions, 8*(1), 9-76.

Chua, B., & Iwabuchi, K. (2008). *East Asian pop culture: Analysing the Korean wave*. Hong Kong, China: Hong Kong University Press.

Dale, J. (2016). Cute studies: An emerging field. *East Asian Journal of Popular Culture, 2*(1), 5-13.

Dator, J., & Seo, Y. (2004). Korea as the wave of a future: The emerging dream society of icon and aesthetic experience. *Journal of Future Studies, 9*(1), 31-44.

Dyer, R. (1997). *White*. London, UK: Routledge.

Fan, Y. (2008). Soft power: Power of attraction or confusion? *Place Branding and Public Diplomacy, 4*(2), 147-158.

Frum, D., & Perle, R. (2004). *An end to evil: How to win the war on terror*. New York, NY: Ballantine Books.

Hall, S. (1980). Encoding/Decoding. In S. Hall, D. Hobson, A. Lowe, & P. Willis (Eds.), *Culture, media, language* (pp. 128-138). London, UK: Hutchinson.

Hong, E. (2014). *The birth of Korean cool: How one nation is conquering the world through pop culture*. New York, NY: Picador.

Iwabuchi, K. (2002). *Recentering globalization: Popular culture and Japanese transnationalism*. Durham, NC: Duke University Press.

Jenkins, H., Ford, S., & Green, J. (2013). *Spreadable media: Creating value and meaning in a networked culture*. New York, NY: New York University Press.

Jin, D., & Yoon, K. (2014). The social mediascape of transnational Korean pop culture: Hallyu 2.0 as spreadable media practice. *New Media & Society*, 1-16.

Jung, S. (2010). Chogukjeok pan-East Asian soft masculinity: Reading Boys Over Flowers, Coffee Prince and Shinhwa fan fiction. In D. Black, S. Epstein, & A. Tokita (Eds.), *Complicated currents: Media flows, soft power and East Asia* (pp. 08.1-08.16). Melbourne, Australia: Monash University ePress.

Jung, S. (2011). *Korean masculinities and transcultural consumption: Yonsama, Rain, Oldboy and K-pop idols*. Hong Kong, China: Hong Kong University Press.

Jung, S., & Shim, D. (2014). Social distribution: K-pop fan practices in Indonesia and the 'Gangnam Style' phenomenon. *International Journal of Cultural Studies, 17*(5), 485-501.

Kim, J. (2015). Despite not being Johnny's: The cultural impact of TVXQ in the Japanese music industry. In J. Choi & R. Maliangkay (Eds.), *K-pop: The international rise of the Korean music industry* (pp. 66-80). New York, NY: Routledge.

Kim, S. (2009). Interpreting transnational cultural practices. *Cultural Studies, 23*(5-6), 736-755.

Kim, Y. (2013). *The Korean wave: Korean media go global*. London, UK: Routledge.

Lie, J. (2012). What is the K in K-pop? South Korean popular music, the culture industry, and national identity. *Korea Observer, 43*(3), 339-363.

Miller, L. (2006). *Beauty up: Exploring contemporary Japanese body aesthetics*. Berkeley, CA: University of California Press.

Murphy, P. (2010). The limits of soft power. In D. Black, S. Epstein, & A. Tokita (Eds.), *Complicated currents–media flows, soft power and East Asia* (15.1-15.14). Sydney, Australia: Monash University ePress.

Nye, J. (2004). *Soft power: The means to success in world politics*. New York, NY: Public Affairs.

Oh, C. (2014). The politics of the dancing body: Racialized and gendered femininity in Korean pop. In Y. Kuwahara (Ed.), *The Korean wave: Korean popular culture in global context* (pp. 53-81). New York, NY: Palgrave Macmillan.

Oh, C. (2015a). Queering spectatorship in K-pop: The androgynous male dancing body and western female fandom. *Journal of Fandom Studies, 3*(1), 59-78.

Oh, C. (2015b). K-popscape: *Gender fluidity and racial hybridity in transnational Korean pop dance* (Doctoral dissertation). Retrieved from University of Texas Electronic Theses and Dissertations.

Radway, J. (1984). *Reading the romance: Women, patriarchy, and popular literature.*

Chapel Hill, NC: University of North Carolina Press.

Ryoo, W. (2009). Globalization, or the logic of cultural hybridization: The case of the Korean wave. *Asian Journal of Communication, 19*(2), 137-151.

Schiller, H. (1991). Not yet the post-imperialist era. *Critical Studies in Media Communication, 8*(1), 13-28.

Shim, D. (2006). Hybridity and the rise of Korean popular culture in Asia. *Media, Culture & Society, 28*(1), 25-44.

Spradley, J. (1979). *The ethnographic interview*. Belmont, CA: Wadsworth.

Tracy, S. (2013). *Qualitative research methods*. Hoboken, NJ: Wiley-Blackwell.

Weiss, R. (1994). *Learning from strangers: The art and method of qualitative interview studies*. New York, NY: The Free Press.

Yang, J. (2012). The Korean wave (Hallyu) in East Asia: A comparison of Chinese, Japanese, and Taiwanese audiences who watch Korean TV dramas. *Development and Society, 41*(1), 103-147.

CHAPTER 4

Neo Culture Technology: Affective Fandom and K-Pop in America

Samantha James, University of Texas-Austin

I realized I was a K-pop superfan while watching "Regular" by NCT 127 for the first time in October 2018. The day the music video was released in English, I woke before my alarm, purposefully set to give me a few precious minutes before the video was posted on YouTube. The ten-member boy group dropped teaser videos and preview photos beforehand that I poured over in anticipation for the release of their first album, *Regular-Irregular*. I could list every member's full Korean name in age order and kept a picture of the group's leader and my favorite K-pop idol, Lee Taeyong, as my phone background. In the weeks leading up to the release of "Regular," and subsequently NCT 127's first full-length album, I read fan theory threads on Instagram about hidden meanings behind the concept for the album and was tagged in Tweets about "streaming goals" where my internet friends and fellow superfans decided how many views we wanted to help the boys reach during the first 24-hours following their music video release. As I anxiously awaited my first comeback, the series of promotional events surrounding the release of a new K-pop album, I knew I was not alone. Fans in the West have been learning the ins and outs of K-pop fandom membership for years and have developed our own rules for being a "good" fan of an art form traditionally underrepresented in Western markets. This chapter looks at the interplay of culture, media, and affect as it plays out in K-pop fandom in the United States.

Korean Pop Music (K-pop) has achieved unprecedented levels of commercial success across the globe (Herman, 2018a), but one of the more surprising aspects of K-pop's ascendance has been its substantial success in Western music markets that have historically shown broad disinterest in Asian music. Groups such as BTS rival even The Beatles on Billboard charts (Caulfield, 2019), and a rapidly expanding fan base is "elevating K-pop from a niche import to a full-blown international movement" (Willingham, 2019). One group that closely represents the K-pop musical genre and cultural movement is Neo Culture Technology, or NCT. Under the label of SM Entertainment, one of the biggest entertainment agencies in Korea ("Top 20 K-pop," 2020) and the company to coin the K-pop production method known as "Culture Technology," NCT as a performance group is pointedly global, with members representing multiple countries, including the U.S. and Canada, and schedules placing a large emphasis on Western markets (Lee, 2016). NCT 127, a subunit of the larger boy group NCT, recently signed with Capitol Records in the U.S. and released a series of songs in English before concluding their two-month-long North American tour (Herman, 2019b). The first of these songs was the title track of their premier full-length album, "Regular." Released in English on October 8th, 2018 alongside an accompanying music video, the Korean version of the song and video were both released three days later, quickly followed by the album (Herman, 2018b). "Regular" flooded global markets, reaching #2 on Billboard's World Albums chart, #16 on Billboard's K-pop 100, and #86 on the Billboard Top 200 chart. The popularity of "Regular" presents an excellent case study for exploring how NCT 127, and K-pop more broadly, have achieved such visibility and influence in Western markets.

To provide context for the resonance of K-pop in America, I first describe how fan communities are created by content creators via affective responses. Then, I discuss the actions taken by fans themselves to create and maintain fandom culture in a digitally mediated world. Finally, I use autoethnography to explain how I fell in love with the art form and use my experience to theorize how K-pop offers Western audiences a vehicle for escapism from our everyday realities.

Affective Fandom

Fans are created through affective connections to objects, groups, or ideas. Fraade-Blanar & Glazer (2017) outline a formula for building an emotional connection as a marketing strategy, stating: "A successful fandom = critical mass + emotional response + platform" (p. 61). The emotional connection marketers desire from a fanbase is actually the embodiment of affect. Affect is the physiological tug that individuals feel surrounding an item, person, organization, idea, performance, team, or any other form of media that leads to conscious and subconscious reaction. Stewart (2007) writes, "affects are not so much forms of significations, or units of knowledge, as they are expressions of ideas or problems performed as a kind of involuntary and powerful learning and participation" (p. 40). Affect corporeally influences one's reactions, positive or negative, which in turn shape ideas, emotions, or connections (Berlant, 2010). When affective elements are shared between individuals, they can energize community formation and galvanize participation in shared activities toward ideological goals (Cisneros, 2015). Fan communities—created by media companies then poached by content consumers—work together to support a cultural product as a result of the energy that tugs them together.

Consumer products such as merchandise or albums are symbols that remind the fan of the first time they interacted with the content (Fraade-Blanar & Glazer, 2017). Content creators build products that resonate with their audience to the point of dedicating some part of themselves to that product, cultivating a level of "stickiness" (Ahmed, 2004) around a symbol that circulates enough to create affect. Fans take it a step further, building communities where affective energy flows that do more than provide economic support. K-pop is an intensification of the phenomenon of community building based on cultural symbols and products. Lee Gyu-Tag said in an interview for *Explained: K-pop* on Netflix that, "In terms of how agencies create the music, K-pop is more product than art. But the fans don't consume it like merely as a product, like a car or a laptop. Rather they're interpreting and finding their own ways of enjoying it" (Posner, 2018). Instead of passively consuming the content, K-pop fans organize into fandoms that take actions such as "streaming parties," to get artists' albums or music videos onto music charts, or crowd-raising funds to buy advertising in

Times Square for their favorite idol's birthday (Herman, 2019b). In a Western context, K-pop fans are compared in levels of fanaticism to the likes of the British Invasion and the popularity of bands like The Beatles (Willingham, 2019). The guttural, embodied, affective connection fans feel with certain artists or groups is what drives their organization into communities of practice with shared rules, expectations, and goals.

Fandom Culture

A fandom is a collection of all of the fans of a certain object of affection ("Fandom," n.d.). Fandoms are a means of organizing ideas, gathering people, and sharing vulnerabilities around love of a certain content form. In many cases, these super collectives are based not solely on the object of their affection, but the relationship built between fans of the same content. There are expectations and self-imposed norms that stitch together fan communities, conversations about what it means to be a "good" fan echoing larger gatekeeping practices in participatory cultures. Gray, Sandvoss, and Harrington (2017) describe the multilevel fascination within fan studies as a way to "help us understand and meet challenges beyond the realm of popular culture because they tell us something about how we relate to ourselves, to each other, and to how we read the mediated texts around us" (p. 7). K-pop fandoms, like other fan organizations, call for active participation and dedication from fans that identify with the group.

For fans of cultural products, such as K-pop, the rules built into fan communities draw upon Bourdieu's (1977, 1986) concept of "cultural capital." "Cultural capital" is made up of normative symbols passed on through generations by those in power that become the standard for recognizing and delineating social hierarchy. The pervasion of these cultural symbols usually occurs in three states: the *embodied* state, as verbal or nonverbal physical cues; the *objectified* state, in cultural products such as art, literature, and technology; and the *institutionalized* state, as seen in formal qualification measures (Bourdieu, 1977). Many American K-pop fan communities want the social capital that aligns with musical success in Western markets. Fans organize to film public flash mobs showing the music's international popularity, engaging in the embodied state. Some fans build large social media followings by creating "collection accounts," the maintenance of which requires them to own every piece of merchandise related to their favorite group or idol, to secure objectified "cultural capital". Fandom leaders devise mass strategies to make sure the "right" song or album wins on music charts in Korea and in the West, attempting earn "cultural capital" at an institutional level. Bourdieu (1986) claims that both dominant groups and non-dominant groups seek "cultural capital" to maintain power and raise their social or monetary status. From the perspective of an American K-pop fan, every Korean artist is in a non-dominant group, since they were not created by the American pop industry in which they now rank ("These 10 Nations," 2019).

Scholars challenge Bourdieu's (1977, 1896) claims that all social groups constantly strive for that which has been defined by the culturally dominant groups. Lo (2015) argues instead that nondominant cultures have their own forms of "unrecognized cultural currency" that better explain the practices valued by underrepresented groups. Traditionally found in racial and/or gender minorities in specific social spaces, this concept better explains the efforts made by Western fans, who make up the minority of the K-pop fandom, interacting to create a social space of our own. Fans in the U.S. have our own form of influencers, who create individual sub-fandoms in specific cities or states in the country. Organizing around K-pop in America includes a different set of norms and expectations; it is a mix of those used by Korean fans and inside jokes or references specific to our Western K-pop fan experiences ("K-pop 101," 2018). American fans participate in fandom, critique one another, and act as a community online through mediated technologies.

Technology and Intercultural Fandom

Digital forms of media and technology change the way fans interact. While the invention of sites like YouTube and Spotify initially popularized K-pop in the United States (Posner, 2018), the art form permeated further into mainstream American culture in recent years. K-pop groups now walk the red carpet at the American Music Awards and the GRAMMYs (Nickolai, 2019), their songs are suggested by Spotify and Apple Music streaming algorithms, and their members appear in video interviews with Forbes, Billboard, Rolling Stone, and Elle Magazine (Benjamin, 2018). The way young American fans engage with K-pop becomes closer in outlet- and content-style to their experience with contemporary Western pop as a genre. Media outlets are relentless, making it harder for even those who chose to avoid K-pop to ignore the genre's ubiquity.

For Westerners who already identify as K-pop fans, the accessibility and permeation of media technologies heightens every aspect of the culture and experience. Traditionally, content creators tightly controlled what their audience saw, heard, and discussed (Jenkins, 2013). However, contemporary media organizations offer new forms of interaction. Slade, Narro, and Givens-Carroll (2015) explain the distinction between "old" fan-creator interactions and new ones, stating "while today's television creator is no longer the omniscient media gatekeeper, they now have the opportunity to be something even more valuable-omniscient communicator" (p. 4). Fans can directly communicate with the people and stories they feel a physiological draw to, both positive and negative. Idols have personal Instagram accounts the artists use to interact with majority Western audiences (Tamondong, 2020) and go on Twitter takeovers, responding to fan questions from around the world. The immediacy of social media strengthens the affective connection between artists and audiences; this provides the groundwork for parasocial relationships. These parasocial relationships (Yates, 2015) are often the underpinning of a modern fan-artist relationship, and as media companies guide the affective quality of the contents and communities they capitalize on that connection. However, the emotional pull toward an idol or group does not stop at the individual fan's relationship with the artist; it often culminates into social communities related to them, especially in a digitally mediated age (Yates, 2015). With technology at the forefront, not only are parasocial relationships heightened at the individual level, but communities organize with parasocialism as their guiding principle. As Gray, Sandvoss, and Harrington (2017) state, "today, following continued technological, social, and cultural changes, fandom is an even more commonplace experience" (p. 1). Fandoms stand at the precipice of pop culture, and K-pop fandoms in the West are more prevalent than ever before.

Autoethnography as a Method

In order to understand why K-pop is growing in popularity across Western audiences, I utilize autoethnography to explore my own journey as an American fan of the art form. Autoethnography is an individual's narrative situated within culture (Adams, Jones, & Ellis, 2015) and provides perspective for the permeation of K-pop into Western culture from the ground up. According to Boylorn (2008), "Autoethnographers look in (at themselves) and out (at the world) connecting the personal to the cultural," (p. 413). Autoethnographic research includes a mix of "aha" moments with mundane "aesthetic moments" (Adams, Jones, & Ellis, 2015) that allow for a deeply reflective look at everyday life. In order to situate my identity as an American fan within the larger conversation surrounding K-pop's success, I provide an in-depth retelling of my experience becoming a superfan.

I use individual narrative as a lens to understand many of the theoretical components of this chapter. Affect is an inherently embodied concept (Ashcraft, 2020) and the cultural experience of fandom is dependent on the identity of the fan in question. Cultures are as fragmented as identities. McGee (1990) emphasized the value different fragments of cultural context bring to a rhetorical text. According to McGee (1990), "the unity and structural integrity we used to put in our texts as they faithfully represented nature is now presumed to be in *us ourselves*" (p. 287). We provide and embody the context for the content we wish to understand. As aca-fans, those who identify as both academics and superfans, we cannot expect consumers of any form of content to do so within a vacuum. Context is important for understanding cultural phenomena, especially music (Matula, 2000). This chapter provides context and an in-depth analysis of the fragments that make up my personal experience in K-pop fandom in order to answer a larger question: Why do Americans love K-pop? I do not intend to speak for all American fans of K-pop; rather, I use my experiences and accompanying questions, emotions, and reactions to theorize the genre's success in a Western context.

Self-reflexivity is vital in order to situate individual experiences as both partial and illustrative of this cultural phenomenon. Jenkins (2013) was the first scholar of Fan Studies to "out" himself as an aca-fan in response to not just the stigma surrounding fandom as an area of research, but the unique experiences each fan has in their relationship to the content they love. My experience as fan-turned-researcher proceeds following Jenkins' (2013) model to include the cultural fragmentation of experience the listener and fan brings to each piece of the text. This chapter emphasizes the human embodiment of fandom in an intercultural context. I begin with my introduction to K-pop as an art form and my transition from a passive observer to an active fan. Then I recount my journey to becoming a superfan of NCT and the escapism from reality which K-pop provided. Finally, I explore how affect and community influenced my first comeback with the release of "Regular."

Embodied Fandom: Autoethnographic Exploration

My first encounter with K-pop came as a surprise. I sat in my best friend's beat up red Honda Civic in fall 2017, deciding where we should go for ice cream and listening to her complain about a recent break-up, when she insisted on showing me a video from YouTube.

"My ex hated that I watch this stuff," she said, "I think you'll like it."

We watched BTS's *DNA* music video as she emphatically pointed out each member and cooed over how talented they are as dancers, rappers, and overall performers. I felt overwhelmed by the saturated color scheme in the video and the up-tempo EDM beat. While I recognized the high production quality of the video and the obvious talent of the group, I did not quite understand her excitement. What made K-pop any different from the music videos released by artists like Ariana Grande and Bruno Mars, other than the language?

Over the next few weeks, text messages from my friend venting about the breakup were interspersed with videos of stunning men and women performing on stage, practicing their intricate dances, or joking around on Korean talk shows I relied on subtitles to understand. I began noticing K-pop artifacts in other facets of my everyday life. Pictures of idols occupied my Instagram Explore page, K-pop memes appeared on my Twitter feed, my Spotify algorithm suggested songs from the "K-pop Daebak" playlist and groups like BTS guest-starred on *Jimmy Kimmel*

Live! and *The Late Late Show with James Corden* (Benjamin, 2018). The cultural phenomenon that permeated into Western pop culture more and more throughout recent years (Wang, 2018) and finally reached a young white woman living in the American Deep South. I began to feel a familiar tug of pride when I recognized the faces of idols on U.S. talk shows and could name the K-pop songs that played on satellite radio stations. I started actively seeking out information about different artists, the egotistic notion that I could learn everything about K-pop "before it was cool" driving my research.

Around that time, I went through my first real breakup as well, and was longing for a distraction from my guilt. K-pop as an art form felt like the perfect escape, an all-encompassing media outlet that required research, dedication, and large amounts of time spent watching beautiful people perform for an increasingly global audience. I followed social media accounts dedicated to specific idols or groups and learned how to be a "good fan," memorizing some Korean slang as well as terms unique to the English-speaking K-pop fan community. I learned the distinction between a "bias," used to describe my favorite member of a specific group, and an "ult," or ultimate bias, who was my favorite K-pop idol in the industry as a whole. I tested myself on the members of each of the major groups and completed countless Buzzfeed quizzes to tell me who my bias was in each one. Following the actions of other American fans via their posts on social media sites, I practiced passive fandom. I lurked on Twitter and Instagram to see what ideas were trending in K-pop and kept up with popular releases on Spotify and YouTube, but still did not consider myself any more a fan of K-pop than I was of other popular genres of music.

In early 2018, however, I stumbled upon a video released in 2016 by Lee Soo-Man (2016), director and owner of the third largest production company in Korea ("Top 20 K-pop," 2020). The scene in the video was similar to that of a product launch by a major technology company: Lee walking across a stage, explaining concepts while a special-effects-laden presentation flashed on the giant screen behind him. The director used this platform to introduce the idea of "New Culture Technology," an extension of his previous method of artist recruitment and media production that emphasized a worldwide audience. One deliverable of this concept was a brand-new boy group, NCT, named after the idea and intentionally comprised of members from countries like Canada, China, Japan, Thailand, and the United States to fulfill the group's stated goal of reaching from "N-City to the world" (Melendez, 2017)! NCT 127, a sub-unit of the new group, was named for the longitude of Seoul, South Korea, and was specifically intended to target Western audiences.

I finally felt like I had an explanation for the way K-pop had become such a large source of joy in my life. The marketing plan introduced by Lee (2016) was designed to reach me in a way that felt natural. I was fascinated by the transparency of it all, the openness with which Lee (2016) explained his methods. While I spent years listening to rumors of American pop stars being trained to act like robots instead of people, Lee (2016) announced idol recruitment and training methods as his modus operandi in plain language. K-pop as a phenomenon was close enough to what I was used to from Western pop to be accessible, yet different enough that becoming a fan required dedication and effort.

Watching this video was a turning point in my fan experience. I became obsessed with NCT specifically, watching all of their music videos and learning the intricacies of the group. NCT debuted in 2016 with six members and has expanded since then to a whopping 21 members by early 2020. The eldest member, Moon Taeil, was born in 1994, and the youngest, Park Jisung, was born in 2002. Their music videos always have a specific concept and their music style is characterized by mixing forms and genres (Melendez, 2017). NCT followed in the footsteps of other famous K-pop acts created by SM Entertainment, and are known for excellent visuals, dancing, rapping, and musical ability. Over half of the group is multilingual, with many members learning Korean as a second or third language. Outside of concerts and music videos, the boys in NCT appear on K-pop talk shows and create behind-the-scenes videos to give us, the fans, more insight into their lives. Johnny, the sole American member of the group, even started his own YouTube series, modeled after the video logs (vlogs) influencers on the platform use to gain internet stardom. After consuming as much NCT content as I could, I finally reached a milestone of K-pop fandom: selecting my first "ult." Mine is a Thai dancer-turned-idol named Chittaphon Leechaiyapornkul- Ten, for short.

As soon as I realized how much I cared about NCT, I immersed myself in the NCT fandom. The goal of the fan community is to support the idol group in any way possible. We watch music videos on repeat, to reach self-determined view count goals on YouTube, and listen to albums for days on end using a variety of platforms to hit streaming targets. We spend money, not just on official albums and merchandise, but on fan-made art and crafts that make us stand out from other fans. I dove in headfirst once I chose to focus on NCT and created social media accounts specifically for communicating in the K-pop fandom. No one cared where I lived or who I was, only that I was an active "NCTzen," the official fandom name for superfans of NCT. I was finally able to immerse myself in fan culture where the most important thing about me was my love for Ten and the rest of the group. All of my accounts used a screen name instead of my real name, and none of the photos on any social accounts were of me. The escapism I hoped for when first learning about the art form had reached new heights, and I was able to completely ignore any other responsibilities or emotions I had in favor of sharing an inside joke with a fellow NCTzen or reposting a photo from a concert that I thought some of my followers would want to see.

After observing for over a year, I felt ready to become an active fan- after all, the boys worked so hard for us that they deserved it. I formed friendships with people I have never met in person, built around our shared love for an idol and K-pop as a whole. I signed up for unofficial group orders orchestrated entirely on social media, in which fans in Asian countries or with Asian addresses purchase large quantities of Korean K-pop merchandise and then ship it back to the U.S. in bulk to lower shipping costs for all fans who participated. I joined group messages designed around certain parameters, including "Ten dance compilations," "NCT Memes" and "Fans over 18." Other fans sent me suggestions for new idol groups to watch out for, playlists to listen to, and definitions for terms I still did not understand. I could tweet my visceral reactions to photos, music videos, and songs without fear of repercussions for being too obsessed or enthusiastic. I found not just an escapist outlet in fandom, but a community of like-minded fans who cared just as much as I did.

Two years after their debut, NCT 127 dropped their first full-length album alongside a title track in both English and Korean. This was the first time I participated in a comeback and all of the events leading up the release of a new album were thrilling. I watched every teaser video that was dropped and looked for spoilers when the members of NCT posted on platforms like V-Live and Instagram. My fandom community planned ahead for weeks, deciding streaming goals and choosing whether or not to preorder the album. The English version of the music video for "Regular" was scheduled to drop before both the Korean version and the rest of the album. The day it was released, I woke before my alarm at four in the morning and watched it live, heart racing.

During the months I spent fawning over NCT, I had never heard them sing in English. It felt different. Instead of observing another culture's content, this music video felt like it was for me. They referenced making money, working hard, and success, all while wearing sparkly suits and shiny jewelry on a set designed to look like the dreamscape version of Seoul. I was reminded of the lyrics of every Western pop song I have ever heard, the tone and message reminiscent of the songs I grew up listening to on the radio. Hearing words like "iced out both my wrists, now I can barely see the time" ("Regular (English Ver.) Lyrics," 2018) come from Taeyong, my bias in NCT 127, felt different in its familiarity. I messaged my fandom friends and gushed about my favorite people singing in a language I could understand. When the Korean version of the song dropped with a distinct music video a few days later, I watched for differences and similarities between the two. I looked up the lyrics to compare them and realized the meanings were different, the message behind the Korean version of the song emphasizing the strength of effective teamwork where the English version highlighted the value of monetary success.

When the full-length album was released the next day, I listened to it on repeat. I supported the group not just by listening to and buying their music, but through grassroots promotion, and shared the videos outside of the fandom with my friends. Around this time, I became more open about my obsession with K-pop and NCT, telling people in my life from outside the fandom and attempting to recruit them by casually sending them videos or recommending songs. Even as I used K-pop and Western K-pop fandom as a way to escape my real-life stressors, I wanted everyone to see how talented and attractive the members of NCT were and how great of an art form K-pop was overall. My ego was back, and I watched with glee as NCT became more and more popular in the West, finding success on international music charts and appearing on the same talk shows BTS had appeared on in years previously. I felt that the group's success in an American market was in part due to my efforts as a fan.

Implications and Future Directions

My experience becoming a fan of NCT 127 exemplified the affective, community-building, and technologically advanced qualities of K-pop that make it so pervasive in an American market. This section connects my experience with conversations surrounding K-pop fandom in the United States on a larger scale, then proposes potential implications and future research on the topic of fan representation in an intercultural context. Pop culture creators generate emotional connections that provide the right amount of escapism from the troubles of daily life. For me, it was a combination of timing, media saturation, and a unique mix of familiar yet unusual content that lead me to identify as an American K-pop superfan. My narrative exemplifies both the success of efforts by content creators to foster an affective relationship between me and the idea of K-pop, as well as the emotional tug of fan communities that led to my continued participation and fan identification. However, these affective relationships have unique impacts and significance in multiple settings.

First, the relationship between fans and content creators is under-theorized. Fans have traditionally held a paradoxical relationship with the creators of the content they love. Despite fanbases being the largest indicator of success for any Western artist, athlete, musician, or franchise (Fraade-Blanar & Glazer, 2017), the "crazy fangirl" and other stereotypes carry a negative connotation even years after Jenkins' foundational work on the subject (Jenkins, 2013). Negative stereotypes about fans are heightened when those fans are young, female, or members of other underrepresented groups in society (Lewis, 1992). Members of underrecognized groups are more likely to participate in actions that replicate larger systems of oppression in order to gain more "cultural capital" (Bourdieu, 1986) or create their own systems of in-grouping and out-grouping aligning with Lo's (2015) "unrecognized cultural currency." Despite recent growth, K-pop as a music style is still disproportionately underrepresented in America, leading American K-pop fans to view themselves paradoxically as members of both a dominant cultural group and an unrepresented one. Fans then enact

Bourdieu's (1986) and Lo's (2015) assumptions simultaneously, participating in self-regulated gatekeeping practices and working to gain "cultural capital" through formal ranking systems. Fans of different K-pop groups often participate in virtual "fan wars," competing to trend negative hashtags about other idol groups or battling to see who can get more votes on music trending apps (Tinaliga, 2018). This chapter calls into consideration both the role fan communities play in creating and maintaining their own systems of control and the position content creators play in defining and upholding those structures.

Next, intercultural and transnational identities must be taken into account when discussing fandom based on a cultural product. K-pop fandom, just like the music itself, does not exist in a vacuum (Matula, 2000). In the United States, Asian voices are largely underrepresented in mainstream media (Force, 2018). Western fans of K-pop have multifaceted identities, and those identities overlap in the context of their fan community. When fandoms act as subcultures, the members of that culture continue to operate within broad structures of oppression. Fans take actions that may earn additional "cultural currency", which in turn leads them to participate in larger hegemonic systems of oppression. I still see comments from long-time K-pop fans about how they would never "out" themselves as super fans to their friends or partners, upholding the mainstream notion that being a fan of something is worthy of shame (Jenkins, 2013). Any research on K-pop in Western cultures calls for a deeper criticism of the overwhelming persistence of Western media over the rest of the world, and fan positioning within a larger context.

Further, certain fan opinions or actions represent larger issues of identity and agency in popular culture. After introducing me to K-pop, my best friend told me that listening to music and watching performances was almost an act of rebellion for her, as she felt that by becoming obsessed with something that was not "for her," a white woman from the American Deep South, she could escape the issues stressing her relationship with her family, her partner, and her other friends. There is long history of Western colonial powers successfully "othering" culturally distinct art forms and consuming content due to its "exotic" or "alien" qualities (Oh, 2017; Noh, 2016). By utilizing the cultural product of another culture as a mode of escapism, Western fans, myself included, risk "othering" in a modern form, regardless of intention. Moreover, Western fans take part in "self-othering" when describing our relationship with K-pop, paradoxically claiming to be in both a minority of Western music fans by liking K-pop, and in a minority of K-pop fans by being from the West ("These 10 Nations," 2019). Western fans consume K-pop from the colonialist privilege of having a majority of the world's content designed for us. Practically speaking, this reminds us to question our own position as fans and scholars of K-pop.

Finally, this research reminds me to question my own identity as a fan of a cultural product that is not my own. Writing about K-pop fandom from the position of a white Western scholar carries certain implications and calls for frequent self-reflexivity. How does my privilege play into my obsession with a group of performers who do not have the same cultural norms as I do? How do the fan communities I have access to and join impact my emotional connection with the content of K-pop and its producers? This chapter was in no way an exhaustive look at the lived experience and affective relationships of all Western K-pop fans. Future researchers should maintain a reflexive mindset in their understanding of how we measure popularity and success of K-pop in any setting, as well as keep in mind our own positioning. Culture is not monolithic, and K-pop culture in no way speaks for the Korean experience. I work to reconcile my own identity as an American fan of K-pop by understanding that, no matter how much research I conduct, I will never fully understand the intricacies of a cultural product tied so closely to national identity (Joo, 2011). My role as an aca-fan is to respect the parts of K-pop culture as well as Korean culture that I do not understand and avoid claims I do not have the right to. Western fans of K-pop must take into account our own perspectives and take a critical look at where we derive our affection. It is our role as researchers and fans to draw the line between adoration and cultural appropriation.

Conclusion

Western K-pop fans have overlapping, heterogenous circumstances that impact our identities and interactions as fans. This chapter shows how a combination of factors fostered my identity as an American

K-pop super fan. I felt a strong affective pull toward the content I was inundated with, dedicated myself to a virtual fan community, and felt connected to others with the barrage of K-pop-related content I was witness to every day. For me, Neo Culture Technology is not just the name of a boy band, but a method of content production that fostered my obsession with K-pop and cultivated a relationship with other fans in my position. Understanding K-pop as form of escapism highlights the need for further research on the relationship between Western fans, identity, and culture.

Recommended Readings

Fraade-Blanar, Z., & Glazer, A. M. (2017). *Superfandom: How our obsessions are changing what we buy and who we are*. London, UK: Profile Books.

Jenkins, H. (2013). *Textual poachers: Television fans and participatory culture* (Updated 20th anniversary ed.). New York, NY: Routledge.

Lo, M. (2015). Conceptualizing 'unrecognized cultural currency': Bourdieu and everyday resistance among the dominated. *Theory & Society*, *44*(2), 125-152, doi:10.1007/s11186-015-9249-4

Oh, D. C. (2017). K-pop fans react: Hybridity and the white celebrity-fan on YouTube. *International Journal of Communication (19328036)*, *11*, 2270-2287.

Stewart, K. (2007). *Ordinary affects*. Durham, NC: Duke University Press.

Additional Sources

Lee, S. M. (2016, February 1). *SMTOWN: New Culture Technology, 2016* [Video]. https://www.youtube.com/watch?v=Ky5NvWsXnn8

SMTOWN (2018, October 8). *NCT 127 엔시티 127 'Regular (English Ver.)' MV* [Video]. https://www.youtube.com/watch?v=gj-VU9oK2Yo

SMTOWN (2018, October 11). *NCT 127 엔시티 127 'Regular (Korean Ver.)' MV* [Video]. https://www.youtube.com/watch?v=Gif0E6jYakM

References

Adams, T. E., Jones, S. L. H., & Ellis, C. (2015). *Autoethnography: Understanding qualitative research*. Oxford; New York: Oxford University Press.

Ahmed, S. (2004). *The cultural politics of emotion*. New York, NY: Routledge.

Ashcraft, K. L. (2020). Senses of self: Affect as a pre-individual approach to identity at work. In A. D. Brown (Ed.), *The Oxford handbook of identities in organizations* (pp. 848-864). Oxford, UK: Oxford University Press.

Benjamin, J. (2018, May 18). A full timeline of BTS in America. *Billboard*. Retrieved from https://www.billboard.com/articles/columns/k-town/8455536/bts-in-america-timeline

Berlant, L. (2010). Cruel optimism. In M. Gregg & G. J. Seigworth (Eds.), *The affect theory reader* (pp. 93-117). Durham, NC: Duke University Press.

Bourdieu, P. (1977). *Outline of a theory of practice*. Cambridge, UK: Cambridge

University Press.
Bourdieu, P. (1986). The forms of capital. In I. Szeman & T. Kaposy (Eds.), *Cultural theory: An anthology* (pp. 47-58). Malden, MA: Wiley-Blackwell.
Bourdieu, P., & Saint-Martin, M. (1974). Scholastic excellence and the values of the educational system. In J. Egglestone (Ed.), *Contemporary research in the sociology of education* (pp. 338-369). London, UK: Methuen & Co Ltd.
Boylorn, R. M. (2008). As seen on TV: An autoethnographic reflection on race and reality television. *Critical Studies in Media Communication, 25*(4), 413-433.
Caulfield, K. (2019, April 22). BTS meets the Beatles and the Monkees in Billboard chart history with 'Map of the Soul: Persona'. *Billboard.* Retrieved from https://www.billboard.com/articles/columns/chart-beat/8507983/bts-beatles-monkees-billboard-chart-history
Cisneros, J. D. (2015). Affect, emotion, and immigration rhetoric, or what happens when a minuteman lives with unauthorized immigrants? In E. J. Hartelius (Ed.), *The ehetorics of US immigration: Identity, community, otherness* (pp. 164-181). University Park, PA: Penn State University Press.
Fandom. (n.d.). *Merriam-Webster.* Retrieved from https://www.merriam-webster.com/dictionary/fandom
Force, T. L. (2018, November 6). Why do Asian-Americans remain largely unseen in film and television? *The New York Times.* Retrieved from https://www.nytimes.com/2018/11/06/t-magazine/asian-american-actors-representation.html
Fraade-Blanar, Z., & Glazer, A. M. (2017). *Superfandom: How our obsessions are changing what we buy and who we are.* London, UK: Profile Books.
Gray, J., Sandvoss, C., & Harrington, C. L. (2017). *Fandom, second edition: Identities and communities in a mediated world.* New York, NY: NYU Press.
Herman, T. (2018a, May 18). K-pop eyes 'next wave' of success in U.S. music industry. *NBC News.* Retrieved from https://www.nbcnews.com/news/asian-america/k-pop-eyes-next-wave-success-u-s-music-industry-n874836
Herman, T. (2018b, October 8). NCT 127 premieres first-ever English-language song 'Regular': Watch the music video. *Billboard.* Retrieved from https://www.billboard.com/articles/columns/k-town/8478863/nct-127-english-song-regular-video
Herman, T. (2019, February 19). NCT 127 set to tour North America for first time: Exclusive. *Billboard.* Retrieved from https://www.billboard.com/articles/columns/k-town/8498880/nct-127-north-american-tour-details
Herman, T. (2019, November 1). Fans raise north of $20,000 for Times Square billboard to keep Wonho in Monsta X. *Billboard.* Retrieved from https://www.billboard.com/articles/columns/k-town/8542117/fans-raise-money-times-square-billboard-wonho-monsta-x
Jenkins, H. (2013). *Textual poachers: Television fans and participatory culture* (Updated 20th anniversary ed.). New York, NY: Routledge.
Joo, J. (2011). Transnationalization of Korean popular culture and the rise of "Pop nationalism" in Korea. *The Journal of Popular Culture, 44*(3), 489-504. Retrieved from https://core.ac.uk/download/pdf/51180588.pdf
K-pop 101: 21 words every fan should know. (2018, March 13). *SBS.* Retrieved from https://www.sbs.com.au/popasia/blog/2018/03/13/k-pop-101-21-words-every-fan-should-know
Lee, S. M. (2016, February 1). *SMTOWN: New Culture Technology, 2016* [Video]. Retrieved from https://www.youtube.com/watch?v=Ky5NvWsXnn8
Lewis, L. A. (1992). *The adoring audience: Fan culture and popular media.* London;

New York: Routledge.

Lo, M. (2015). Conceptualizing 'unrecognized cultural currency': Bourdieu and everyday resistance among the dominated. *Theory & Society*, *44*(2), 125-152.

Matula, T. (2000). Contextualizing musical rhetoric: A critical reading of the pixies' "Rock music". *Communication Studies*, *51*(3), 218-237.

McGee, M. (1990). Text, context, and the fragmentation of contemporary culture. *Western Journal of Speech Communication*, *54*, 274-289.

Melendez, M. (2017, June 30). NCT 127 discuss the group's unique concept, breaking into U.S. & more. *Billboard*. Retrieved from https://www.billboard.com/articles/columns/k-town/7850237/nct-127-kcon-ny-america-interview

Nickolai, N. (2019, February 11). BTS makes history at the Grammys as first K-pop presenters. *Variety*. Retrieved from https://variety.com/2019/music/news/bts-grammys-present-awards-kpop-1203130948/

Noh, S. (2016). Subversion and reification of cultural identity in global fandoms. *gnovis*, *17*(1), 13. Retrieved from http://hdl.handle.net/10822/1043000

Oh, D. C. (2017). K-pop fans react: Hybridity and the white celebrity-fan on YouTube. *International Journal of Communication*, *11*, 2270-2287.

Posner, J. (Creator). (2018, May 30). K-pop. (Season 1, Episode 16). [Tv series episode]. In Klein, E. & Rozansky, K. (Producers), *Explained*. Vox.

Regular (English Ver.) Lyrics. (2018). *Genius Lyrics*. Retrieved from https://genius.com/Nct-127-regular-english-ver-lyrics

Regular (Korean Ver.) Lyrics. (2018). *Genius Lyrics*. Retrieved from https://genius.com/Nct-127-regular-korean-ver-lyrics

Slade, A. F., Narro, A. J., & Givens-Carroll, D. (Eds.). (2015). *Television, social media, and fan culture*. Lanham, MD: Lexington Books.

Stewart, K. (2007). *Ordinary affects*. Durham, NC: Duke University Press.

Tamondong, H. (2020, April 3). Daebak! These are the 10 K-pop idols with the most followers on Instagram. *Cosmopolitan*. Retrieved from https://www.cosmo.ph/entertainment/kpop-idols-most-instagram-followers-a4575-20200315

These ten nations are the biggest K-pop stans of 2019, based on YouTube views. (2019, August 22). *Koreaboo*. Retrieved from https://www.koreaboo.com/lists/ten-nations-biggest-idol-stans-2019-kpop-radar-youtube-views/

Tinaliga, B. (2018, May 18). "At war for oppa and identity": Competitive performativity among Korean-pop fandoms. *USFCA master's projects and capstones*. Retrieved from https://repository.usfca.edu/capstone/768

Top 20 K-pop entertainment companies–Best of 2020. (2020, January 28). *Soulz*. Retrieved from https://seoulz.com/top-20-k-pop-entertainment-companies-best-of-2020/

Wang, A. X. (2018, August 21). How K-pop conquered the West. *RollingStone*. Retrieved from www.rollingstone.com/music/music-features/bts-kpop-albums-bands-global-takeover-707139/

Willingham, A. J. (2019, April 14). BTS! We haven't seen boy-band fandom like this since the Beatles. *CNN*. Retrieved from https://www.cnn.com/2019/04/12/entertainment/bts-kpop-album persona-soul-who-is-trnd/index.html

Yates, B. L. (2015). It's social, not parasocial: Understanding the impact of the internet on building community among Bruce Springsteen fans. *Atlantic Journal of Communication*, *23*(5), 254-268.

CHAPTER 5

"Oppa, Gangnam Style!": The Accidental Persuasion of Asian Creativity, Authenticity, and Masculinity in American Pop Music

Chen Yang, Robert Morris University

In 2012, almost every American had heard a song called *Gangnam Style* performed by South Korean singer, songwriter, and record producer Park Jae-Sang, best known by his stage name Psy. The music video debuted on YouTube on July 15th 2012 and went viral instantly, earning more than 460 million views. As the No. 1 digital song in America in 2012 (Sinha-Roy, 2012), *Gangnam Style* is not only the first song by which an Asian musician successfully achieved wide popularity in America and across the world, but also the first Korean song that features its viral dance moves, i.e., the horse-riding dance. Along with Psy's rise on the international pop music stage, one factor that caught U.S. audience's attention is his Asian male identity as many Americans referred to Psy as "the Asian guy doing the horse-riding dance." The fact that Psy is an Asian man from South Korea singing and rapping in Korean made his success too odd a phenomenon to be deciphered. In a sense, his image as an Asian male music artist is something new to Americans, a persona that is still underrepresented and often misconstrued. A meme circulating online put Psy alongside North Korean leader Kim Jong-Un, with the subtitle saying "can you believe they are both Korean?"

Despite being a member of Korean Wave, Psy is not the typical K-pop artist with a perfectly tall slim body and a cute baby face. Nor was his music created with an intention to conquer the U.S. market like many other K-pop stars. Because Psy's superstardom is such a unique case in K-pop, this article analyzed the visual and auditory semiotics embedded in *Gangnam Style* in an effort to find out how this

Korean megahit managed to obtain a foothold in the deeply racialized American pop music industry.

White Hegemonic Masculinity in America

Each culture and society assigns men specific social roles they play, and the constructs of masculinity vary across social and cultural contexts. Due to the fact that gender studies in the 1990s mainly concentrated on femininity, the studies of masculinity have been ignored till recent years (MacKinnon, 2003). In a traditional sense, masculinity of a man is established as a financial source of a heterosexual family and a leader of the household (Chapman, 1988). In a capitalist society, individuals are forced to act upon the gender identity prescribed by the society and to reinforce the existing gender boundary (Lorber & Farrell, 1990). Therefore, any violation of this prescribed gender role could be mocked, marginalized, or even punished. This dominant gender boundary was later developed into the discourse of hegemonic masculinity by many gender scholars (e.g., Connell, 1987; Hanke, 1990, 1998; Miller, 2001; Nakayama, 1994; Vavrus, 2002).

Connell (1987) defined hegemonic masculinity as the privileged status of males in a Western society, which puts women and minority others in a subordinate position and allows men to maintain their social power and control. Trujillo (1991) also argued that hegemonic masculinity is defined through occupational achievement in an industrialized capitalist society. It is no surprise that hegemonic masculinity bears a hallmark of whiteness from the beginning. White male corporate executives and politicians are typical manifestations of hegemonic masculinity and embody aspects of transnational business masculinity by controlling dominant social institutions (Connell, 2000). Later on, America's traditional constructs of white masculinity changed with Hugh Hefner's introduction of Playboy to the mainstream media. As Chapman (1988) argued, Playboy celebrates a bachelor's life based on the accumulation of material and the consumption of women, which removes a man's familial obligations and assigns him social privileges over women and other men. Hefner's bachelor masculinity created alternative constructs of white masculinity by challenging the traditional man as a family patriarch.

Hegemonic masculinity as an idealized cultural construct has found its way into the common sense of a society (Trujillo, 1991). The American entertainment industry, as a mirror of the society, not only reflects and reinforces hegemonic masculinity in a capitalist society, but also objectifies these masculinity constructs and makes profits out of them. This is because masculinity sells as well as women's beauty. Previous literature has explored and discovered hegemonic masculinity in Hollywood movies (Bucholtz & Lopes, 2011), TV show (Henson & Parameswaran, 2008), sports (Trujillo, 1991), pop music (Calhoun, 2005; Eastman, 2012) and many other entertainment media. As some scholars (Carrigan, Connell, & Lee, 1985; MacKinnon, 2003) have argued, men with typical hegemonic masculinity can be fictional figures that help sustain a cultural ideal, a fantasy that can only be achieved by a small portion of men but is likely to be promoted by the mass media.

Masculinity conveyed in Asian pop culture has also been investigated in communication and cultural studies. Several scholars (e.g., Geng, 2016; Jung, 2009; Louie; 2012) explored the newly emerging representations of male image in Japanese and Korean pop music, discovering a discrepancy in the ideal forms of masculinity between Western and East Asian cultures. They labelled this unique Pan-East Asian masculinity "soft masculinity." As a majority of K-pop boybands (e.g., Big Bang, Exo, and BTS) feature young men with pale skin tone, tall slim bodies, dyed hair, and colorful outfit, Ainslie (2017) argued that Korean Wave is redefining what attractive men should be like across Asia. On the other hand, Korean Wave's influence on Western masculinity may not be as pronounced as in Asian regions. In a survey of 772 young Americans, Song and Velding (2020) found out U.S. audiences viewed K-pop bands as neither highly masculine nor feminine, showing a tendency to conform to hegemonic masculinity as the most idealized form. Thus, today's masculinity reproduced by the U.S. media and entertainment industry still contains a prevailing discourse of hegemonic whiteness and, accordingly, reflects a racialized social hierarchy that centers on white masculine manifestations in reality.

Hegemonic Appropriation of Black Masculinity

African American culture has found its way into American pop culture due to white audience's demand for its complementary reinforcement of white masculinity and for increasing profits in a wider population. Black masculinity is closely linked to African Americans' limited access to social power as well as their authenticity in music creation. In a white-dominated masculinity discourse, financially challenged and socially underprivileged black males have no channel to assert their voices and identities in conventional institutional venues. Music has become an alternative platform for black men to establish and advocate their masculinity (Skeggs, 1993). Along with other fashion elements developed from the African American urban community (e.g., baggy pants, Black Vernacular, and graffiti), black masculinity represented in hip-hop culture is condensed into the slang expressions of being "cool" and later having "swag." In rap music, it is typically embodied by the skill of delivering bold artistic lyrical flows to demonstrate men's big ego and by men showing off their power over women, money, and other material resources.

More than thirty years ago, rap music, along with break dance and graffiti, was considered as a vulgar "street art" or "ghetto culture" by the mainstream media and only enjoyed its popularity among a limited audience, mainly African Americans (George, 2001). In 1986, rap duo Run DMC's collaboration with Aerosmith in the remake of "Walk this Way" topped the charts, reaching a milestone for hip-hop's integration into mainstream pop music (Edgers, 2016). Since then American pop has taken a strong signature of black masculinity. The growing influence of hip-hop culture proves that hegemonic masculinity mainly embodied by white Americans entertains the idea of adding black masculinity as a supplement to maximize audiences and profits in both white and black communities. However, the endorsement of black music and its associated masculinity by white America is a paradox. "The historical love of black music by whites in the United States has always been troubled by the fact of blackness itself" (White, 2011, p. 10). This led to two consequences: the justification of white faces as standardized pop icons and the objectification of African American masculinity by constructing black men as primitive, aggressive, and dangerous. The former was demonstrated by white musicians' hegemonic appropriation of black music as white men do not have much trouble in justifying their position as a generic embodiment of masculinity. White (2011) argued that Elvis Presley appropriation of black masculinity by erasing the visible sign of blackness, i.e., the act of masking, has made him the first all-American masculine music icon. While white musicians gained fame by appropriating black male subjectivity, mass media are also obsessed with the objectification of black masculinity. In other words, black masculinity in the U.S. media has long been ideologically associated with hyperphysicality that involves physical strength, hyper(hetero)sexuality, and physical violence (Davis, 1983), and black men are more likely to be depicted as "violent, uneducated, sexualized, (and) incompetent" in media (Jackson & Moshin, 2012, p. 9).

Asian Masculinity in American Pop Culture

Because the tradition of regarding a male as a family patriarch and a carrier of heritage is prevalent in Asian countries, the social identity of a masculine Asian male figure is narrowly defined, leading to Asian American's less influence and their perpetuated marginalized position in pop culture. This is demonstrated by the fact that many Asian parents want a son instead of a daughter so that their family names can be passed on, and Asian families hold higher expectations for boys in their academic achievement and career development than for girls. Compared to black masculinity, America found Asian masculinity of being straight-A students and model citizens too insipid to be a profitable supporting act for white manliness.

The marginalization of Asian men in mass media has its political and historical roots too. According to Said (1979), the term Orient was coined by white Europeans to express a relationship of the Occident's power, domination, and hegemony over the Orient and to sustain and relive their romantic, exotic, and remarkable haunting memories and experiences in Asia. In order to draw a boundary between the exotic East and the familiar West, the Orientalist discourse necessitates the feminization and emasculation of Asian men as weak and submissive so that Europeans' colonial possession over Asian resources can be maximized. Early U.S. immigration and labor policies reinforced the marginalization of Asian masculinity by building up the anti-Asian resentment against Chinese and Japanese immigrants, ultimately strengthening America's perception of an Asian male as Oriental first and then a man. The salient foreign image of Asians consolidated America's repulsion and rejection of Asian masculinity as peripheral and alien. Previous literature (e.g., Espiritu 1997; Wilkins et al., 2011) argued that Asian men have long been marginalized and even excluded from the dominant white American masculinity as the media tend to depict Asian men as "nerds", "geeks", "model minorities", "homosexuals," and "eunuchs" with Asian females constantly construed as exotic, subservient, and sexual. Although Asian men did establish their masculine identity of strength, wisdom, and swiftness through Kung Fu movies with Bruce Lee and his successors, the Asian philosophy of inner peace, humbleness, silence, and self-containment in these movies is inherently inconsistent with swag and ego symbolized in American hip-hop, leading to white and black audiences' misinterpretation of Asian men as weak and cowardly. Aside from martial arts movies, Asian male icons are generally missing, and the pop music industry is no exception.

Appropriation of American Masculinity in *Gangnam Style*

The thrive of Korean Wave in East Asia largely relies on the adoption of Western music genres (i.e., hip-hop, rock, disco, R&B, and more) rather than on traditional Asian music. Because America and European countries are still the major contributor and trendsetter of contemporary pop, K-pop artists inevitably bear the stigma of being copycats and stealers when trying to appeal to the U.S. market. Unsurprisingly, prior to Psy, many K-pop artists found it hard to enter North America and ended up focusing on fans in Asia only. There are also gender differences. In 2009, BoA achieved medium success in the U.S. with her album entering the Billboard 200. In the same year, Wonder Girls even hit the chart with their Billboard Hot 100 song "Nobody." But in comparison to their female counterparts, many talented and multilingual K-pop male artists (e.g., Rain and Kangta) had been underappreciated by U.S. audiences.

Prior to Psy, there were very few Asian male figures in the contemporary history of American pop music including *American Idol* reject William Hung and *Freestyle Friday* champion and battle rapper MC Jin. Psy's success seems to follow a similar pattern, yet in various ways breaks away from his predecessors. Although the Korean song talks about the lavish lifestyle in Seoul's Gangnam district, international viewers are less concerned about the meaning of lyrics due to the language barrier, but focus more on the symbolic representations of image and sound beyond words. These symbols include body language, facial expression, outfit, choreography, video scenario, vocal delivery, and music style. The masculinity performances in this music video are evident.

First of all, Psy's posture and gesture bears strong resemblance to the idealized masculine image in U.S. rap music. His protuberant body is similar to many well-known American rappers (e.g., Notorious B.I.G., Fat Joe, and Rick Ross) as large body types are considered as a common manifestation of masculinity in hip-hop. In the music video, Psy engaged in a dance battle in a parking lot with another guy. Scholars (e.g., Kee, 2016; Hoffmann, 2007) have argued that dance battles are an important manifestation of black masculinity as African Americans living in harsh conditions frequently resort to the use of force to survive and settle disputes. Furthermore, Psy's exaggerated way of walking in the horse stable scene represents an often seen body movement in rap videos called "swag walk". This act is greatly elevated by his aggressive hand gestures and the gigantic explosion in the background alongside his mean-mugged delivery of "*Oppa Gangnam Style.*"

Facial expression is an important element of Psy's masculinity performances. In the music video, Psy demonstrates a non-verbal presentation of angry facial expressions known as "mean mugging." Mean mugging, frequently practiced in American hip-hop videos, "rejects feminization and vulnerability through the withholding of emotion but is nonetheless a powerful affective display that telegraphs hypermasculinity and potential aggression" (White, 2011, p. 44). At the beginning of the video, Psy displays an intimidating and almost evil look with his eyes hiding behind sunglasses; he shows the same intimidating look every time he shouts out "Oppa *Gangnam Style*!" furiously, even at the face of a female dancer.

Furthermore, the reiteration of male heterosexuality greatly enhances Psy's masculinity performances. In one scene, Psy walks with two young women side by side while laying his arms on their shoulders. This scene conveys a distinguishable message of hyperheterosexuality by boasting his possession of beautiful women. In another scene, the camera zooms on a female dancer's buttock while Psy is gazing and yelling at it. This is a typical scenario in American rap videos, demonstrating men's objectification of, obsession with, and dominance over female bodies.

Intensive lyrical flows, another signature of masculinity performance in rap, are repeatedly heard in the song. Although Psy's rap in Korean does not make any sense to most Americans, many listeners think the song's rapping style and beats arrangement are as catchy as LFMAO's "Sexy I Know It." In addition, the phrase "*Gangnam style*" bears much similarity in spelling to "gangsta style", a hardcore rap music genre, which mistakenly elevated American audience's interpretation of the masculinity discourse in this song. Last but not least, the only understandable line to an English speaker "Oh, sexy lady!" once again reinforces Psy as a heterosexual masculine Asian man.

The semiotics in the *Gangnam Style* music video reveal that Psy's music heavily adopts the recurring elements in mainstream American pop and features intensive masculinity performances idealized by Western rappers, which subconsciously caters to the taste of U.S. audiences. Although these performances have been normalized in the Western masculine culture, they did not meet well with many conservative viewers in Asia. For example, quite a few Chinese Internet viewers called the song "immoral, of low taste, and vulgar" and some even suggested boycotting such music (Feng, 2012).

The Persuasion of Asian Creativity, Authenticity, and Masculinity in *Gangnam Style*

Considering Psy's history of studying music in Boston University and Berkley College of Music, one would not be surprised at how skillfully he has integrated these Western musical elements and masculinity discourses into K-pop. Nevertheless, the fact he can sell K-pop back to the U.S. audiences is something phenomenal. Because the U.S. pop music scene has such a rigidly divided racial hierarchy, an Asian male pop artist, in order to appeal to the general American audiences, should not only be talented but also capable of validating his "realness" as a minority. While many other Asian musicians have struggled with the justification of their creativity, authenticity, and masculinity in the United States, Psy managed it in an unconventional way.

First, Psy's persuasion discourse for Asian creativity is built upon the challenge to audience's expectations for a stereotypical Asian man. With the scarcity of social roles assigned to Asian Americans, U.S. audiences are used to linking Asian masculinity with the concept of a salaryman (Dasgupta, 2000), a boring traditional Asian male patriarch working hard to obtain material wealth and social prestige. Prior to Psy, few American audience would expect a middle-aged stocky Korean guy to deliver fast rap lyrics and throw such smooth rhythmic dance moves. Although Psy's appearance and body type resembles much of a middle-aged salaryman, his performance deviates from the stereotypical humble, peaceful, asexual Asian man who is a father, a husband, and a white-collar workaholic. In the music video, Psy's flagrant hyperheterosexuality approaches Hefner's playboy-like "bachelor masculinity," an Asian male image rarely depicted in the U.S. pop culture. Even in Hollywood movies, the few Asian action figures may easily beat up hooligans but hardly get any women. For example, the film "Romeo Must Die" originally had the Chinese actor Jet Li kissing R&B star Aaliyah as an ending, but the kissing scene was replaced with a friendly hug due to criticism from a pre-screening urban audience (Vargas, 2007).

Furthermore, there are numerous scenes in the video that push the boundary of Americans' expectations for what an Asian man can do. For example, Psy raps while sitting on toilet with his pants down, sings while lying in an elevator with another man standing behind and thrusting his pelvis, and does silly dance moves while wearing out-of-place short pants and riding a speedboat. Slapstick in music video is nothing new as many U.S. pop artists, such as Lonely Island and Eminem, have tried it in their music video. But in 2012, it was still rare and shocking for U.S. audience to see an Asian man doing all these goofy wacky things as mass media have mainly depicted Asians to be the "successful," "hardworking," or "obedient," "passive" model minority (Kawai, 2005; Kim, 2013, Zhang, 2010) and, consequently, Asian masculinity has been centering on the discourse of social role conformity and group affiliation (Lebra, 1976; Sugimoto, 2004). In this sense, not only did Psy's presence shatter the society's expectations of an Asian man as an uptight family patriarch and a boring money-earning machine, but also demolished Asian people's stigma of being incompetent and uncreative in music and dance.

Second, Psy's persuasion discourse for Asian authenticity is realized by alienating *Gangnam Style* from the dominant American pop scenario. In the hip-hop world, the discourse of masculinity has always been space bounded (e.g., Forman, 2002; White, 2011), which can be a key feature of credibility many talented Asian musicians struggle to establish. With rap music's straight-no-chaser hardcore urban life narrative, any impersonators of the black authenticity claiming their attachment to ghetto life will be called into question (Kitwana, 2002). Therefore, black masculinity is oftentimes intertwined with authenticity as black hip-hop artists and filmmaker constantly draw boundaries between the authentic and inauthentic (Dyson, 1996). This connection resulted in the abundant Afrocentric representation of ghetto life as in the narrative of real blackness (e.g., Boyd, 1997; Costello & Wallace, 1990; Jackson, 2006; Krims, 2000). Eminem's rise as a rap icon has everything to do with his origin as he claims to be a poor white boy growing up with a single mother in a ghetto area of Detroit (Calhoun, 2005). When White (2011, p. 38) commented "mediated references to place and space allow those who do not live in geographical zones where black expressive behavior is part of the performance of the everyday to re-create spaces of racialized play outside these zones," he was referring to white music artists adopting black music styles.

While Eminem, Elvis Presley, and other white performers can easily adopt black authenticity to become mainstream music icons, Asian artists have a major hurdle to jump, i.e., justifying their authenticity. This is due to the prevailing profile of Asian Americans being fresh-off-the-boat and "forever foreign" immigrants who speak broken English (Reyes, 2007). For example, Eminem's Asian equivalent, MC Jin, faced a totally different fate. MC Jin was born in America; he has street credibility as he joined underground rap battles and distributed mixtapes in NYC; his lyrical rhymes are full of wisdom and boldness. Jin's challenge to the centralized perception of Asian Americans catapulted him to overnight fame. Nevertheless, his music career also encountered major hurdles due to his Chinese/Asian origin: unlike

Eminem, MC Jin moved to Hong Kong after his debut album flopped in America. This shows America is yet to embrace a rap hero that bears an "alien" label. An article in the New York Times commented on the absence of Asian pop musicians in the United States as follows, "Asian-American artists and scholars say that racial stereotypes—the image of the studious geek, the perception that someone who looks Asian must be a foreigner—clash with the coolness and born-in-the-U.S.A. authenticity required for pop stardom" (Navarro, 2007).

Psy, nevertheless, avoided these common embarrassments facing Asian musicians and succeeded in selling U.S.-inspired K-pop rap back to America. This is because he never intended to bow down to the American market by singing and rapping in English. Despite the fact that *Gangnam Style* heavily adopted elements of American pop from rapping style and beat arrangement to masculinity performance, Psy tactfully, though not intentionally, justified his Asian authenticity in music and masculinity by simply being Korean and performing for Korean-speaking listeners. Gangnam, the place the song is based on, is a district in Seoul, which estranges the song's setting from a typical American social context. Along with its original horse-riding dance moves, *Gangnam Style* subtly convinced America that it is original exotic Asian dance music imported from South Korea and yet simultaneously cater to their cultivated taste for Americanized masculinity.

Psy's rapping in Korean conveyed his confidence in music creativity and his rejection of the default English-speaking rule for most international pop stars. This unconventional approach potentially prevented his music from the American critics' judgmental attitudes and subconsciously eliminated U.S. audiences' cynicism with an Asian rapper who heavily borrowed Western music and masculine styles. As a music video shot in Korea, made by Koreans, and for Korean audiences, *Gangnam Style* is not intended to compete with white or black masculinity in the American pop music scene. Therefore, its Asian masculinity appears hilarious, exotic, and non-threatening to the existing hegemonic masculinity structure and solicits a less repulsive reaction among U.S. audiences.

Third, Psy did not just sell a full package of U.S.-inspired Asian masculinity, but a mixed bag of Asian masculinity and Asian goofiness. To some extent, *Gangnam Style* exploited Asian stigma by playing the beaten role of a nerdy and physically unattractive Asian man. For instance, the music video starts and ends with Psy's goofy cartoon persona popping up. His horse-riding dance is original and creative, but audiences may also find these animal-inspired moves as cheesy and laughable as William Hung's off-key singing. Besides the prevailing discourse of male heterosexuality, there is even a scene implying homosexuality or sexual ambiguity, in which Psy rests his head on another naked man's shoulder at a sauna. All the slapstick makes *Gangnam Style* more than just a music video with pure masculinity discourse, but also a visual comedy mocking and celebrating the stereotypical Asian goofiness.

In terms of physical attractiveness, Psy is not considered to be handsome or sexy compared to the majority of K-pop stars, more or less contributing to the widespread perception of an undesirable Asian man in the Western media. Psy's slightly blown figure and chubby face may have unintentionally perpetuated the stigma of an awkward-looking unattractive Asian man like his Asian predecessors in American pop, i.e., the nerdy William Hung and chubby Lin Yuchun. Paradoxically speaking, this mixture might be a shortcut strategy for Asian males to make a dent in U.S. mass media because many scholars (e.g., Atkinson, 2003; Ferrell, 2001; Lasn, 1999) have identified mockery as a method of "culture jamming," an effective rhetorical weapon to challenge the dominant power structure and ideology.

Gangnam Style and Asian Musicians' Dilemma

The phenomenon of *Gangnam Style* reveals a continuous pattern of Asian pop stars' rise on the Western pop music stage and may give further suggestions for K-pop's thrive in North America.

First, Asian musicians, male artists in particular, have remained invisible in the U.S. for a long time because the racial filter of the entertainment industry intentionally or unintentionally limits their accessibility to the power and resources of mass media. It is no coincidence that both William Hung and MC Jin gained their fame by appearing on reality TV shows because the perpetuated myth of a physically undesirable and musically incompetent Asian male could have disqualified many Asian pop artists in their attempts to sign a mainstream record label. This has led to the dilemma that

Asian musicians have very few platforms to showcase their talents, contributing to the vicious cycle of absence of Asian faces in American pop music. Consequently, Asian pop artists had to take advantage of every valuable second on traditional media (i.e., TV and radio) to impress the audience and to maximize their media exposure in a limited timeframe, which makes slapstick or mockery a shortcut for overnight fame. However, this is not necessarily true after *Gangnam Style* as Psy has opened Western media's eyes for the potential cultural and market values of K-pop. The recent frequent appearances of K-pop groups, such as BTS, in various American award shows are a clear demonstration of this change.

Second, the spread of K-pop in North America is generating an emerging pop culture among a niche audience, mostly younger and minority audiences. Yet there is still a long way to go before K-pop becomes a mainstream music genre or generates an everlasting music icon in the U.S. market. Previous Asian pop stars' success has been more or less built on the "eyeball economy" or "shock value," such as the hilarious reinforcement of Asian stigma by William Hung, or the shocking challenge to that stigma by MC Jin, or a well-integrated combination of both by Lin Yuchun and Psy. This shock value may create stars or hits overnight, but they tend to fade away with audiences' increasing aesthetic fatigue. William Hung's off-key singing is not something new in daily life. But the fact that it is the first time an Asian stigma has ever been projected on reality TV made him a hard-to-come-by entertainer. The same is with MC Jin when his battle skills in "Freestyle Friday" shattered the deeply rooted concept of a permanently foreign and culturally irrelevant Asian American. Nevertheless, none of them was able to elevate their overnight fame into the next level of being a mainstream pop icon. Despite *Gangnam Style*'s global success, Psy's superstardom was short-lived as he has not been able to dominate the U.S. music charts after three minor hits (i.e., Gentleman in 2013, Hangover in 2014, and Daddy in 2016). Yet his international success definitely opened the door for succeeding K-pop stars (e.g., Got7, BTS, Girl's Generation, and Twice) targeting the U.S. market and has contributed to the increasing visibility of K-pop in the U.S.

Third, the Internet provides K-pop musicians with a new platform free from the rules defined by the racialized hierarchy of traditional media. In particular, globalized distribution of digital music on the

Internet has spurred the popularity of K-pop in America. With the accelerating Internet speed and accessibility, online streaming services (i.e., YouTube, Spotify, Vevo, and etc.) and social media fan culture have made the sharing and distribution of music across borders faster, cheaper, and more convenient. In the last decade, numerous independent musicians without a major record label contract have successfully launched and grown their music career by using social media as a cost-efficient promotional channel, including Ok Go, Justin Bieber, Ed Sheeran, Pentatonix, and more. The fact that many YouTube singers became famous by covering hit songs and making music videos proves that signing a mainstream record label is no longer the only gateway to a successful music career.

Doubtless, the Internet is speeding up the rise of Asian music sensations in the U.S. as it took three years from MC Jin in 2001 to William Hung in 2004 but numerous Asian musicians have sprung up in the cyberspace recently. Many talents of Asian decedent (e.g., Jason Chen, Timothy DeLaGhetto, Awkwafina, and David Choi) also grasped a fair share of U.S. audiences. Lin Yuchun was just a reject from a Taiwanese TV talent show before someone posted a clip of his singing Whitney Houston's "I Will Always Love You" on YouTube, which got viral instantly and received more than 10,000,000 views in 2010 (1music4hall, 2010). Psy's success started from millions of hits on YouTube before he could sign a major U.S. music label and collaborate with American rappers such as MC Hammer and Snoop Dogg. With *Gangnam Style*'s huge success, American music fans in the younger generations are awakening to more and more hip-hop artists of Asian decedent (e.g., Rich Brian, Tim DeLaGhetto, G-Dragon, Kris Wu, Jackson Wang, and Far East Movement), mostly from the platform of YouTube. U.S. record labels also began to seek opportunities with talented K-pop stars. For example, the famous hip-hop label Cash Money signed an $11.3 million deal with the American Korean R&B group Aziatix. However, Aziatix did not release any album under the label, forcing them to leave the company (Nini, 2015). It seems K-pop's best bet to break into the U.S. market is still YouTube besides other social media and streaming/digital media.

Reconsidering the Popularity of *Gangnam Style* in the United States

The value of this analysis not only lies in *Gangnam Style*'s extreme popularity, but also in the pervasive discourses of white masculinity and hegemonic appropriation the song's success is built amid. Although white musicians appropriated black music styles and masculinity, it does not mean whites want their own hegemonic masculine status to be challenged or replaced. On one hand, the objectification of black men as violent, hypersexual, and crime-prone beings automatically eliminates their eligibility as the media-genic candidate for the standardized male icon. On the other hand, Asian appropriation of black masculinity and music style could pose a threat to white masculinity and originality in music and is less likely to be embraced by white audiences. Consequently, the repetitious depiction of a feminized, homosexualized, and emasculated Asian man in mass media is a reaction to that threat, serving the purpose of maintaining and reinforcing white Americans' position as the generic masculine role model while perpetuating Asians as the lesser man.

Gangnam Style is a crossover of a visual comedy and a hip dance song, which Americans find entertaining in that their stereotypical perceptions of Asian men are shattered and mocked at the same time, and in that U.S. audiences find joy in experiencing both exotic Korean elements and Americanized masculinity discourses synchronically. Psy's viral popularity showcased the audience's complicated attitude towards the marginalized and stigmatized image of an Asian male, partly obsession and partly annoyance. For one thing, *Gangnam Style* reveals Asian pop artists' awkward position of being stuck with the ongoing discourse of persuasion for authenticity. For another, it offers some suggestions for K-pop and Asian musicians targeting the American market. In order to win over the U.S audiences, adopting American music elements and masculinity traits is necessary, but it is far from enough. As Cheah and Kim (2014) argued, *Gangnam Style*'s viral popularity in the U.S. is due to the fact Psy's performance posed no threat to the "centralism" of the much racialized white American culture. Since Asian music artists do not enjoy the privilege of hegemonic appropriation as their white peers do, K-pop stars will have to do it in a subtle and innocuous way by either alienating themselves from the strictly defined American social and cultural locus or by challenging and mocking the dramatized Asian stigma simultaneously. Because Psy differs from most K-pop artists who are typically teenage heartthrobs featuring sexy looks and slim bodies with perfectly trained vocal skills and choreography (such as BTS, Exo, and Got7), *Gangnam Style* marks a breakthrough for K-pop and Asian pop in general as it paved the way for a new era of Korean Wave by rejecting Western traditional mainstream media and record companies as the only model and standard for international stardom.

Recommended Readings

Jackson, R. L., & Moshin, J. E. (Eds.). (2012). *Communicating marginalized masculinities: Identity politics in TV, film, and new media*. New York, NY: Routledge.

Kim, Y. (2013). Representation of people of Asian descent in mainstream mass media within the United States. *Multicultural Education Review, 5*(2), 20-48.

Shek, Y. L. (2006). Asian American masculinity: A review of the literature. *The Journal of Men's Studies, 14*(3), 379-391.

Taylor, G. (2004). *Buying whiteness: Race, culture, and identity from Columbus to hip-hop*. New York, NY: Palgrave Macmillan.

White, M. (2011). *From Jim Crow to Jay-Z: Race, rap, and the performance of masculinity*. Champaign, IL: University of Illinois Press.

Zhang, Q. (2010). Asian Americans beyond the model minority stereotype: The nerdy and the leftout. *Journal of International and Intercultural Communication, 3*, 20-37.

Additional Sources

Aziatix. (2014, December 31). *Hi everyone-we are announcing that we have decided to officially part ways with Cash Money Records* [Facebook post]. Retrieved from https://www.facebook.com/aziatix/posts/hi-everyone-we-are-announcing-that-we-have-decided-to-officially-part-ways-with-/776095302471054/

CGTN. (2017, September 9). *Prejudice against race and hip-hop: MC Jin's storytelling at CGTN* [Video]. YouTube. Retrieved from https://www.youtube.com/watch?v=VthkXsS7oT4&t=775s

Harvard University. (2013). *"Gangnam Style" singer PSY visits Harvard* [Video]. YouTube. Retrieved from https://www.youtube.com/watch?v=wJKjsb_A8M4

Psy [@psy_oppa]. (n.d.). Tweets [Twitter profile]. Retrieved from https://twitter.com/psy_oppa

Psy. (n.d.). *Home* [Facebook page]. Facebook. Retrieved from https://www.facebook.com/officialpsy/

Rolli, B. (2020, April 7). BTS just broke a major YouTube record formerly held by Psy. *Forbes*. Retrieved from https://www.forbes.com/sites/bryanrolli/2020/04/07/bts-dna-youtube-record-psy-gangnam-style/#cae4d427e2f2

References

1music4hall. (2010). *Taiwanese Lin Yu Chun sings "I Will Always Love You" Live* [Video]. YouTube. Retrieved from https://www.youtube.com/watch?v=aA-tOsM6F4Y

Ainslie, M. J. (2017). Korean soft masculinity vs. Malay hegemony: Malaysian masculinity and Hallyu fandom. *Korea Observer, 48*(3), 609-638.

Atkinson, J. (2003). Thumbing their noses at 'the man': An analysis of resistance narratives about multinational corporations. *Popular Communications, 1*(3), 163-168.

Boyd, D. (1997). *Am I black enough for you?: Popular culture from the 'hood and beyond.* Bloomington, IN: Indiana University Press.

Bucholtz, M., & Lopes, Q. (2011). Performing blackness, forming whiteness: Linguistic minstrelsy in Hollywood film. *Journal of Sociolinguistics, 15*(5), 680-706.

Calhoun, L. R. (2005). "Will the real slim shady please stand up?": Masking whiteness, encoding hegemonic masculinity in Eminem's Marshall Mathers LP. *The Howard Journal of Communications, 16*(4), 267-294.

Carrigan, T., Connell, B., & Lee, J. (1985). Toward a new sociology of masculinity. *Theory and Society, 14*(5), 551-604.

Chapman, R. (1988). The great pretender: Variations on the new man theme. In R. Chapman & J. Rutherford (Eds.), *Male order: Unwrapping masculinity* (pp. 225-248). London, UK: Lawrence and Wishart.

Cheah, J., & Kim, G. J. (2014). *Theological reflections on "Gangnam Style": A racial, sexual, and cultural critique.* New York, NY: Palgrave Macmillan.

Connell, R. W. (1987). *Gender and power.* Oxford, UK: Polity Press.

Connell, R. W. (2000). *The men and the boys.* Cambridge, UK: Polity Press.

Costello, M., & Wallace, D. F. (1990). *Signifying rappers: Rap and race in the urban present.* Hopewell, NJ: Ecco Press.

Dasgupta, R. (2000). Performing masculinities? The 'salaryman' at work and play. *Japanese Studies, 20*(2), 189-200.

Davis, A. (1983). *Women, race and class.* New York, NY: Vintage.

Dyson, M. E. (1996). *Between god and gangsta rap: Bearing witness to black culture.* New York, NY: Oxford University Press.

Eastman, J. T. (2012). Rebel manhood: The hegemonic masculinity of the southern rock music revival. *Journal of Contemporary Ethnography, 41*(2), 189-219.

Edgers, G. (2016). The collaboration that altered music-and popular culture. *The Washington Post.* Retrieved from https://www.washingtonpost.com/graphics/lifestyle/walk-this-way/

Espiritu, Y. L. (1997). *Asian American women and men: Labor, laws, and love.* Thousand Oaks, London, and New Delhi: Sage Publications.

Feng, Q. (2012). Many Chinese netizens find 'Gangnam Style' vulgar. Retrieved from http://english.peopledaily.com.cn/90782/7970737.html

Ferrell, J. (2001). *Tearing down the streets: Adventures in urban anarchy.* New York, NY: Palgrave.

Forman, M. (2002). *The hood comes first: Race, space and place in rap and hip-hop.* Middletown, CT: Wesleyan University Press.

Geng, S. (2016). Changing masculinities in East Asian pop culture. *East Asia Forum Quarterly, 8*(2), 3-5.

George, N. (2001). *Buppies, b-boys, baps, and bohos: Notes on post-soul black culture.*

Da Capo Press.

Hanke, R. (1990). Hegemonic masculinity in thirtysomething. *Critical Studies in Mass Communication, 7*(3), 231-248.

Hanke, R. (1998). The "mock-macho" situation comedy: Hegemonic masculinity and its reiteration. *Western Journal of Communication, 62*(1), 74-93.

Henson, L., & Parameswaran, R. E. (2008). Getting real with "tell it like it is" talk therapy: Hegemonic masculinity and the Dr. Phil Show. *Communication, Culture, & Critique, 1*(3), 287-310.

Hoffmann, F. W. (2007). *Rhythm and blues, rap, and hip-hop*. New York, NY: Facts on File.

Jackson, R. L. (2006). *Scripting the black masculine body: Identity, discourse, and racial politics in popular media*. Albany, NY: SUNY Press.

Jackson, R. L., & Moshin, J. E. (Eds.). (2012). *Communicating marginalized masculinities: Identity politics in TV, film, and new media*. New York, NY: Routledge.

Jung, S. (2009). The shared imagination of Bishonen, pan-East Asian soft masculinity: Reading DBSK, Youtube.com and transcultural new media consumption. *Intersections: Gender and Sexuality in Asia and the Pacific, 20*. Retrieved from http://intersections.anu.edu.au/issue20/jung.htm

Kawai, Y. (2005). Stereotyping Asian America: The dialectic of the model minority and the yellow peril. *Howard Journal of Communications, 16*(2), 109-130.

Kee, P. S. (2016). The Korean tradition of humor in Psy's "Gangnam Style". *Korean Journal, 56*(1), 5-32.

Kim, Y. (2013). Representation of people of Asian descent in mainstream mass media within the United States. *Multicultural Education Review, 5*(2), 20-48.

Kitwana, B. (2002). *The hip hop generation: Young blacks and the crisis in African American culture*. New York, NY: Basic Civitas Book.

Krims, A. (2000). *Rap music and the poetics of identity*. New York, NY: Cambridge University Press.

Lasn, K. (1999). *Culture jamming*. New York, NY: Harper Collins.

Lebra, T. S. (1976). *Japanese patterns of behavior*. Honolulu, HW: University of Hawaii Press.

Lorber, J., & Farrell, S. A. (1990). *The social construction of gender*. Thousand Oaks, CA: Sage Publications.

Louie, K. H. (2012). Popular culture and masculinity ideals in East Asia, with special reference to China. *The Journal of Asian Studies, 71*(4), 929-943.

MacKinnon, K. (2003). *Sex and gender: Maleness and masculinity*. New York, NY: Oxford University Press.

Miller, T. (2001). *Sportsex*. Philadelphia, PA: Temple University Press.

Nakayama, T. K. (1994). Show/down time: "Race," gender, sexuality, and popular culture. *Critical Studies in Mass Communication, 11*(2), 162-179.

Navarro, M. (2007). Missing: Asian-American pop stars. *The New York Times*. Retrieved from http://www.nytimes.com/2007/03/04/world/americas/04iht-singer.4787848.html?pagewanted=all&_r=0

Nini. (2015). *Aziatix announces departure from Cash Money Records*. Retrieved from https://www.hellokpop.com/news/aziatix-announces-departure-from-cash-money-records/

Reyes, A. (2007). *Language, identity, and stereotype among Southeast Asian American youth: The other Asian*. Mahwah, NJ: Lawrence Erlbaum.

Said, E. W. (1979). *Orientalism*. New York, NY: Random House.

Sinha-Roy, P. (2012). Pink tops Billboard Album Chart, 'Gangnam' No. 1 digital song. *Reuters*. Retrieved from http://www.reuters.com/article/2012/09/26/entertainment-us-chart-pink-idUSBRE88P1FP20120926

Skeggs, B. (1993). Two minute brother: Contestation through gender, race, and sexuality. *Innovation in Social Science Research, 6*(3), 299-322.

Song, K. Y., & Velding, V. (2020). Transnational masculinity in the eyes of local beholders? Young Americans' perception of K-pop masculinities. *Journal of Men's Studies, 28*(1), 3-21.

Sugimoto, Y. (2004). *An introduction to Japanese society*. Cambridge, UK: Cambridge University Press.

Trujillo, N. (1991). Hegemonic masculinity on the mound: Media representations of Nolan Ryan and American sports culture. *Critical Studies in Mass Communication, 8*(3), 290-308.

Vargas, J. A. (2007). "Slanted screen" rues the absence of Asians. *The Washington Post*. Retrieved from http://www.washingtonpost.com/wp-dyn/content/article/2007/05/24/AR2007052402573.html

Vavrus, M. D. (2002). Domesticating patriarchy: Hegemonic masculinity and television's 'Mr. Mom'. *Critical Studies in Media Communication, 19*(3), 352-375.

White, M. (2011). *From Jim Crow to Jay-Z: Race, rap, and the performance of masculinity*. Champaign, IL: University of Illinois Press.

Wilkins, C. L., Chan, J., & Kaiser, C. J. (2011). Racial stereotypes and interracial attraction: Phenotypic prototypicality and perceived attractiveness of Asians. *Cultural Diversity and Ethnic Minority Psychology, 17*(4), 427-431.

Zhang, Q. (2010). Asian Americans beyond the model minority stereotype: The nerdy and the leftout. *Journal of International and Intercultural Communication, 3*(1), 20-37.

CHAPTER 6

To Lose Your Path is the Way to Find That Path: The BTS Narrative, Mental Health, and US Fans

Hannah Christine Fassbender, **Xzavior Rain Sweeny**, & **Cheryl L. Nicholas**, Pennsylvania State University at Berks

The music helped me sympathize with our young generation and also empathize with them. I'd like to create and write more music that represents them.

J-Hope, *Elle* Interview (2017)

In May 2019, Kpop boy-band Bangtan Sonyeondan, which means Bulletproof Boy Scouts, but more commonly known as BTS, stayed five weeks in the number one position on the Billboard Artist 100 chart (Zellner, 2019). The band already had three number one albums on the Billboard 200 charts in the last year, a feat which propelled them to the ranks of UK and US bands such as The Beatles and The Monkees. They are the first Korean pop music (K-pop) band to spend 1-year on the Billboard 200, with their album *Love Yourself: Answer* while simultaneously breaking several other records on the Billboard charts (Benjamin, 2019). In 2019, they attended and presented an award at the 61st GRAMMY Award ceremony in the United States. BTS is reported to have over 40 million followers on social media and a combined net worth of nearly 60 million (Winifred, 2019). Their transnational fandom, known as ARMY (acronym for "adorable representative MC for youth") has significantly out-performed the fan-bases of top US-Western musicians on various social media platforms (Blake, 2018). BTS' meteoric rise in the US charts, along with their widespread popularity globally is so captivating that popular online US news magazines (such as CNN and *The Guardian*) have recently labeled them the "biggest" or "best boy-band in the world."

BTS comprises seven young men from South Korea, aged 28 to 23. They are from oldest to youngest, with associated stage-name: Kim Seokjin (Jin), Min Yoongi (Suga), Jung Hoseok (J-Hope), Kim Namjoon (RM), Park Jimin (Jimin), Kim Taehyung (V), and Jeon Jeongguk (Jungkook). They were initially formed as a hip-hop group under Big Hit Entertainment in 2013 but have since evolved to include into their repertoire a variety of different music genres, from pop and gangsta-rap, to punk and R&B. While their music style may appear distinctive, BTS is also well-known for socially conscious messages that imbue their music and rhetoric.

BTS' success has been easily linked to the Korean wave—*Hanryu/Hallyu* in the Korean language—which references the swell of Korean pop culture in global markets. Since its beginnings in East Asia in the 1990s, Hallyu has grown, bringing considerable international visibility to Korean media products (Kim & Kim, 2011). Jin (2016) claims that since 2008, Hallyu has evolved to focus more strongly on platforms that appeal to digital and social media, with a younger consumer base, and stronger investment in genres such as K-pop, video games, and animation. This new-Hallyu also has a wider geographic appeal, with pronounced movement into Europe, Central Asia, and the Americas. Hallyu's recent momentum in countries outside of East Asia, has drawn the attention of Western media pundits and scholars, who also recognize the influence of new technology such as streaming and social media on Hallyu's progress in the West. Longenecker and Kim (2018) have argued, for instance, that the surprise success of PSY's "Gangnam-Style" and the more recent momentous accomplishments of BTS in the United States can be attributed to YouTube streaming.

The growing corpus of scholarship on the global expansion of Hallyu in general (for example, Jin, 2016; Kim & Kim, 2011; Lee & Normes, 2015), and K-pop music in particular (for example, Kim, 2018b; Kim, 2019; Lee & Jin, 2019) is noteworthy. There has been less focus, however, and as attested by the need of this volume, on the influence of Hallyu/K-pop in Western cultures or of its appeal to Western consumers. More so, the remarkable infusion of Korean culture in Western countries such as the United States, the United Kingdom, and France unravels longstanding notions about the Western/US domination of global culture and provides a unique opportunity to engage with the complex interplay of global-local forces' influence on the West.

This study of BTS's music attempts to address these research needs. BTS' successes in the US create an opportunity to better understand how Korean popular culture operates and engages with/in US culture. BTS' messages on mental health in their music videos are of particular interest here. As this chapter argues, mental health 'narratives' found in BTS' music videos are distinctively appealing to US (young adult) audiences, since these videos transcend language barriers, offering a space for community and connection.

K-Pop, BTS, and Mental Health

The inclusion of socially conscious mental health messaging in BTS' music and rhetoric was not happenstance. Their music reflects stances and struggles related to mental health in the larger K-pop music industry. Jung (2017a) states that there has been, since the early 1990s, a distinct shift in K-pop music spearheaded by Seo Taiji and Boys. Seo Taiji introduced newer musical styles and choreography (inspired by US/Western hip-hop, rap, and metal) while incorporating fashion and lyrics that appealed to younger people. Seo Taiji offered a hybridized (US-Korean style) that challenged censorship limits and promoted self-expression along with social consciousness. Taiji's influence came at an interesting time, since the two decades before the 90s saw much of Korean music broadcasting regulated or heavily scrutinized by the government in defense of patriotism and the moral code. Moreover, the emergence of a new youth generation (called *Sinsedae* or Generation X) paved the way for Seo Taiji and Boys and other similar groups to (re) shape Korean popular music. *Sinsedae* were middle-class and affluent. Living in urban areas, they grew up consuming American (popular) culture such as, television, fast food, music, and fashion (Jung, 2017a, b).

In the late 1990s, three powerhouse music studios—SM Entertainment, JYP Entertainment, YG Entertainment—emerged to methodically create idol groups (Shin & Kim, 2013). Members of idol groups, which persist in Korea, are selected through auditions and are subject to highly disciplined grooming, enmeshed in a rigid studio culture that demands "perfection" in all areas, from physical appearance to dance moves and musicality. Padget (2017), citing "slave contracts," notes of the difficulties faced by idol group members while trying to cope with the high standards placed on them, since studios exert strong control over the idols' performance (music, dance), brand and marketing, as well as their everyday lifestyle/behaviors. Additionally, such controls streamlined the idol groups to represent the studio's interests, thus erasing the idols' personal messages of self-expression and social consciousness (as initially introduced by Seo Taiji). Padget reveals that there have been several idols who suffered from depression, anxiety, and even physical injury due to these pressures. Mental health related tragedies, such as the 2017 suicide of Kim Jong Hyun from the band SHINee, became public discourse focusing on mental health issues, not only among K-pop idols, but also more generally in South Korea.

Despite the developing interest in mental health issues in Korea, such subjects have rarely appeared in popular Korean music. This is perhaps where BTS stands out amongst other K-pop bands. BTS' music, lyrics, and public communication address topics germane to the mental health of Korean youth; from life pressures and cultural expectations, depression and suicide, to identity issues and social/communal support. These messages are also appealing to their US/global fans. Industry and entertainment publications have recognized these efforts, citing BTS as "helping to erase the stigma associated with mental health issues like depression" (Galla, 2018, p. 7) and that the band breaks social taboos about mental health when they "tell their fans to fight back and remain alive" (Kim, 2018a, para 11). In its official website, Big Hit Entertainment, BTS' recording company, proudly labels itself "Music and Artist for Healing" and along with BTS as its main front, promotes the "Love Myself" campaign that features self-care and mental well-being (Big Hit Entertainment, n.d.). Even popular Western news sites such as *TIME*, have recognized these efforts, noting, "With BTS there has been the ongoing "Love Yourself" narrative, paired with their work with the U.N. and their openness on topics like mental health" (Bruner, 2019). Anecdotal data from Western/global fans sites and web-posts attest to these claims; fans have fervently claimed BTS' role in helping them cope with mental struggles or strive for better mental health. While BTS' messages on self-care and mental health are well publicized in popular media venues and within fan communities, their work has received little academic attention. Most scholarly work on BTS focuses more broadly on their fan-culture (for example, Chang & Park, 2019;

Jung, 2017b), with some notable exceptions, such as Achmad, Fitriani, & Hanifa's (2019) study on self-esteem in lyrics from the *Love Myself* campaign.

BTS' US Fans and Mental Health

Mental health issues are also a relevant topic for young Americans, and as argued here, an important factor in why BTS' message and music are appealing to US audiences. Mentally vulnerable youth are known to have a high consumption of and intense relationships with music (North & Hargreaves, 2006). A study done by the U.S. Department of Health and Human Studies through the National Institute of Mental Health in 2017 found that one in five US adolescents has experienced some sort of mental disorder. Mental health issues are particularly common in school-aged students, and many begin with symptoms by age fourteen. There are many reasons that school-aged children have a high risk of having a mental health disorder; a study by the Pew Research Center (DeSilver, 2016) found that parents were most concerned with their children being bullied, followed closely by their children struggling with anxiety or depression.

Moreover, the number of young people experiencing mental difficulties seem to be growing (Mojtabai, Olfson, & Han, 2016). These trends mirror global trends of growing mental disorders among adolescents.

While there is still a stigma around mental illness in the United States, it is not quite as taboo a topic as it tends to be in many other countries. Additionally, mental health is an increasingly important public health issue which has garnered the attention of Western artists and celebrities. In 2017, for instance, American rapper, Logic, released a song titled "1-800-273-8255" featuring popular American musicians Alessia Cara and Khalid. The track title is the phone number for the National Suicide Prevention Lifeline, and the song imitates a phone call between a hotline worker and someone contemplating suicide. This song spent 42 weeks on the Billboard Top 100 and peaked at number 3 (Billboard, 2019). Other famous American musical artists like Shawn Mendes, Khalid, Lil Uzi, Kendrick Lamar, Lady Gaga, Alessia Cara, and Billie Eilish have also had popular hits that relate to mental health issues. US music fans seem to be drawn to music that deals with mental well-being. This is unsurprising as there have been numerous studies linking music to mental health in young people (see McFerran, Garrido, & Saarikallio, 2016).

Similarly, BTS has been particularly successful with US fans because of how they address mental health in their music and public persona. Yoon (2018) claims that for young Western fans, K-pop can provide "a resource to symbolically negotiate their social and material problems" (p. 386). Longenecker and Lee (2018) assert that BTS fulfills their US fans' social and psychological needs; as explained by uses and gratifications research (see Katz, Blumer, & Gurevitch, 1973), fans are attracted to media that serves a purpose or satisfies a need, be it for personal- and social-integration, cognitive and affective demands, or even to relieve tension. Specifically, BTS fulfills mental health and social well-being needs of their US fans in two major ways, through 1) community inclusion and 2) celebrity connection.

BTS' communication with fans along with the potency of their fan virtual community—ARMY—epitomizes the idea of *community inclusion*. ARMY offers fans a powerful base for social interaction and connection. There have been several studies that have attested to the ARMY's fan efficacy, brought about by their cultural, political, and even economic clout (e.g. Chang & Park, 2019). ARMY has been argued to be responsible for much of BTS' advancement in the United States. Ju (2019) states that in 2017, ARMY launched an online campaign in the US, along with 'tactical manuals,' to promote BTS through local radio stations and among well-known deejays. Importantly, the relationship between BTS and ARMY, and within members of ARMY, is characterized by public expressions of care and love, supporting the claim for mental well-being. BTS express their care and affection through their extensive social media presence and "heartfelt recognition" of their fanbase, including noting how certain songs are written for their fans and checking in to see if their fans are satisfied or happy. Longenecker and Lee (2018) cite an interview with Bang Shi-Hyuk, CEO of Big Hit Entertainment in *Joon Ang Daily*, where Bang asserts that for ARMY, BTS is "a shoulder to lean on" (p. 115).

Longenecker and Lee (2018) argue that BTS fans can have "imaginative emotional connections" with BTS members, so much so that their songs may attend to deeper psychological needs. This *celebrity connection* is another important factor in how US fans are drawn to BTS. Studies on parasocial relationships in fandoms show how fans imagine a "real" relationship with the celebrity, often referencing them as they would an actual social relationship. Caughey (1984) explains how most of these relationships help fans compensate or replace unsettling everyday experiences. These relationships can also give fans an escape by offering them an ideal self-image. Citing Hills (2013) research, Longenecker and Lee show that fans do not merely have a connection to the band's material, rather they have a profound connection to the musicians themselves, where the fans "anchor" their own narratives to that of the celebrity. This connection fosters both a sense of solidarity with BTS members and with ARMY/other fans. Correspondingly, Ju (2019) claims that ARMY is connected to a "narrative of growth" in the BTS universe. The BTS universe (or BU) is colloquially named by fans and prominent BTS players, such as CEO Bang Shi-Hyuk, as the composite space of all things BTS.

Ju (2019) discusses Lee Jeeheng's critical analysis of the BTS universe, noting that BTS creates their own imaginary world through their songs and music videos. In the BTS universe, BTS members are engulfed in narratives of despair, mental duress, and tragedy. They eventually overcome these struggles, become self-aware, and discover self-love. BTS fans attach their own narrative to that of BTS, "growing together" to overcome social and psychological hardship. This growth narrative unifies BTS fans, particularly young adult fans who struggle with mental health.

These arguments about US audiences' mental health needs, as fulfilled by community inclusion and celebrity connection in BTS' celebrity, music, and fandom, operate as a touchstone to this study on BTS' music videos. As next discussed, music videos, unlike other forms of music media (e.g. CDs, streaming services), are particularly efficacious with US audiences in conveying mental health messages.

Music Videos and Access

BTS' messages, especially those with strong affect such as the "growing together narrative," are potent when available in audio-visual formats. As earlier noted, multimedia audio-visual messages in social media sites such as YouTube have prompted BTS' successes in the US and globally. Their appeal to US audiences is simple; visual channels are highly relevant in cases where linguistic channels pose barriers. Additionally, music videos operate on both visual and aural channels, and as such can offer a stronger platform for messages that have high affect. In this format, BTS' narratives about mental health and "growing together" can be easily accessed by US audiences.

In addition, BTS' messages of mental wellness and self-love are attractive to US audiences when packaged with American music elements, from music genres (e.g. rap, rock, electronic) to dance styles (e.g. jazz, hip-hop, contemporary) and English lyrics. Cultural hybridization, where global and local forces are continually negotiated, is germane to K-pop's worldwide/US success (Ryoo, 2006). Longenecker and Lee (2018) add, "Incorporating American musical elements into K-pop songs illustrates the case of hybridization ... this helps K-pop find a smooth transition to acceptance by the American audience" (p. 112-113). Music videos are thus an ideal media to analyze BTS' messages on mental health.

Data Collection and Analysis of BTS' Music Videos

At the time of this analysis in March 2019, BTS had made thirty-five music videos in the span of their career, since 2013 (not including extended/dance/special, and Japanese versions of the original Korean music videos). Twenty of the thirty-five music videos were selected for analysis. The videos selected (Table 1) were title track videos and highly popular videos based on YouTube views. The music videos were obtained from the Big Hit Entertainment's official YouTube page, Bangtan TV/Big Hit Labels (Ibighit, 2019).

The first part of the analysis (content analysis) was focused on proportion and type of *negative* and *positive* mental health messages found visually (text, mise-en-scène, editing) in the videos. The second part of the analysis (textual analysis) explored narrative themes around mental health that emerged from those messages. First, it was necessary to define qualifiers of positive and negative mental health messages. The qualifiers were determined by watching the selected music videos in multiple viewings while inductively generating classifications for positive and negative mental health depictions, until saturation was reached. The inquiry yielded more categories for negative qualifiers (12) over positive qualifiers (5), and it was decided that these categories would remain to keep the integrity of the initial findings. Negative and positive qualifiers found are listed in Table 2.

Coding criteria was developed for the next level of analysis. Coding was based on how much time (in seconds) was dedicated to these positive and negative qualifiers. Two of the researchers/authors (Fassbender and Sweeny) were trained to code the music videos based on the coding criteria, reaching an intercoder reliability of > 0.85. They watched and coded the twenty music videos separately and four videos together, focusing first on positive qualifiers and then re-watching the videos for negative qualifiers. A textual analysis was then incorporated to explore narrative themes, based on how the primary positive and negative qualifiers were depicted (based on the results of the content analysis).

Results

The results indicate that BTS music videos have a high propensity to visually represent mental health issues, with approximately 55-66% of the 20 videos analyzed being associated with mental health messages. These percentages are approximate since certain categories (e.g. rebellion) could be coded simultaneously. Importantly, there are

Table 1. Music Videos Analyzed

No More Dream (2013)	*We Are Bulletproof pt.2* (2013)	*N.O.* (2013)	*Danger* (2014)
Boy In Luv (2014)	*I Need U* (Original Version) (2015)	*Dope* (2015)	*Run* (2015)
Epilogue: Young Forever (2016)	*Fire* (2016)	*Save Me* (2016)	*Blood, Sweat, & Tears* (2016)
Spring Day (2017)	*Not Today* (2017)	*Come Back Home* (2017)	*DNA* (2017)
Mic Drop (Steve Aoki Remix) (2017)	*Euphoria* (2018)	*Fake Love* (2018)	*Idol* (2018)

Table 2. Mental Health Qualifiers

Negative Mental Health Qualifiers	
Depression	Signs of sadness such as frowning, crying, despondent stares, apathy
Anxiety	Portrayals of tenseness or anxiousness, hesitation, fearful looks
Medication	Use of medication to treat mental health issues, or portrayals of over-medication and the use of medicine
Suicide	Attempting to end or ending one's own life
Self-Hatred	Directing hatred towards one's self, self-violence, negative facial expressions when looking at one's self
Anger	Acting aggressive or using aggressive body language or facial expressions
Rebellion (negative)	Pushing back against systems in place and stereotypes, disobeying authority figures, breaking laws, or rules, getting arrested, or chased by police
Uncertainty	Lack of knowing what to do or how to proceed, lost, wandering aimlessly, blurriness
Loneliness	Being alone or isolated/isolating one's self
Violence/ Destruction	Being destructive, harming others or objects
Bullying	Putting down others, abusing others, harming others emotionally or physically
Masking	Hiding who one is or shying away from revealing one's true self, use of masks, sunglasses, hats that cover the eyes, costumes, or hiding from others
Positive Mental Health Qualifiers	
Friendship/ Community	Love between friends/community, sharing activities with friends/ community, thinking/dreaming about friends/community, showing concern for, supporting, and helping friends/ community with difficult issues
Hard work	Dedication to work and one's goals, doing jobs, roles of workers, studying, exercising, being determined to succeed, not giving up, career-based outfits, portrayal of careers
Love	Romantic feelings or gestures towards another person
Happiness	Joy in life, an outward expression of happiness in life, wearing bright colors, positive settings, and smiling
Rebellion (positive)	Pushing back against systems in place and stereotypes, doing what is right. Breaking rules or showing disobedience for a positive goal

also distinct differences in mental health messages of BTS music videos related to chronology; that is, their messages on mental health change over time. The music videos analyzed (Table 3) are situated into three categories: a) Early videos, from 2013-2014; b) Middle videos, from 2015-2016; and c) Later videos, from 2017-2018.

Early Videos (5 videos, 2013-2014)

The early works of BTS show overwhelming negative mental health trends with minimal amounts of positive qualifiers (50% of negative/ 10% positive). The few representations of positive mental health are about positive-rebellion, love, and hard-work. The overarching themes, however, are violence/destruction, (negative and positive) rebellion, masking, and anger.

Many of these early music videos show BTS rebelling against repressive systems of power. Specifically, in the *N.O.* music video, BTS is shown breaking classroom rules and revolting against the strictly regulated education system. The members appear visibly upset and they outwardly express anger towards the education system; they destroy a classroom. This behavior against the education system was coded as both negative and positive rebellion. The method of rebelling is violent, and therefore negative. The goal of the rebellion, however, is positive, that is to revolt against an oppressive system.

In BTS' first three music videos released, RM wears sunglasses throughout his screen time. Other members wear black or spiked face masks to cover (parts of) their faces. Masking is prevalent in these early videos. This physical hiding is something BTS has acknowledged in more recent works, pointing to the inability to show one's true self, or the need to hide from the world/others.

Finally, in many of the solo shots, BTS members scowl or appear angry while singing. Anger is shown in a myriad of ways, often interlinked with the other negative qualifiers such as rebellion and violence. BTS was coded as having a higher level of aggression associated with their displays of anger compared to their later videos. The colors in these early videos (such as in clothing and setting) also lean towards darker and more gloomy hues.

Table 3. Chronological Categories of Music Videos

Song title	Seconds per video dedicated to negative mental health	Seconds per video dedicated to positive mental health
	Early Videos (2013-2014)	
No More Dream	128/290	4/290
We Are Bulletproof pt.2	158/233	5/233
N.O.	144/243	23/243
Danger	115/291	12/291
Boy In Luv	127/282	101/282
Mental health representation-early videos	672/1339 50% negative mental health	145/1339 10% positive mental health
	Approximate overall mental health representation: 60%	
	Middle Videos (2015-2016)	
I Need U (Original)	216/333	79/333
Dope	7/256	156/256
Run	184/450	218/450
Epilogue: Young Forever	92/205	54/205
Fire	100/294	89/294
Save Me	80/217	67/217
Blood, Sweat, & Tears	114/364	32/364
Spring Day	124/329	111/329
Not Today	47/291	36/291
Mental health representation-middle videos	964/2739 35% negative mental health	842/2739 31% positive mental health
	Approximate overall mental health representation: 66%	
	Later Videos (2017-2018)	
Come Back Home	177/271	15/271
DNA	0/256	39/256
Mic Drop (Steve Aoki remix)	160/274	26/274
Euphoria	134/533	216/533
Fake Love	167/319	29/319
Idol	25/232	48/232
Mental health representation-current videos	663/1885 35% negative mental health	373/1885 20% positive mental health
	Approximate overall mental health representation: 55%	

Middle Videos (9 videos, 2015-2016)

The middle videos represent the largest of three categories analyzed, and this category indicates a distinct shift in BTS' representation of mental health, with the number of negative mental health qualifiers dropping to 35% and the positive qualifiers rising to 31%. Moreover, and perhaps more significantly, this segment relates more directly to mental health disorders or consequences (i.e. depression, anxiety, suicide, self-hatred). The middle videos also have the highest number of positive qualifiers in comparison to early and later music videos. The positive qualifiers are presented as friendship, happiness, and hard work.

While there is a smaller percentage of the depiction of negative mental health compared to the early videos, what is portrayed is particularly poignant and strategic. Each member of the group is shown struggling with some form of mental health issue, and their struggle can be found thematically in many of the videos in this time frame. V is shown fraught with anxiety due to his abusive alcoholic father. He wanders the city in torment instead of going home. Suga is depicted as depressed and suicidal; he lights himself on fire while in a hotel room. Also depressed and suicidal is Jimin, who tries to drown himself. J-Hope is shown looking at his reflection in contempt and disdain. There are also several scenes where members are depicted in mental health institutions.

The use of medication to treat mental health is present in these videos. J-Hope is seen taking pills, often in handfuls, indicating an abuse of self-medication. BTS members are also portrayed significantly as isolated and alone. There is a consistent pattern of members experiencing strong mental distress due to such isolation. This tendency is particularly relevant when compared to BTS' later videos that show friendship/community to counter mental struggles.

In these middle videos BTS are still shown as being violent/destructive, as well as rebelling against oppressive legal and social rules. BTS break the law by spraying graffiti on public walls and cars, and they encounter the police when doing so. Objects are still being blown up or set on fire and BTS members get into verbal or physical fights. A key finding in these videos, however, is that while still present, these negative behaviors appear to be toned down compared to earlier videos. Displays of violence and destruction are more inward-directed, directed towards members of the band, or people close to the band; for example, the videos show Jungkook being jumped by a stranger on the street, and in the *Not Today* video, all seven BTS members are seen running away from a shooter.

It is in these middle videos that friendship emerges as a significant and consistent theme. When the band members are together, they are happier than when they are apart. Many of these videos juxtapose scenes of an isolated BTS member struggling with negative mental health issues, with scenes of that same member happy when with other members of the group. This theme continues in the later videos but is not quite as amplified.

Later Videos (6 videos, 2017-2018)

Later BTS videos continue the trend in switching between negative and positive mental health messages. While it might be the case that the percentage of positive health messages here is lower (at 20%) than that of the middle period, the quality of those messages is different as they reflect a stronger ethos for mental wellness. Compared to the middle period, the amount of negative mental health messages is comparable (35%) but qualitatively, the negativity is assuaged or presented with an interesting spin. Negative mental health depictions follow earlier themes of masking, loneliness, anger, depression, anxiety, and violence/destruction. BTS members appear to still be involved in negativity, but interestingly, in these later videos there are more instances when the negativity does not implicate them; for example, in the middle videos, both Suga and Jimin attempt suicide by self-immolation and drowning, but in 2017's *Fake Love* similar scenes occur but instead of inflicting harm, the flames and water circle both members, not touching them. Moreover, in the later videos BTS members appear to be less encumbered by mental despair and they perform less self-harm, especially when they are with other members of the group. Like the earlier videos, negative mental health outcomes happen when BTS members are isolated or alone. There are also brighter/lighter colors and textures incorporated into these videos, indicating shift or break away from darker times.

The videos in this later period show a higher tendency for BTS members to be seen together. In these scenes, they are depicted in mundane 'friendship' behaviors, such as hanging out, joking, and showing support/camaraderie (embracing, leaning into each other). They are happy together. Friendship/community (and happiness related to friendship/community) is the most common positive mental health theme coded in all the later videos. The message is distinct: that (BTS) friends/community can help each other overcome or cope with mental health problems; or more so, that mental wellness is associated with being part of a friendship/community, and we should support that friendship/community, keeping it intact.

BTS' later videos are also packaged as part of a larger campaign on mental wellness and self-care. Their music compilation *Love Yourself*, released over the span of 2017-2018, features three albums: *Her, Tear*, and *Answer*. BTS has been very clear that the overarching message of this compilation is about caring for ourselves and others (the community). These messages are available in related music videos, as analyzed.

US Audiences and the BTS Narrative on Mental Health

This study shows that BTS music videos visually contain a significant amount of positive and negative mental health messages. The content analysis demarcates their negative and positive mental health messages, pointing to a drop in negative messages and a rise in positive messages starting with BTS videos in 2015. The closer textual analysis, however, offers perhaps the more significant findings, yielding an underlying narrative about mental health, implicating BTS and their US followers. This BTS narrative offers a compelling justification for celebrity connection and community inclusion.

An important part of the BTS narrative is the distinct depiction of mental health suffering, from anxiety and depression to suicidal tendencies. BTS ventures into areas considered taboo in K-pop music to bring into sharp detail the dire struggles of those afflicted with mental illness. Their story, however, does not end here. BTS offers a solution—support from friends/community—to help counter and cope with these mental struggles. Such support, for their fans, is easily available in ARMY; BTS' fan-community. According to Chang and Park (2019), the ARMY is unlike ordinary fan communities; with a tribe-like stance in their social media and internet engagements, they advocate for individual perspective and voice, operating with(in) the backdrop of strong community support and connection. Chang and Park claim that the ARMY's rhetoric is particularly appealing to Western/global audiences. The messages of friendship/community connection in current BTS music videos work in tandem with the larger culture and dialogues of support in ARMY.

BTS' narrative on mental health is one that not only acknowledges mental health issues but empathizes with people suffering from those issues. Such understanding and consideration towards mental health dispositions are enticing to audiences who are themselves struggling with mental health. BTS' public and musical persona, as advocates for mental health and self-love, is crucial here, as it is this that their fans latch on to. Tajfeld and Turner's (1979) social identity theory (SIT), and other theories of identity, has been used by several scholars (see summary in Lamont & Hargreaves, 2019) to explain how young music fans categorize themselves and participate in behaviors based on shared social identities. SIT postulates that parts of our self-concept stem from our in-group membership.

US fans find further identification with band members based on the implicit meta-narrative of BTS' own struggles and mental duress of being in and navigating the limelight. In the music videos, the BTS narrative relied heavily on visuals of BTS members engulfed in symbols that represent mental illness (e.g. masks, pills, darkness, and fire) and mental well-being (e.g. bright colors, hugs, smiling faces). The interaction between BTS and symbols of mental health/wellness is what drives the BTS' narrative and become critical points for introspection. Sandvoss (2005) states that these critical points are distinctive, as they offer fans opportunities for self-examination, where fans can mimic or see themselves in those objects. In so doing, fans "superimpose attributes of the self, their beliefs and value systems and, ultimately, their sense of self on the object of fandom" (p. 104). Therefore, meanings are not necessarily situated in the music videos, but emerge from fans' interaction with these critical points in the BTS narrative. There is distinct influence in these negotiations, as Sandvoss asserts, "It is, then, precisely because objects of fandom can be so radically appropriated by fans to service their own self-reflection, that they gain the ability to profoundly shape the fan" (p. 112-113).

As explained earlier in the chapter, fans can find a deep emotional bond with the celebrity (Hills, 2013; Longenecker & Lee, 2018), and in some cases they form a parasocial relationship with that celebrity. Parasocial relationships can easily work alongside "narratives of growth" as discussed by Ju (2019). When fans' realities about relationships with celebrities are imagined to be real, similarly imagined are perceived struggles, and methods of overcoming those struggles. The music videos are clear in showing these struggles and triumphs. Thus, through the BTS narrative, BTS and their fans are "in it together," pointing to both celebrity connection and community inclusion as the basis for managing mental well-being. Moreover, BTS' crusade for mental health and well-being, extolled in the media and strident in their public discourse, further validates what fans already experience through the music videos. In these ways, these (positive and negative) visual representations of mental health form an overarching story that works to spread BTS' messages on mental health, while breaking language barriers, making their message more accessible in the US/Western contexts.

Conclusion

Audio-visual messages in social media such as YouTube, have prompted the success of Korean groups such as BTS in the US, and globally. US audiences are attracted to media that address issues considered important or that bring fulfillment, within a platform of access and cultural hybridity. Mental health is an important issue among young people in the United States, and it is contended here that mental health messages in BTS music videos make BTS particularly appealing to US youth.

The music videos tell a story of BTS' journey grappling with mental health; from early times of loneliness, despair and destruction, bound by stifling social rules and expectations, to dealing with different types of mental disorders that can cause harm, and finally a possible breakthrough, in finding solace and support through friendship/community. The BTS narrative, as this story is referred to here, offers fans a space to attend to mental health needs through community inclusion and celebrity connection; it is a place for negotiation and refuge.

This chapter examined mental health messages in BTS music videos—finding the BTS narrative on mental health—to better understand BTS' appeal to US audiences; however, the focus of the study is limited. More research, preferably from the perspective of the US fan (using interviews and/or field methodologies) can benefit this research trajectory and add a deeper and multilayered conversation about US audience mental health needs as fulfilled by BTS/K-pop. More research is necessary as we enter another chapter of the BTS narrative.

On April 12, 2019 BTS released *Map of the Soul: Persona,* and on February 20, 2020, BTS released their album, *Map of the Soul: 7,* featuring twenty tracks, which includes five remakes. These albums are already making waves in the US, garnering the dedication and support of BTS' US fan base. In a review on Billboard.com (Herman, 2020), *Map of the Soul: 7* is described as self-reflective and fulfilling; with BTS looking back on their seven-year career while "optimistic in facing both past and future shadows ... [and] rife with potential regarding whatever comes their way" (para. 15). The *Map of the Soul* series offers a potentially new layer to BTS' interaction with their US fans. It is left to see where these albums take the BTS narrative, and if mental health still plays a prominent role.

Recommended Readings

Kim, D. K., & Kim, M. S. (Eds.). (2011). *Hallyu: Influence of Korean popular culture in Asia and beyond.* Seoul, Korea: Seoul National University Press.

Kim, G. (2019). *From factory girls to K-pop idol girls: Cultural politics of developmentalism, patriarchy, and neoliberalism in South Korea's popular music industry.* Lanham, MD: Lexington.

Kim, S. Y. (2018). *K-pop live: Fans, idols, and multimedia performance. Stanford, CA: Stanford University Press.*

Lee, H., & Jin, D. (2019). *K-pop idols: Popular culture and the emergence of the Korean music industry.* Lanham, MD: Lexington.

Longenecker, L., & Lee, J. (2018). The Korean wave in America: Assessing the status of K-pop and K-drama between global and local. *Situations: Cultural Studies in the Asian Context. 11*(2), 105-127.

Additional Sources

ARMY (USA) Official Webpage. Retrieved from https://www.usbtsarmy.com/

BTS Official Website. Retrieved from https://ibighit.com/bts/eng/

BTS YouTube Channel. *Bangtan TV/Big Hit Labels.* Retrieved from https://www.youtube.com/channel/UCLkAepWjdylmXSltofFvsYQ

References

Achmad, D., Fitriani, S., & Hanifa D. (2019). Love Myself campaign: Exploring Branden's sic-pillars of self-esteem in BTS songs. *Proceedings of the 28th International Conference on Literature: Literature as a Source of Wisdom*, Banda Aceh, Indonesia. doi:10.24815/.v1i1.14409

Benjamin, J. (2019, November 6). BTS has the very first K-pop album to spend 1 year on the Billboard 200. *Billboard: Chart Beat.* Retrieved from https://www.billboard.com/articles/business/chart-beat/8542957/bts-love-yourself-answer-1-year-billboard-200-first-kpop-album

Big Hit Entertainment. (n.d.). *Music and artist for healing.* https://www.bighitcorp.com/eng/

Billboard. (n.d.). *Logic: Chart history.* Retrieved from https://www.billboard.com/music/logic/chart-history/hot-100/song/1024604

Blake, E. (2018, April 4). The strength of K-pop fandom, by the numbers. *Forbes.* Retrieved from https://www.forbes.com/sites/emilyblake1/2018/04/04/k-pop-numbers/#2563ec2448ab

Bruner, R. (2019, October 9). The mastermind behind BTS opens up about making a K-pop juggernaut. *TIME.* Retrieved from https://time.com/5681494/bts-bang-si-hyuk-interview/

Caughey, J. L. (1984). *Imaginary social worlds: A cultural approach.* Lincoln, NE: University of Nebraska Press.

Chang, W., & Park, S. E. (2019). The fandom of Hallyu, a tribe in the digital network era: The case of ARMY of BTS. *Kritika Kultura, 32*, 260-285.

DeSilver, D. (2016, January 14). Dangers that teens and kids face: A look at the data. *Pew Research Center.* Retrieved from http://www.pewresearch.org/fact-tank/2016/01/14/dangers-that-young-people-face-a-look-at-the-data/

Galla, B. (Ed.). (2018). *Music spotlight special collector's edition: BTS* (p. 7). New York, NY: Centennial Media.

Herman, T. (2020, February 1). BTS' new album Map of the Soul: 7 shines light on shadows and the act's career. *Billboard.* Retrieved from https://www.billboard.com/articles/news/bts/8551615/bts-map-of-the-soul-7-album-analysis

Hills, M. (2013). Back in the mix: Exploring intermediary fandom and popular music production (pp. 16-36). In M. Duffett (Ed.), *Popular music fandom: Identities, roles, and practices.* New York, NY: Routledge.

Ibighit. (2019, December 5). *Bangtan TV.* [Video Files]. https://www.youtube.com/user/ibighit

Jin, D. Y. (2016). *New Korean wave: Transnational cultural power in the age of social media.* Urbana, IL: University of Illinois Press.

Ju, H. (2019). Premediating a narrative of growth: BTS, digital media, and fan culture. *Popular Entertainment Studies, 10*(1-2), 19-33.

Jung, E. Y. (2017a). Seo Taiji syndrome: Rise of Korean youth and cultural transformation through global pop music styles in the early 1990s. In H. Shin & S.

A. Lee (Eds.), *Made in Korea: Studies in popular music* (pp. 143-154). New York, NY: Routledge.

Jung, H. (2017b). *Transcultural media and the soft power of the Korean wave: A reversed ethnographic approach to U.S. fans' reception of Korean popular culture* [Unpublished doctoral dissertation]. University of Texas, Austin.

Katz, E., Blumler, J., & Gurevitch, M. (1973). Uses and gratifications research. *The Public Opinion Quarterly, 37*, 509-523.

Kim, D. K., & Kim, M. S. (Eds.). (2011). *Hallyu: Influence of Korean popular culture in Asia and beyond.* Seoul, Korea: Seoul National University Press.

Kim, G. (2019). *From factory girls to K-pop idol girls: Cultural politics of developmentalism, patriarchy, and neoliberalism in South Korea's popular music industry.* Lanham, MD: Lexington.

Kim, H. S., & Kim, H. S. (2008). Risk factors for suicide attempts among Korean adolescents. *Child Psychiatry & Human Development, 39*, 221-235

Kim, J. H. (2018a, May 29). How BTS are breaking K-pop's biggest taboos. *Rolling Stone.* Retrieved from https://www.rollingstone.com/music/music-news/how-bts-are-breaking-k-pops-biggest-taboos-628141/

Kim, S. Y. (2018b). *K-pop live: Fans, idols, and multimedia performance.* Stanford, CA: Stanford University Press.

Lamont, A., & Hargreaves, D. (2019). Musical preference and social identity in adolescents. In K. McFerran, P. Derrington, & S. Saarikallio (Eds.), *Handbook of music, adolescents, and wellbeing* (pp. 109-118). Oxford, UK: Oxford University Press.

Lee, H., & Jin, D. (2019). *K-pop idols: Popular culture and the emergence of the Korean music industry*. Lanham, MD: Lexington.

Lee, S., & Nornes, A. (Eds.). (2015). *Hallyu 2.0: The Korean wave in the age of social media.* Ann Arbor, MI: University of Michigan Press.

Longenecker, L., & Lee, J. (2018). The Korean wave in America: Assessing the status of K-pop and K-drama between global and local. *Situations: Cultural Studies in the Asian Context, 11*(2), 105-127.

McFerran, K., Garrido, S., & Saarikallio, S. (2016). A critical interpretive synthesis of the literature linking music and adolescent mental health. *Youth & Society, 48* (4), 521-538.

Mojtabai, R., Olfson, M., & Han, B. (2016). National trends in the prevalence and treatment of depression in adolescents and young adults. *Pediatrics, 138*(6).

North, A. C., & Hargreaves, D. J. (2006). Problem music and self-harming. *Suicide and Life-Threatening Behavior, 36*, 582-590.

Padget, F. (2017, February 20). What are the difficulties of being a Korean pop idol and to what extent do they outweigh the benefits? *Academia.edu.* Retrieved from http://www.academia.edu/download/52242864/difficulties-korean-pop_2.pdf

Ryoo, W. (2009). Globalization, or the logic of cultural hybridization: The case of the Korean wave. *Asian Journal of Communication, 19*(2), 137-151.

Sandvoss, C. (2005). *Fans: The mirror of consumption.* Malden, MA: Polity Press.

Shin, S., & Kim., L. (2013). Organizing K-pop: Emergence and market making of large Korean entertainment houses, 1980-2010. *East Asia: An International Quarterly, 30*(4), 255-272.

Tajfel, H., & Turner, J. C. (1979). An integrative theory of intergroup conflict. In W. G. Austin & S. Worchel (Eds.), *The social psychology of intergroup relations* (pp. 33-37). Monterey, CA: Brooks/Cole.

U.S. Department of Health and Human Services, National Institute of Mental Health. (2019, February). *Mental illness*. Retrieved from https://www.nimh.nih.gov/health/statistics/mental-illness.shtml

Winifred, D. (2019, May 26). What is BTS's net worth? *Showbiz cheat shee*t. Retrieved from https://www.cheatsheet.com/entertainment/what-is-btss-net-worth.html/

Yoon, K. (2018). Global imagination of K-pop: Pop music fans' lived experience of cultural hybridity. *Popular Music and Society*, *41*(4), 373-389.

Zellner, X. (2019, May 23). BTS becomes first group to spend 5 weeks at No. 1 on Billboard artist 100 chart. *Billboard*. Retrieved from https://www.billboard.com/articles/columns/chart-beat/8512920/bts-first-group-to-spend-5-weeks-no-1-billboard-artist-100-chart

CHAPTER 7

My First Taste of K-Drama, *Boys over Flowers*: Analysis of an Autoethnography

Hayley Rummel & **Do Kyun David Kim**,
University of Louisiana at Lafayette

When a person tells a story, the storyteller intentionally or unintentionally organizes the contents into a certain pattern that represents and explains her/his experience (Cortazzi, 1994). As such narrative analysis has been employed in numerous studies that explore cultures and social movements, this study attempted to investigate the diffusion of K-dramas among American viewers by using the method of narrative analysis that interprets a personal story. This grassroots perspective helps researchers and readers make sense of this new cultural phenomenon of K-dramas in many western countries, expanding both understanding of a subjective individual's experience and shared experience among American K-drama fans in the United States.

The First Experience of the K-Drama, *Boys over Flowers*: A Personal Narrative

During the summer break before my first semester of college, I decided that I would enjoy my break to the fullest extent. This included spending much of my break binge-watching television shows on the streaming service, Netflix. As I was scrolling through my recommended list that Netflix creates based on our previously watched items, I came across a thumbnail for a Korean drama called, "Boys Over Flowers", that caught my eye. The background was baby pink and there were four attractive young guys on the front along with a cute girl in the center. I decided to read the description because I had never watched a Korean show or movie before and it said something along the lines of, "This adaptation of the hit manga series follows unassuming high school student Jan Di as she stands up to—and eventually falls for—a spoiled rich kid whose clique reigns over their exclusive private school." This intrigued me because there are different versions of a rich boy falling in love with the underprivileged girl in American dramas, but I was so fascinated with the idea of this happening in a different country with this twist of the clique in this exclusive school. How would that story work? I just wanted to watch something different from all of the shows I had seen before and I figured why not try watching a show from a completely different country? I decided to watch the first episode and see if I liked it; I had no idea that the first episode was going to be such a wild ride.

The episode opens with a compilation of news clips talking about the Shinhwa Group that is the most successful corporation in South Korea. The news clips go on to talk about how the founder of the group asked the president if he could build a school for his grandchildren instead of accepting a medal of honor. Thus, Shinhwa School was born; an elite school for Korea's wealthiest children that provides education from kindergarten into university. This school is only for the best of the best and will accept no less into its ranks.

I have grown up in a city with many private schools, but none were to the level of exclusivity that was being described in this opening scene. If a sort of school like this existed in my city there would be many people that were upset by the superiority being flaunted so arrogantly in front of them. It made me want to know more about this school and the kind of children that are allowed to attend. This wealthy lifestyle is so far away from my realm of existence, so I wanted to see the type of people that are so wealthy, famous, or influential that they attend a school that was basically built for them.

We later see a young man opening his locker in Shinhwa School and discovering a red card with gold skull and crossbones and the letter and number, "F4", on the front. Immediately after seeing this card, he tries to run past a group of other students who begin to brutally beat him. Meanwhile, Geum Jan-di is riding her bicycle to the school to make a dry-cleaning delivery as her family owns a dry-cleaner business. The young man is being beaten up in a bathroom stall to the point where he stumbles out covered in blood and begins to make his way to the roof of the building. As he is going to jump off, Jan-di arrives with his laundry delivery and tries to convince him not to jump off. When he does, Jan-di runs and grabs him so that he doesn't fall to his death. This whole time I am thinking to myself that this makes it look like bullying is a huge issue in wealthy Korean schools. It appears as though the children of the rich can do whatever they want to. Granted, I knew that this show was probably exaggerating since I know that most American television shows do so, but I knew nothing of Korea or Korean culture. For all I knew, this portrayal of bullying, the brutality, and the acceptance of it could be completely accurate.

Next thing I remember, Jan-di is being invited to go to Shinhwa on scholarship as her stunt had caused a media storm like no other. People were protesting at the gates of the school about how it is cruel to allow this kind of bullying to take place, that a school built for the rich is unfair as Korea strives for equal opportunity and the right for all children to get a good education. The chairwoman of Shinhwa decided that Jan-di would fix the media problem on her own by attending the school. Jan-di was less than thrilled as she didn't want to attend a school filled to the brim with obnoxious, spoiled, rich kids.

Jan-di comes from a poor family that lives in an apartment at the top of their dry cleaner. They live a very modest life and live day-to-day with no real opportunity to change their standing. So, Jan-di had no desire to attend a school that is so different from what she has grown up with. However, her family was so excited to the point that they were dancing around the house and saying how proud they were. Her mother even threatened to drag her to the school by her ear if she didn't want to go. I think it goes without saying that Jan-di did end up going to the school as she was not going to continue trying to fight the wishes of her family since her mother, father, and little brother were all pressuring her to go. This fits my preconceived expectations of how a Korean family would react to their child getting a full-ride scholarship to a prestigious school.

It is a well-known stereotype that Asian families care the most about education than anything else, so this excitement from the family fits in perfectly with that stereotype. Another stereotype that the family portrayed was the mother's push for Jan-di to try and impress one of the rich young men at the school so that she could marry into a higher status. This seems old-fashioned to me, but the stereotypes I knew of

Asian parents made me believe that this is an accurate depiction of an Asian mother's desire for their daughter to marry up. I always wondered if those stereotypes were completely inaccurate, so it was interesting seeing them portrayed on a Korean television drama. It doesn't make me think that the stereotypes are 100 percent accurate, but it does give me the impression that they aren't completely off the mark. I wanted to see if there were any other stereotypes shown on the show because it made me curious about if those stereotypes are perpetuated by more than just American television shows.

The show continued with Jan-di being an outcast at the school as all of the other students couldn't understand the idea of a scholarship student being at their school. Her ignorance of their wealthy world is shown very quickly with the arrival of the "F4". Four very attractive young men arrive through the front doors of the school with a bright light streaming in behind them as if to hint at their "angelic" beauty. It turns out that "F4" is short for "Flower Four" as they are four beautiful young men that also happen to be the wealthiest, most talented, and smartest. The leader of the four is Gu Jun-Pyo, the future inheritor of the Shinhwa Group. He is vain, arrogant, and vile to all those that oppose his authority or status in the school. This is seen when he stains another student's shirt since it was the same shirt he was wearing. The other members of the group include Yoon Ji-Hu, grandson of the former president of Korea who is extremely musically talented, So Yi-Jung, a skilled potter whose family owns Korea's largest art museum, and Song Woo-bin, future inheritor of the largest construction business in Korea that has deep ties to organized crime. This group of young men elicits screams of excitement and a stampede of students just by walking through a door. Jan-di scoffs at how they all act and mumbles to herself about how it isn't right how they act like absolute jerks. She is overheard by three girls who I can only assume are the president, vice-president, and secretary of the "F4 Fan Club". They use English words more heavily than any other character on the show by saying things like "oh my god", "terrible", and "whatever." They lay into Jan-di about how she shouldn't disrespect the "F4" and how they will let her slide today since she doesn't know of their world since she is merely a commoner.

This lack of acceptance by these girls was not something that I have never seen or experienced in my own life. I have witnessed people who treat someone as less than because they have less than they do. It is something that has been done to me as I knew several people in school as well as people I have served in my jobs that talk down to others because of their status. The fact that these girls are so obsessed with this group of young men that they can't understand how some "commoner" could disrespect them, especially since she is of such a low status.

Each of the "F4" knows their status and acts accordingly, but Jun-Pyo is the most malicious out of all of them, especially to Jan-di since she directly challenges him. Jan-di shoves ice cream into his face after he tries to force her only friend at school to lick ice cream off of his shoe. He is infuriated by this "commoner's" challenge. So, he delivers an "F4" death card to her locker and her nightmare begins. She is teased and bullied relentlessly, but she does not back down and remains strong. The end of the episode was a cliffhanger showing Jan-di being attacked in a locker room by three male students and ends in a freeze-frame of her screaming face. My first reaction to the ending of this first episode was, "What the hell is going on?"

Regardless of how confused I was by the rollercoaster that was this episode, this show had me hook, line, and sinker. I was fully prepared to dedicate the next couple weeks of my life to working and watching this drama. There was so much thrown into this first episode that just reeled me in and wouldn't let me go. Why are the members "F4" so irrefutable in their hold on this school? Why does Jan-di refuse to back down when it would make her life easier? What happened to the guy that tried to kill himself? Is somebody going to help Jan-di and save her from her attackers? So many questions were running through my head and this was only the first, hour-long episode of the show. Naturally, I immediately started watching episode two, then three, then four, and next thing I knew two weeks had passed and I finished all 25 episodes in the series. I couldn't remember the last time I was so invested in a group of characters and their stories. This show truly stuck with me and began my love for K-dramas.

Since "Boys Over Flowers," I have watched countless K-dramas. However, "Boys Over Flowers" will always remain my favorite because of the storyline and the characters, as well as the nostalgic feeling I get when I go to rewatch the series for the third time. Looking back on my experience watching, I realize that one of the reasons I enjoyed watching and continue to enjoy watching K-dramas is because of the differences between Korean culture and American culture as portrayed in the entertainment. I loved the language from the Korean slang they use that is at times so different from American slang, to expressions, to even simple greetings. The relationship dynamics were also so different in how they all interacted with each other. There is a distinct difference in tone, greeting, etc. when communicating with someone of higher status or authority or even in a different school class.

I was also fascinated by the dramatics of the shows for things that normally wouldn't be a big deal in America. For example, kissing is a massive occurrence in K-dramas as compared to an American drama. There is a slow-motion panoramic shot of the two characters kissing with the show's theme song blasting in the background; this scene lasts for a minimum of a full minute to two minutes. Kissing in American television is not nearly as dramatic as it is in these K-dramas. I found it hilarious that these actors had to keep their lips together with a straight face for the length of time that they did. Relationships also move much more slowly in K-dramas than they do on American television. It takes half a season, so around ten to twelve episodes, for the two main characters to admit their feelings for each other or kiss. In American television shows it takes much fewer episodes, in my viewing experiences.

Another massive difference in K-dramas is the length or number of seasons. I have never watched a K-drama that had more than one season. That season is usually much longer than an American television series. Most American shows have several seasons that last 12 to 14 episodes, while K-dramas have the one season that can be anywhere from 20 to 30 episodes. Korean drama producers squeeze so much into that one season, however, so that the show doesn't feel unfinished in the end. I almost always get an ending that provides me with some closure from the K-drama that leaves me satisfied with how the story ended. "Boys Over Flowers" did exactly that by giving me an ending set a few years in the future from where all of the drama ended. It showed me the characters all finding happiness in their respective couples while remaining friends, after all, they went through together. It doesn't get better than that. Countless times I have watched different American television drama series that I didn't realize was not renewed for another season after a particularly frustrating cliffhanger. So, I am attracted to the style of K-dramas in that I will usually get closure from them.

I cannot speak for every young American female, but I think that K-dramas certainly have great potential to be some of the most entertaining shows to watch among young American females. It isn't because the acting is phenomenal, not that the characters are super unique, not even that they only require 25 episodes of dedication to watch, but it is because they are different. When watching K-dramas I don't just enjoy some sweet romances, intense action, and gut-wrenching drama. I also get to learn a little bit more about Korean culture. It may not be an accurate depiction of all aspects of Korean culture, but I still get to experience something different than the culture I have grown up around. I get to experience how another group of people lives their lives. They speak a different language, eat different food, study differently, dress differently, and so many other things that I find so intriguing. I also enjoy the fact that I can bring some of these things I learn to other people. There are times where I will tell my friends about the funny expression they used in a K-drama, or I fix my makeup in a more Korean style and get so many compliments. All of these things just add more substance to my outlook on cultures outside of my own. So, my mom can make fun of my K-drama obsession all she wants, but I don't think it will come to an end any time soon.

Narrative Analysis as a Method

Narrative analysis is an analytic method that researchers interpret a narrative (story) that is told within a context of research topic shared in everyday life (Allen, 2017). Research that employs this analytic method mostly explores diverse, yet equally substantial and meaningful interpretations of a narrative. Related to this methodological nature, narrative analysis aims to reveal the complexity of human experience and provide an in-depth understanding of social, cultural, and historic contexts that are embedded in a narrative (Sharp, Bye, & Cusick, 2019). While there is no set approach to analyze a narrative inquiry, a combination of various approaches can be employed to analyze a story as Polkinghorne (1995) suggested the use of both narrative analysis and paradigmatic analysis: Narrative analysis focuses on revealing the constructed story of an individual, while paradigmatic analysis of narratives utilizes both inductive and deductive means to identify shared and/or contrasting themes out of narratives. This study also combined narrative analysis and paradigmatic analysis to expand our understanding of how K-dramas have diffused among American viewers.

Results and Discussion

Through analyzing an autoethnographic narrative written by an American woman who is in her early 20s, this study identified noteworthy factors explaining why the popularity of K-dramas has notably increased among Americans. As a result of narrative analysis, this study found online television streaming services, narratives engagement that creates a parasocial interaction between viewers and the lead actors/actresses, a relatively shorter number of episodes, Generation Z's cultural openness, and intercultural trend/experience as influencing factors. All these factors are not mutually exclusive but interwoven and interplayed to create a K-drama fandom especially among American women.

Online Television Streaming Services

As described in the autoethnographic narrative above, many American television viewers were first exposed to K-dramas through online streaming services. The advancement of media technology accelerated the international exchange of media contents, breaking the limitations of physical boundaries. The adoption of online streaming services is now as influential as an increasing number of people cut their cable services (Tefertiller, 2018). This exemplifies how the rapidly growing mobile video technology transforms the pattern of people's media content consumption from fixed TV and video players to Internet-based mobile devices (Chan-Olmsted, Rim, & Zerba, 2013). Specifically, as of November 2019, Netflix had 158 million subscribers worldwide, and 271 online video streaming services were available in the United States (Barnes, 2019). This new media consumption behavior with online streaming technology drastically changed the global media landscape and substantially affected the exposure of K-dramas to the U.S. viewers.

Before television streaming service providers legally offered K-dramas, approximately six million people watched K-dramas in America through illegal online streaming websites (Lee, 2015). Noticing the increasing K-drama consumption, some online streaming service providers developed legal streaming websites by obtaining licenses from Korean media and entertainment companies and accelerated the diffusion of K-dramas rapidly among their viewers, providing more convenient platforms to watch K-dramas. For example, DramaFever, launched in 2009, was subscribed by 200,000 individual viewers in just a month after beginning their legal K-drama streaming service. It climbed to four million in four years (Lee, 2015).

The co-founder of DramaFever, Bak, mentioned that 85 percent of DramaFever viewers were non-Asian viewers with 45 percent being Caucasians and 25 percent being Latinos (Ambrosino, 2014). However, coupled with Caucasians and Latinos, Asian Americans were also a major group of K-drama consumers. Based on interviews with 15 female undergraduate students who identified themselves as Asian American, Ju and Lee (2015) found that K-dramas awakened their pan-ethnic identity as a member of the East Asian community. In general, streaming service providers, such as Netflix, Hulu, and Amazon Prime, are well aware of the large market of non-Western entertainment products and strive to provide more international contents to their subscribers (Lee, 2015).

Romance and Parasocial Interaction

How do K-dramas draw viewers in and keep them coming back? This study also found that K-dramas' narratives are one of the main factors that attract American viewers. Especially, K-dramas are loved by female viewers across different cultures because of their common desire toward a universally attractive theme, *sweet love*, with interesting plots (Ju, 2020). The touching theme of sweet love feeds into viewers' romantic feelings, which relates to their innate social and psychological needs.

Several previous studies show that romance dramas are historically one of the most popular genres in literature, theater, as well as popular culture media. Related to this, the romance portrayed on television is often able to avoid some cultural boundaries that people have in their minds to different cultures (Innocenti & Pescatore, 2014). A romance-centered plot often has underlying subplots with interesting supporting characters that can present realistic conflicts in socio-cultural values, life issues, competitive conditions, and other living problems (Ju & Lee, 2015). Such an emotional realization of a loving relationship draws viewers in different cultures through the story, which is commonly observed when television viewers watch a romantic drama. They can fulfill a longing for romantic love while also adhering to real-life issues. Most K-drama viewers admitted to being interested in the variations of romantic stories and settings as well as the verbal and nonverbal interactions that occurred between characters (Ju, 2020).

Viewers also referenced the attraction they had to main and/or supporting characters. Theoretically, such a relationship between audiences and a television drama is called a *parasocial relationship*. A parasocial relationship refers to symbolic, one-sided emotional ties that television audiences create with media characters or celebrities (Horton & Wohl, 1956). Audiences form parasocial relationships for various reasons. For example, parasocial relationships are a means to fulfill audiences' needs for interaction, mostly because of their unmet social need with others (Nordlund, 1978). According to Rubin, Perse, and Powell (1985), this imaginary social interaction resulted from the viewer's perception of the media persona as real or similar to a real person.

Many viewers continue watching K-dramas due to the affection they had for the lead actors or actresses (Ju, 2020). Most often, they would center on the lead actors' or actresses' physical appearance, tenderness, and attractive personality. They referenced the mindful, sensitive approach the lead had to love and their preference for the honest tenderness as opposed to sexual chemistry so often focused on in American dramas. A general manager of DramaFever explained how television viewers create a parasocial relationship while watching K-dramas (Orsini, 2018):

> *here's a very interesting world that can be built around this storyline: it can be fantasy, it can be history. But what makes us stand out from a content point of view is we focus on the development of the lead characters' romance. That, coupled with interesting world-building, offers a reason for fans to get really interested in and 'ship' the characters. That, in a nutshell, is the secret sauce of our content.*

Structure of K-Dramas with a Short Number of Episodes

As told in the autoethnographic narrative above, the relatively shorter number of episodes of K-dramas than American television dramas or soap operas appeals to American viewers. This structural feature allows television viewers to complete watching all episodes at once. Researchers have also noticed this unique television watching behavior with K-dramas. It is called *binge-watching* (Mikos, 2016; Hills, 2007; Jenner, 2017; Tryon, 2015). Binge-watching is, as it sounds, the television watching behavior that a viewer watches all episodes of a show back-to-back and finish it at once or in a few days. In other words, it is a consecutive watching of a K-drama from the beginning episode to the last one. People often do this over the weekend or during their vacation, reserving a day or two only for watching a K-drama series. This process of binge-watching directly affects television viewers' deeper connections to the drama's narrative, also creating parasocial relationships with characters in the drama (Hills, 2007; Mikos, 2016; Jenner, 2017). One of the main reasons that K-drama viewers show the binge-watching behavior is most K-dramas only have one season with a shorter number of episodes and a clear conclusion, while American dramas continue over multiple seasons. Therefore, viewers of American television dramas may be tired of a long number of episodes and of waiting for the next season, while K-drama viewers can experience the show in its entirety within a shorter period and do not have to wait for a new season or other continuation of the show, as they are completely finished in one season.

Generation Z: A New Generation and a New Culture-Making

The main group of K-drama consumers in the United States seems to be young female populations as the narrative of this study presents "my mom can make fun of my K-drama obsession." This finding also demonstrates the generational difference in media consumption. To some extent, a prominent group of Korean popular culture consumers in the United States as seen in many other western countries is people belonging to Generation Z (Premack, 2018). Over the 20th century, society generated several names that represented changing generations (Dimock, 2019): Baby boomers for those who were born right after

World War II (Born 1946-1964), Generation X (Born 1965-1980), & Millennials (Born 1981-1996). The first generation included entirely in the 21st century is Generation Z, which is comprised of those who were born in the late 1990s through the early 2010s. Interestingly, the previous titles of generation are associated with historic events or trends, such as World War II, rapid economic or market change, and 9/11 terrorism, Generation Z is not much related to a significant historic event but represented by their unique culture.

According to a report published by McKinsey & Company (Francis & Hoefel, n.d.), Generation Zs are represented by their use of mobile communication technologies, more social connections with diverse groups across different religions, races, cultures, nationalities, and other social categories, more fluid identities, and ethical choice in their consumption, such as considering climate change and preserving nature. Especially, they are more culturally open-minded and multicultural (Williams, 2015) as they were born in the age of the Internet and digital/mobile communication. They are exposed to and enjoy multi-cultural contexts and communicate with people with diversity. Besides, their education level is higher than in previous generations. All these attributes of Generation Zs contribute to their openness to different cultures and creating a new global culture.

Related to such a new cultural environment constructed by the new generation, Schulze (2013) viewed K-dramas as a catalyst for culture-making, using a notable term, K-dramaland. It is an imagined world created through narrative tropes in K-dramas. As international viewers watch K-dramas, they participate in a culture-making process that they are usually unaware of. They see certain behaviors, characteristics, and stories on K-dramas and come to K-dramaland with commonalities viewers can find and share with others. While some international viewers may classify traits they see on K-dramas as just part of Korean culture, people of K-dramaland classify what they experience with K-dramas—behaviors, phrases, locations, plotlines, character personalities, class representations, and more—as the K-dramaland culture. This shows that while K-dramas are products of the Korean culture, K-drama as a genre has developed its own culture that is not necessarily associated with the traditional Korean culture.

Many international K-drama fans do not feel comfortable defining something as being part of Korean culture, but they classify relevant commonalities into K-dramaland culture which is a product of the fandom (Schulze, 2013). In other words, instead of taking the step to defining their experiences as being unique to Korean culture, the viewers may think of K-dramas as existing in their own realm. The K-dramaland seems an example of the world in which Generation Zs live and where they create their own culture, which is a driving force in the diffusion process of K-dramas in the United States.

Intercultural Experiences through Watching a TV Show

According to Kramsch (1993) and Byram (1991), one of the most important aspects of intercultural experiences is to decenter an individual's original or firm cultural identity and give oneself the ability to experience another paradigm, as a person in a different culture might see the world. Especially, understanding other cultures through an artistic form, such as television dramas, has been a universal way to expand the understanding of others or other cultures. More specifically, according to Bredella (2003), the arts are a great way to have an intercultural experience as people allow for imaginative immersion and self-reflection that can be as influential and rewarding as a person-to-person intercultural experience.

Film and television are art forms that have been major tools for seeking intercultural experience. While it can be difficult to have direct contact with a culture of interest, people can more easily access films and television series from other cultures and experience different cultures (Corbett, 2003). With the power of moving image arts including films and television dramas (Ryan & Kellner, 2005), it is no surprise that many Western television viewers find themselves experiencing a different culture through watching K-dramas.

The narrative of this study also revealed that an American K-drama fan was intrigued by having intercultural experience through watching K-dramas. As described in her story, she was aware that television dramas often exaggerate reality. However, she mentioned she "got to learn a little bit more about Korean culture" that is somewhat different from the American culture. In other words, although television viewers are aware of fictional aspects of television dramas as K-dramas are not directly related to true Korean culture, K-dramas are a great access point for American viewers to catch a glimpse of Korean culture. Such intercultural experiences help people gain knowledge about foreign cultures, while also reflecting on one's own culture (Byram, Gribkova, & Starkey, 2002).

Conclusion

This chapter has sought reasons why K-dramas have been popularized among American viewers through an in-depth analysis of an auto-ethnographic narrative written by a white American woman in her early 20s. Based on the in-depth analysis of a personal narrative that helps listen to the research subject's voice and cultural experience truthfully (Bochner, 1994; Denzin, 1989), this narrative analysis revealed that the popularity of K-dramas is triggered and fertilized by the global trend of online streaming media watching behavior, the narrative engagement that connects romantic characters in K-dramas and viewers, a limited number of episodes that enables people to binge-watch a K-drama, new generation's openness to other cultures, and a trend of (media) globalization that has introduced and exchanged different cultures throughout the world. These elements of popularity are not mutually exclusive but interplay with one another to construct a K-drama media culture (e.g., K-dreamland) among Americans. Especially, as the consumers of television dramas or soap operas are mostly females, K-dramas have been shared among female viewers who were more emotionally involved with the stories and the characters of K-dramas (Ju, 2020).

In comparison to K-pop songs and K-films, K-dramas as a genre of popular media culture are relatively new to Americans. Therefore, it is questionable how K-dramas could be further disseminated and gain popularity among more Americans in the future. However, it is certain that K-dramas have many differences in comparison to American television dramas, while continuously growing its popularity. Therefore, K-dramas give media and popular culture researchers many scholarly agendas in terms of exploring how this international media genre can thrive or languish in different cultures and countries.

Recommended Readings

Ju, H. (2020). Korean TV drama viewership on Netflix: Transcultural affection, romance, and identities. *Journal of International and Intercultural Communication, 13*(1), 32-48.

Kim, D. K., & Kim, M. S. (2011). Hallyu: Influence of Korean popular culture in Asia and beyond. Seoul, Korea: Seoul National University Press.

Morris, M. W., Chiu, C. Y., & Liu, Z. (2015). Polycultural psychology. *Annual review of psychology, 66*, 631-659.

Said, E. W. (1979). *Orientalism*. New York, NY: Vintage.

Schulze, M. (2013). Korea vs. K-dramaland: The culturalization of K-dramas by international fans. *Acta Koreana, 16*(2), 367-397.

Additional Sources

Korea Culture and Tourism Institute. (2020). *Research reports*. Retrieved from https://www.kcti.re.kr/eng/user/main.do#none

Ministry of Culture, Sports and Tourism and Korean Culture and Information Service. (n.d.). *Hallyu*. Retrieved from http://www.korea.net/AboutKorea/Culture-and-the-Arts/Hallyu

Moon, K. (2020). The 10 best Korean dramas to watch on Netflix. *TIME*. Retrieved from https://time.com/5835519/best-korean-dramas-netflix/

References

Allen, M. (2017). Narrative Analysis. *The sage encyclopedia of communication research methods* (Vols. 1-4). Thousand Oaks, CA: SAGE Publications, Inc.

Ambrosino, B. (2014, December 21). Here's why millions of Americans are binge-watching Korean dramas. *Vox*. Retrieved from https://www.vox.com/2014/9/24/6832951/heres-why-millions-of-americans-are-binge-watching-korean-dramas

Barnes, B. (2019, November 18). The streaming era has finally arrived. Everything is about to change. *The New York Times*. Retrieved from https://www.nytimes.com/2019/11/18/business/media/streaming-hollywood-revolution.html

Bochner, A. P. (1994). Perspectives on inquiry II: Theories and stories. In M. L. Knapp & G. R. Miller (Eds.), *Handbook of interpersonal communication* (pp. 21-41). Thousand Oaks, CA: Sage.

Bredella, L. (2003). For a flexible model of intercultural understanding. In G. Alred, M. Byram, and M. Fleming (Eds.), *Intercultural experience and education* (pp. 31-49). Multilingual Matters.

Byram, M. (1991). Teaching culture and language: Towards an integrated model. In D. Buttjes & M. Byram (Eds.), *Mediating languages and cultures: The social and intercultural dimension restored*, (pp. 17-30). Multilingual Matters.

Byram, M., Gibkova, B., & Starkey, H. (2002). Developing the intercultural dimension in language teaching. A practical introduction for teachers. Council of Europe.

Chan-Olmsted, S., Rim, H., & Zerba, A. (2013). Mobile news adoption among young adults: Examining the roles of perceptions, news consumption, and media usage. *Journalism & Mass Communication Quarterly, 90*(1), 126-147.

Corbett, J. (2003). *An intercultural approach to English language teaching*. Multilingual Matters.

Cortazzi, M. (1994). Narrative analysis. *Language Teaching, 27*(3), 157-170.

Denzin, N. K. (1989). *Interpretive biography*. Newbury Park, CA: Sage.

Dimock, M. (2019, January 17). Defining generations: Where Millennials end and Generation Z begins. *Pew Research Center*. Retrieved from https://www.pewresearch.org/fact-tank/2019/01/17/where-millennials-end-and-generation-z-begins/

Francis, T., & Hoefel, F. (n.d.). "True Gen": Generation Z and its implication for companies. *McKinsey & Company*. Retrieved from https://www.mckinsey.com/industries/consumer-packaged-goods/our-insights/true-gen-generation-z-and-its-implications-for-companies

Hills, M. (2007). From the box in the corner to the box on the shelf. *New Review of Film and Television Studies, 5*(1), 41-60.

Horton, D., & Wohl, R. R. (1956). Mass communication and para-social interaction. *Psychiatry: Journal for the Study of Interpersonal Processes, 19,* 215-229.

Innocenti, V., & Pescatore, G. (2014). Changing series: Narrative models and the role of the viewer in contemporary television seriality. *Between, 4*(8), 1-15.

Jenner, M. (2017). Binge-watching: Video-on-demand, quality-TV and mainstreaming fandom. *International Journal of Cultural Studies, 20*(3), 304-320.

Ju, H. (2020). Korean TV drama viewership on Netflix: Transcultural affection, romance, and identities. *Journal of International and Intercultural Communication, 13*(1), 32-48.

Ju, H., & Lee, S. (2015). The Korean wave and Asian Americans: The ethnic meanings of transnational Korean pop culture in the USA. *Continuum: Journal of Media & Cultural Studies, 29*(3), 323-338.

Kramsch, C. (1993). *Context and culture in language teaching*. Oxford, UK: Oxford University Press.

Lee, S. (2015). *Hallyu 2.0: The Korean wave in the age of social media*. Ann Arbor, MI: University of Michigan Press.

Mikos, L. (2016). Digital media platforms and the use of TV content: Binge-watching and video-on-demand in Germany. *Media and Communication, 4*(3), 154-161.

Nordlund, J.-E. (1978). Media interaction. *Communication Research, 5*(2), 150-175.

Orsini, L. (2018, January 9). Korean media hits the big time in North America. Retrieved from https://www.forbes.com/sites/laurenorsini/2018/01/08/korean-media-hits-the-big-time-in-north-america/

Polkinghorne, D. E. (1995). Narrative configuration in qualitative analysis. *International Journal of Qualitative Studies in Education, 8*(1), 5-23.

Premack, R. (2018, July 12). Millennials love their brands, Gen Zs are terrified of college debt, and 6 other ways Gen Zs and millennials are totally different. Retrieved from https://www.businessinsider.com/gen-zs-habits-different-from-millennials-2018-6

Rubin, A. M., Perse, E. M., & Powell, R. A. (1985). Loneliness, parasocial interaction, local television news viewing. *Human Communication Research, 12,* 155-180.

Ryan, M., & Kellner, D. (2005). The politics of representation. In T. E. Wartenberg and A. Curran (Eds.), *The philosophy of film: Introductory text and readings* (pp. 213-224). Oxford; Malden: Blackwell.

Schulze, M. (2013). Korea vs. K-dramaland: The culturalization of K-dramas by international fans. *Acta Koreana, 16*(2), 367-397.

Sharp, N. L., Bye, R. A., Cusick, A. (2019). Narrative analysis. In P. Liamputtong (Ed.), *Handbook of research methods in health social sciences*. Singapore: Springer.

Tefertiller, A. (2018). Media substitution in cable cord-cutting: The adoption of web-streaming television. *Journal of Broadcasting & Electronic Media, 62*(3), 390-407.

Tryon, C. (2015). TV got better: Netflix's original programming strategies and binge viewing. *Media Industries Journal, 2*(2), 104-116.

Williams, A. (2015, September 18). Moreover, Millennials, here comes Generation Z. *The New York Times*. Retrieved from https://www.nytimes.com/2015/09/20/fashion/move-over-millennials-here-comes-generation-z.html

CHAPTER 8

A Mirror Image of the Self as Other: The Korean Adoptee as a Hybrid Consumer of K-Culture

Aino Rinhaug, University of California Los Angeles

In the summer of 1974, 6 month-old Kweon Hee Ra traveled from Seoul, via Tokyo and Amsterdam, to Oslo, Norway. She arrived at the airport at Fornebu, on the outskirts of Oslo, where her adoptive mother boarded the plane to pick her up. Over the next few months, Hee Ra changed her name, citizenship, language, family, and home—in short, she became a Norwegian citizen. Growing up in the suburbs of Oslo in the late 70s and 80s, a Korean adoptee had little, if any, exposure to anyone or anything non-Western. Her neighborhood was overwhelmingly White. Whenever asked to draw a picture of her family at school, Hee Ra would portray every member as blond and blue-eyed. Only occasionally would she draw Asian faces, mostly as caricatures of herself and her younger sister. In her inner eye, Hee Ra saw herself as White. Later, with the heightened self-awareness of adulthood, she began to focus more on the unique traits that distinguish her adoptee identity and to nourish a greater curiosity about her ties to both Norway and to Korea. Increasingly, she came to see questions of who she was, and where she belonged, as inextricably connected to a consciousness that required constant attempts to synchronize her Western and Asian selves.

The story of Kweon Hee Ra, which outlines my own background as a Korean adoptee to Norway and adoption researcher, serves as an introduction to a particular adoptee identity formation. In the course of this chapter, it is the sense of double belonging and of being positioned in between two countries and cultures that will guide the exploration of adoptee consumption of, and contribution to, K-culture.

Brief History of Korean Adoption

The present Korean diaspora comprises approximately 7 million people, or 10 % of the population of the Korean peninsula's 70 million (Kim, 2011). The history of international adoption from Korea to the West is intricately connected to the post-Korean War era of the 1950s. Since the end of the war, an estimated 200,000 Korean-born individuals have been sent abroad, mostly to the US, but also to Scandinavia (Norway, Sweden, Denmark), The Netherlands, France, Belgium, Germany, Australia, and Canada (Hübinette, 2005; Oh, 2015). The Korean international adoption program began as an expatriation of orphaned mixed-race babies and young children who were ostracized by the racially homogenous Korean society. In 1956, the American missionary couple Harry and Bertha Holt founded Holt International Children's Services, whose work was supported by the Korean government's willingness to change laws and regulations to facilitate international adoptions. It was believed that adoption would alleviate the country's poverty and child abandonment; as a result, the placement of a large number of full-Korean babies and children increased (Oh, 2015). The curve peaked a few decades later, between 1984-88, with a staggering 6,500-9,000 adoptions per year, a number, which, according to Una Kim (2002), represented 1-1.4 % of the country's annual living births (as cited in Hübinette, 2004). Within an adoptee discourse of gratitude, visions of the American dream illustrated notions of adoption as a better alternative to life in Korea and, by the same token, helped advance the belief in Western superiority (McKee, 2019). Systematically, Korean-born adoptees were placed at the intersection between ongoing international Cold War diplomacy and domestic US family politics involving race relations (Kim, 2007; Kim, 2010; Oh, 2015).

At the Margins of K-Culture

Since the 1990s, there has been an increasing amount of scholarly and creative work, largely conducted by the adoptees themselves, centering on the topic of international adoption and adoptees. Many adoptees return to Korea for shorter or longer periods of time, motivated by a desire to seek answers about their past and to look for birth parents.

Technology, social media, and TV have played a key role in facilitating access to a vast amount of information about Korean culture, history, and language. This trend of returning Westernized Koreans has prompted major Korean television networks to produce popular reality shows featuring Korean adoptees and their experiences in their birth country (Jin, 2016). In particular, *Ode to my father* (국제시장) (Yoon, 2014), is a powerful film on the topic. These televised homecomings of ethnic Koreans, who are not Korean nationals and are culturally Western, provide an opportunity to examine the intricate figure of the Korean adoptee, including their narratives of separation and adoption (Park 2010). Portrayed in this context, adoptees come to function as mediators between the local and the global (Woo, 2012).

This added "global" dimension represented by adoptees contributes to the continuous transformation and expansion of *Hallyu*'s boundaries and definitions. As consumers increasingly came to exert more power over content production, K-pop acts and K-dramas took on a more hybrid character (Elfving-Hwang, 2013). Consequently, Korean popular culture—or "K-culture"—came to be regarded as a *genre* in its own right, including not only drama and music, but also fashion, beauty, food, and lifestyle (Lee 2013). These cultural productions and products allow a modified, adapted cultural content, which cater for the local needs, while, at the same time, retain the unique characteristics of "Korean-ness" (Ju, 2014). In this way, K-culture can both uphold an essentialist, nationalistic view on Korean culture, a harbor for the specifically Korean spirit, identity, and character (Lee, 2013), and also expand the conversation about what constitutes Korean identity (Kim, 2019) and belonging in a globally oriented discourse.

Furthermore, as a link between the local and the global aspects of "K-culture," the transnational audience of adoptees constitutes a singular perspective on *Hallyu*'s globalization project. If *Hallyu*'s "glocal" intention is to probe into the hybridity of "Koreanness," then that interrogation finds a striking resonance in adoptee discourses on transnationality and belonging. It would seem incredibly potent, therefore, to attempt to draw a line between current discourses and tendencies of K-culture and those of a global adoptee community. Like most foreign viewers, with little or only superficial knowledge of the Korean language and culture, adoptees' ability to engage with K-culture rests largely on the experience of translations, their curiosity for something different and unfamiliar (Dutch, 2019). And yet, whether the Korean-born adoptee is invited to appear on a TV show or takes the position of a TV-viewer of a K-drama, in both cases, he or she is invited back to the country of birth, to a historical, cultural, and discursive world with which there exists an undeniable relation by way of the often undisclosed narrative of the adopted self. In many instances, as a consequence, a Korean-born adoptee may come to negotiate his or her identity and belonging via the carefully mediated representations of Korea and Koreans, of whose larger historical and cultural discourse the adoptee nonetheless forms an ineluctable part.

At the Margins of Europe

As a case study, this chapter sheds light on Scandinavian adoptees as consumers of K-culture. In order to introduce this particular set of viewers, a few remarks on Nordic countries (seen largely as a whole) and their relation to Korea are in order. Geographically at the margins of Western Europe, Scandinavia has relatively few citizens of Korean origin, but enjoys long-standing historical ties to Korea (Hübinette, 2012). In one of the few preliminary studies of Scandinavian *Hallyu* fans available, Hübinette's findings suggest that there are two groups of K-pop fans in Sweden: The first is non-white, of a working-class background, and often second-generation immigrants of non-Western parents. The second group is educated, middle-class and lives in larger urban areas. Most, but not all, are of Pacific-Asian origin, adopted Asians, Asian migrants, mixed race Asians, and people from Chile, Turkey, India and North Africa (Hübinette, 2012, 2018). Presumably due to the scarcity of Korean nationals and the geographical distance from Korea, as Hübinette points out, in Scandinavian countries, Asians have often been exposed to ridicule, racism and derogatory comments, based on total ignorance and/or unfounded negative perceptions about Asian nations and culture. Recently, however, and especially since 2012, when PSY's *Gagnam Style* became a megahit around the globe, the Korean globalization project appears to have finally broken its last barrier to becoming mainstream, even in Northern Europe. Aided by the advent of streaming channels, social media and a more globally oriented youth culture, commonly held perceptions about Asians,

Koreans in particular, are changing. Consequently, the Scandinavian K-pop fanbase has gone from being small and niche-like to becoming broader and more numerous.

However, with increasing interest in the mechanisms that help maintain the multi-billion dollar industry of *Hallyu*, comes starker criticism, even by die-hard fans. The "Koreaboos" (e.g. non-Korean fans of K-culture) of Norway offer a striking example of this new scrutiny (Pak, 2019). A small, but significant fan community in their own right, the Koreaboos of Norway, mostly young women, focus largely, but not exclusively, on K-pop. Most importantly, although fans of *Hallyu*, the Koreaboos critique many aspects of Korean pop culture that seem unacceptable from a Nordic perspective: excessively sexualised portrayals of young women on stage, increased suicides by young K-stars in recent years, or disclosure of unbearably harsh working conditions within the industry, to mention a few, are most likely to put the entire K-industry machinery in a very bleak light indeed; something, which, in turn, questions the longevity of K-pop fandom in Northern European countries. The Koreaboos of Norway, therefore, exemplify an important skeptical dimension of *Hallyu* fan culture, one that could point to fundamental, incompatible differences between the local producers and manufacturers and their "glocal" fanpool.

Given how remote Scandinavian audiences are vis-a-vis Korea and Korean culture, it is equally likely that the Scandinavian adoptees will approach K-culture with skepticism, criticism and disaffection. Indeed, it would seem most likely that the tendencies in some current K-dramas may reflect this more critical position and perspective of adoptee consumers.

Self as Other: The Orphan as a K-Drama Heroine

In recent years, quite a few K-dramas, such as *Coffee Prince* (2007), *I'm Sorry, I Love You* (2004), *Kill Me, Heal Me* (2015), explicitly address adoption as a social issue pertaining to contemporary Korean society. In one highly successful K-drama, *When the Camellia Blooms* (동백꽃 필 무렵) (2019), originally broadcast on KBS2 and curated by Netflix, the plot resonates with the adoptee experience on different levels. The story revolves around a charismatic single mother, Oh Dong-baek (Gong Hyo-jin), who lives with her 8-year old son, Pil-gu (Kim Kang-Hoon) in the fictional town of Ongsan, where she runs a bar-turned-restaurant, *Camellia*. Not only is Dong-baek a single mother, therefore an outcast in the eyes of the Ongsan townsfolk, she also grew up as an orphan herself, abandoned at seven by her mother. Her unassuming life in Ongsan is complicated by the fact that a warm-hearted local policeman, Hwang Yong-sik (Kang Ha-Neul) is in love with her, in spite of her difficult situation. Crucially, *When the Camellia Blooms* positions the single-parent and the orphan—both personified by Dong-baek—at the center of a plot, that offers an acute portrayal of contemporary Korea. Ongsan is a world full of secrets and plots, in which everyone has something to hide. Most importantly, it offers a context for a reconsideration of the contemporary Korean woman, mother and, by extension, family constellation. It is clear that the character of a single parent challenges traditionally held ideas of a hetero-normative Korean family (Kim, 2017). The drama, which features a range of broken families, questions traditional female roles and highlights social difficulties experienced by an orphan. Over the course of the drama, the heroine slowly emerges as a dynamic character who grows stronger and more confident as the plot progresses, an orphaned adult, who grows into possession of her own narrative and truth.

The dramatic representation of Dong-baek as a struggling orphan resonates immediately with many adoptees' experiences of loss. Her memories of being abandoned have formed her as an individual for 27 years. As an orphan, she has been bullied her entire life; in addition, her mother's absence has left Dong-baek extremely vulnerable and angry. The relationship between mother and daughter comprises anger, frustration, and sadness, elements common to adoptee narratives of abandonment. As a recent study of transcultural K-drama viewership has shown, consumption of the genre is permeated by an affective affinity with plotlines and characters (Ju, 2019). For many Korean adoptees, it is precisely this emotional connection with the K-drama heroine that may function as productive recognition of self-as-other.

The Adoptee Consumer Perspective

Although adoptees are similar to other Western consumers of K-culture insofar as their understanding of content and meaning is mediated by translation, adoptee consumption differs in other respects. Through the lens of a semiotic paradigm, reminiscent of Stuart Hall's (1980) communicative model, the production and consumption of K-drama occurs by way of a complex circuit structure that includes two additional components: circulation and reproduction. If, in this regard, K-drama is the message form, produced by the multi-billion dollar *Hallyu* industry, then meaning is that which is actually being received and consumed by the viewer. Central to this conveyance of meaning—a process of continuous semiotic negotiations between the producer and receiver of a message—is the idea of *encoding and decoding* of a discursive event. What is clear from the above is that the message produced and the message received are not symmetrical in the case of Scandinavian adoptee consumption and interpretation of K-culture generally and K-drama specifically. The probability for misunderstanding is high, given the adoptee's upbringing in a society that accepts constructs regarded as controversial in Korea (independent women, gender equality, single-parent households, etc), coupled with her lack of Korean cultural and linguistic literacy. This inability to decode the myriad of environmentally- coded signs in a K-drama production prevents the adoptee consumer from participating seamlessly and operating within the productive dominant code. Instead, the adoptee can engage interpretatively with the plot and the K-drama, from the perspective of an alternative decoding, within a discursive framework of an alternative life story, namely that of an autobiographically-oriented adoptee transnationality. To borrow Legrand's notion of adoption as "blood dislocation and genealogical bewilderment" (Marre & Briggs, 2009, p. 247), adoptee consumption of K-culture is informed by, and intensifies, an affective yearning towards a hypothetical Korean life and potential aspects of an identity that was uprooted and disrupted by the adoptee's removal from her birth-culture. Significantly, as media theorist John Fiske (1992) has noted, consumption or reception becomes itself the moment of production, whereby the adoptee enters into a continuous renegotiation of her image in the face of the self as the other.

Producing Self as Other: Negotiating an Adoptee Discursive Identity

The guiding assumption of this chapter is that when adoptees involve themselves actively as consumers of K-culture, they participate as interpreters of their own roles at the receiving end of the production circuit. This seemingly passive position may, however, prove prolific when it comes to negotiating, debating, or expanding the boundaries of what global Korea and Koreans may come to signify in K-culture. As one adoptee consumer of K-pop in Sweden has aptly explained, consumption of K-pop functions as part of a personal "decolonisation process" (Hübinette, 2012, p. 43). Broader studies of adoptee consumers and participants in K-culture production are needed to understand more fully how adoptees operate as a specific media-interpretative community (Alasuutari, 1999), increasingly defined by activism and engagement in their own transnational cause. Adoptees of Korean origin have come to question what happened in the past, critically engage post-adoption processes, report on misinformation and on falsification of documents, interventions that currently are helping shape Korean nationality and identity as well as their own sense of belonging. As consumers of K-culture, this global audience of adoptees can, therefore, be characterized as a participatory audience (Jenkins, 2006). As Jenkins argues, participatory audiences function as producers of their own media content, so that, consequently, boundaries between producers and consumers blur to a greater degree. In this way, adoptee producers of narratives about Korea and Koreanness operate in the margins of *Hallyu*, demarcating a potentially new emancipating discursive practice.

Evidence of this social practice spurred by adoptee activism is illustrated by a growing number of literary works by adoptee authors (Ivenäs, 2018, Rinhaug, 2010, 2012). One particularly powerful example of this cultural form is a novel by Norwegian author, Anne Kyung-Sook Øfsti, *Si at vi har hele dagen/Tell me we have all day* (2014). Kyung-Sook Øfsti herself was one of the first Korean adoptees to arrive in Norway in June 1965 when she was three years old. The novel's story is told through the voices of two women—*Rebekka* (a Norwegian adoptee and psychologist by profession) and *I-Sook* (a South Korean woman living in Seoul, separated, and old enough to be Rebekka's mother). Rebekka is planning to return to Korea in an attempt to find her late sister Marion's biological mother and inform her of her daughter's death. While growing up in a small Norwegian town, Rebekka viewed her birth country in a light as foreign as did her sister and Norwegian-born parents. Rebekka leaves for Korea and finds herself in situations where it becomes clear that she both is and is not, Korean. Her changing sense of identity is registered first as an inner bodily experience that deepens as she sees her outward appearance in harmony with the crowd:

> A new and different feeling of belonging spreads through my body. I look like everyone else, and they look like me. An aesthetic yearning that I didn't know I had is revealed to me: I turn around and look behind me; not a single white face, not one line of contrast in the field of view, only a billowing sea of black and brown (Øfsti, 2014, pp. 87-88, trans. Viola Bao).

Rebekka, in Seoul, is seemingly immersed in Korea, overwhelmed by a sensation of much longed-for sameness, a first real experience of seamlessly blending in with other Koreans. In the course of her return journey to Korea, she shifts from being perceived as ambivalent, unsettling, and different (by Scandinavians) to becoming identifiable, recognizable, and meaningful (by Koreans). However, precisely because she is *not* identical to others, due to her Westernized upbringing, what happens in the novel (and to adoptees returning to Korea in real life) is a distortion of meaning, in the sense that the "message" is rendered through the perspective of the adoptee, or *a second-order observation*, to speak from a systems-theoretical standpoint (Luhmann, 2013). From this point of view, Rebekka is only capable of perceiving herself as she is observed by someone else. In the same way, as discourse, she, Rebekka, becomes open to re-interpretation, subject to constant distortion of meaning.

Acts of consumption and production of meaning, processes of moving in and out of differentiating sign-paradigms, can become even more salient by adding to the adoptee equation the sensory language of the body. For example, Rebekka's embodied memories of her birth country are reawakened by her return to Korea, each sensory experience bringing forgotten parts of her past vividly to life. At the sight of a beach house in Busan, she suddenly remembers spoken words of Korean; and when she eats kimchi with I-Sook's family, a kind of dissociation occurs; it is Rebekka's body that reacts and remembers:

> First, I can taste the salty, savory, then my head feels dizzy, a hint of something forgotten, but known spreads around in my body, sharply, distinctly, without images. So this is what it's like to remember, I think to myself.
>
> - Must have eaten it before, I say, and take one more bite.
>
> - All Koreans have eaten kimchi, I-Sook says.
>
> (Øfsti, 2014, p. 79, my trans.)

The act of consumption—portrayed as eating kimchi, or an act of literally internalizing the quintessential culinary symbol of Korea—operates on an individual as well as on a collective level: "All Koreans have eaten kimchi," I-Sook tells Rebekka. This statement of the self-evident includes Rebekka and other adoptees—the marginalized ambivalent signs—in the official discourse of her birth country. While many non-Korean K-culture fans can be seen to search for "Korean-ness"—for example a Korean meal—because they intend to recreate an experience of a K-drama scenery (Dutch, 2019), Korean adoptees returning to Korea are more likely to search for a *real* Korean meal, for food and other sensory experiences, as a key to access affective authenticity in order to become a part of, immersed in and identified—if only momentarily—as "Korean."

Adoptees as Diasporic Koreans and Consumers of Ethnic Media

Having explored the dynamic of adoptees as a part of the larger diasporic Korean community, and in particular how K-culture—and specifically K-drama—is consumed by the adoptee audience and reciprocated by a productive response, I wish now to turn to a reconsideration of the adoptee position within a diasporic audience, especially with regard to the themes of "homeland" and "belonging." To support the argument, I will rely on a concept of "diaspora" dependent on a connectivity enabled by contemporary transnational dynamics (Tsagarousianou, 2004). In her article, Tsagarousianou argues that the concept of diaspora ought to be rethought as imagined communities, continuously reconstructed and reinvented, rather than premised on ethnicity, mobility, and displacement. Media technologies and diasporic media are fundamental in the reproduction and transformation of diasporic identities.

To many members of the Korean diaspora, including adoptees, living with difference and transnationality as an often marginalized group, their often ritual engagement with and consumption of *Hallyu* is still based on K-culture—however globally oriented—as "ethnic media," which can provide a sense of familiarity, of a yearning and longing for "home" (Kim, 2011). However, the communicative encounter between the ethnically produced artefact and uprooted, adoptee consumer has the potential of pushing the boundaries of what it entails to belong to a "place" or even "places," and "of going back" to an "original place." These concepts are continuously negotiated within the global adoptee community and are fueled by the encounter with *Hallyu* productions across a range of media systems. When the consumption of ethnic media leads to a creative response by the diasporic adoptee subject, then concepts of "home" can be debated within the framework of a new discourse of transnationality. Adoptees demonstrate their intention of shying away from an "old" diaspora typology and instead emancipate their creative discourses in order to foster a novel idea of what "home" and "belonging" might be. In a sense, this notion of "in-betweenness," mentioned at the beginning of the chapter, comes to represent an emancipatory site, a space, even "home," to which the diasporic self belongs. From this perspective, diasporic "longing" is perhaps not necessarily directed towards the past or even to "origin." Rather, it is a yearning and an acknowledgment of the enormous creative potential held in transnationality, whose perspective is outward-looking, directed towards the present and the future.

Although it is unlikely that Korean Wave production companies make dramas and other K-culture artefacts with the adoptee consumer in mind, it is also clear that as a particular audience of *Hallyu*, Korean adoptees represent fluid consumers of K-culture and hybrid spectators of K-drama. A greater attention will need to be paid in future studies to this particular aspect of audience and reception research. For now, my aim has been to show how K-culture can trigger a productive response in the adoptee consumer, whose experience of transnationalism is authenticated in her ability to pivot on the paradoxical possibility that *sameness equals difference*. As the Korean adoptee continues to explore his or her "Koreanness," the mirror image, a reflection of someone observing the observer, is precisely a translation of oneself as another, one *who could have been*. As Stuart Hall suggests, the notion of identity formation is a process of becoming rather than being, not according to "who we are" or "where we came from," so much as what we might become, how we have been represented and how that bears on how we might represent ourselves (Hall, 1996). Similarly, "home" must be anchored, not necessarily in an idea of what has been left behind, but rather imbued with a sense of an "experiential construction [...] relevant to the present constitution of subjectivity and internal coherence" (Kim, 2011, p. 144). Even if the Korean Wave proves to have few chances of lasting a long time in Scandinavian countries, due to stark differences in cultural norms (e.g. class and gender hierarchies) (Pak, 2019), Westernized adoptees who engage as consumers of K-culture can nonetheless find resonance in each others' ongoing interpretations of Koreanness and, as such, make their own contributions to a participatory audience, creative, long-lasting and global in the truest sense of the word.

Recommended Readings

Jin, D. Y. (2016). *New Korean wave. Transnational cultural power in the age of social media*. Urbana, IL: University of Illinois Press.

Kim, E. (2010). *Adopted territory: Transnational Korean adoptees and the politics of belonging*. Durham, NC: Duke University Press.

Kim, Y. (2011). *Transnational migration, media and identity of Asian women: Diasporic daughters*. New York, NY: Routledge.

McKee, K. D. (2019). *Disrupting kinship. Transnational politics of Korean adoption in the United States*. The Asian American experience. Urbana, IL: University of Illinois Press.

Park, J. Y. & Lee, A.-G. (Eds.). (2019). *The rise of K-dramas. Essays on Korean television and its global consumption*. Jefferson, NC: McFarland & Company.

Additional Sources

International Korean Adoptee Association. https://ikaa.org

Korea Adoption Services. https://www.kadoption.or.kr/en/intro/opening.jsp

Overseas Koreans Foundation. http://www.mofa.go.kr/eng/wpge/m_5722/contents.do

References

Alasuutari, P. (1999). Introduction: Three phases of reception studies. In P. Alasuutari (Ed.), *Rethinking the media audience* (pp. 1-21). London; Thousand Oaks: Sage Publications.

Dutch, J. R. (2019). Consuming K-drama cuisine. The intersection of fans, fandom, and food in the search for a real Korean meal. In J.-Y. Park & A.-G. Lee (Eds.), *The rise of K-dramas. Essays on Korean television and its global consumption* (pp. 6-25). Jefferson, NC: McFarland & Company.

Elfving-Hwang, J. (2013). South Korean cultural diplomacy and brokering 'K-culture' outside Asia. *Korean Histories*, *4*(1), 14-26.

Fiske, J. (1992). British cultural studies and television. In R. C. Allen (Ed.), *Channels of discourse, reassembled* (pp. 284-326). London, UK: Routledge.

Hall, S. (1980). Encoding/Decoding. In S. Hall, D. Hobson, A. Lowe & P. Willis (Eds.), *Culture, media, language* (pp. 117-127). London, UK: Routledge.

Hall, S. (1996). Introduction: Who needs identity?. In S. Hall & P. du Gay (Eds.), *Questions of cultural identity* (pp. 1-17). London, UK: Sage Publications.

Hübinette, T. (2004). Korean adoption history. In E. Kim (Ed.), *Community 2004. Guide to Korea for overseas adopted Koreans* (pp. 12-19, 25-47). Overseas Koreans Foundation.

Hübinette, T. (2005). *Comforting an orphaned nation: Representations of international adoption and adopted Koreans in Korean popular culture*. (Ph.D. dissertation). Stockholm University. Stockholm.

Hübinette, T. (2012). The reception and consumption of hallyu in Sweden: Preliminary reflections and reflections. *Korea Observer*, *3*(43), 503-525.

Hübinette, T. (2018). Who are the Swedish K-pop fans? Revisiting the reception and consumption of hallyu in post-*Gagnam Style* Sweden with an emphasis on K-pop. *Culture and Empathy*, *1*(1-4), 34-48.

Ivenäs, S. (2018). Travelling home: The Scandinavian transnational adoptee identity on the move. *Scandinavian-Canadian Studies/Études Scandinaves au Canada*, *25*, 154-173.

Jenkins, H. (2006). *Convergence culture. Where old and new media collide*. New York, NY: New York University Press.

Jin, D. Y. (2016). *New Korean wave. Transnational cultural power in the age of social media*. Urbana, IL: University of Illinois Press.

Ju, H. (2014). Transformations of the Korean media industry by the Korean wave: The perspective of glocalization. In Y. Kuwahara (Ed.), *The Korean wave. Korean popular culture in global context* (pp. 33-51). New York, NY: Palgrave Macmillan.

Ju, H. (2019). Korean TV-drama viewership on Netflix: Transcultural affection, romance and identities. *Journal of International and Intercultural Communication*, 1-17.

Kim, E. (2007). Our adoptee, our alien: Transnational adoptees as specters of foreignness and family in South Korea. *Anthropological Quarterly*, *80*(2), 497-431.

Kim, E. (2010). *Adopted territory: Transnational Korean adoptees and the politics of belonging*. Durham, NC: Duke University Press.

Kim, J. H. (2019, March 26). The K-drama adoption element [Blog post]. Retrieved from https://blog.kocowa.com/the-k-drama-adoption-element/

Kim, U. (2002). Dark side of Korean adoption. *Um & Yang*, *11*(1), 23-28.

Kim, Y. (2011). *Transnational migration, media and identity of Asian women: Diasporic daughters*. New York, NY: Routledge.

Kim, Y. (2017). The Korean wave: Korean popular culture in a digital cosmopolitan world. In Y. Kim (Ed.), *Routledge handbook of Korean culture and society* (pp. 269-282). London; New York: Routledge.

Lee, H.-K. (2013). Cultural policy and the Korean wave. From national culture to transnational consumerism. In Y. Kim (Ed.), *The Korean wave. Korean media go global* (pp. 185-198). London; New York: Routledge.

Legrand, C. (2009). Routes to the roots: Toward an anthropology of genealogical practices. In D. Marre & L. Briggs (Eds.), *International adoption. Global inequalities and the circulation of children* (pp. 244-255). New York, NY: New York University Press.

Luhmann, N. (2013). *Introduction to systems theory* (P. Gilgen, trans.). Cambridge; Malden: Polity Press. (Original work published 2002).

Marre, D., & Briggs, L. (2009). *International adoption: Global inequalities and the circulation of children*. New York, NY: New York University Press.

McKee, K. D. (2019). *Disrupting kinship. Transnational politics of Korean adoption in the United States*. The Asian American experience. Urbana, IL: University of Illinois Press.

Øfsti, A. K-S. (2014). *Si at vi har hele dagen*. Oslo, Norway: Gyldendal.

Oh, A. H. (2015). *To save the children of Korea*. Stanford, CA: Stanford University Press.

Pak, N. (2019, March). The "Koreaboos" of Norway and their take on the Korean wave. *The Hankyoreh*.

Park, S. Y. (2010). Transnational adoption, "Hallyu", and the politics of Korean popular culture. *Biography. Personal Narrative & Political Discourse*, *33*(1), 151-166.

Rinhaug, A. (2010). Adoptee aesthetics: A gendered discourse. *Race/Ethnicity: Multidisciplinary Global Contexts*, *4*(1), 9-27.

Rinhaug, A. (2012). Adopted. Crossing (out) boundaries of adoptee kinship and belonging. In P. Gates & L. Funnell (Eds.), *Transnational Asian identities in pan-Pacific cinemas. The reel Asian exchange* (pp. 191-204). London; New York: Routledge.

Tsagarousianou, R. (2004). Rethinking the concept of diaspora: Mobility, connectivity and communication in a globalized world. *Westminster Papers in Communication and Culture*, *1*(1), 52-66.

Woo, H. K. (2012, September). Reading transnationality in a national context: *Hallyu* in Korean audition programs. Paper presented at the Political Popular: Intersection of Democracy and Popular/Public Culture in South Korea conference, University of California-Irvine.

Yoon, J. K (Director). (2014, December 17). 국제시장 [Ode to my father] [Film] CJ Entertainment.

CHAPTER 9

Bonding over K-Drama: Cross-Cultural Influence of K-Pop Culture in South Asian Immigrant Diasporic Families

Rukhsana Ahmed, University at Albany, State University of New York
& **Zerin Mahzabin Khan**, Virginia Tech

The prevalence and widespread use of Information and Communication Technologies (ICTs) have contributed to the diffusion of ethnic media across borders, enabling diasporic communities to sustain communication and develop communities, both locally and transnationally (Karim, 2003; Ahmed & Veronis, 2019). Transnational media refer to the communication and flow of information across boundaries and involve what Marshall McLuhan envisioned as "shrinking of the distance between people globally and increase of cross-cultural understanding" (Kern-Stone & Mishra, 2019, p. 8). Existing migration research has examined immigrants' use of media in a variety of contexts in order to understand how transnational media influence migration decisions, create and sustain communication links across borders (Karim, 1998), build, maintain, and promote diasporic identities and communities (Karim, 2003, 2007; Karim & Al-Rawi, 2018), and facilitate migrants' settlement (Ahmed & Veronis, 2017). While transnational media play an important role in migration and settlement processes (Matsaganis, Katz, & Ball-Rokeach, 2011), diversity also bring about changes in media by way of "people [crossing] borders and [establishing] themselves in new places [and thus bringing] with them new languages, cultures, and traditions" (Kern-Stone & Mishra, 2019, p. 5).

South Asians constitute one of the fastest growing immigrant groups in the United States, increasing in population from 3.5 million to 5.4 million from 2010 to 2017 (Haniffa, 2019). Because of their diverse national origins and immigration experiences, South Asian diasporas have enjoyed a significant cultural presence in the U.S. (Leonard, 1997). As such, it is important to explore their cultural experiences, since "cultural flows diffuse identities, generating new possibilities for intercultural dialogues" (Tzanelli, 2011, p. 384). Ibrahim and colleagues (1997) noted that South Asian culture in the United States is shaped by social class, education, experience with sexism, racism, and exclusion, as well as the identification with one's own culture and ethnicity. The sociohistoric culture of South Asian Americans shape several consistent values and beliefs such as humility, self-control, and respect for elders, family, and the community (Ibrahim, Ohnishi, & Sandhu, 1997). South Asian collectivist cultures value strong family ties (Triandis, 1995; Chadda & Deb, 2013), and family members play a central role in any form of decision-making (Ayyub, 2000). Zaidi and colleagues (2016) underscored the existence of opposing cultural value systems between South Asian immigrants and host country populations, which leads to the adherence of conflicting lifestyles (p. 232).

It is evident from existing literature on South Asian immigrant families that "second-generation [South Asian] youth are at the crossroads of negotiation between cultural traditions and host versus heritage cultural and familial expectations" (Zaidi, Couture-Carron, & Maticka-Tyndale, 2016, p. 235), thus increasing the potential for intergenerational conflict (Khanna et al., 2009; Tummala-Narra & Deshpande, 2018). It is worth noting that through transnational interactions in mediascapes, one of the five dimensions of the global flows of culture (Appadurai, 1996), immigrants "reconcile their lifestyles and customs in a new social context" (Skop, 2013, p. 81). For example, in the case of South Asian immigrants, Durham (2004) found that second-generation youth consume ethnic media to connect with family members or friends from the South Asian diaspora. Diasporic identity and transnational media use with a focus on second generation ethnic minorities (Georgiou, 2006; Oh, 2015) have also received scholarly attention. Despite composing one of the largest immigrant groups in the United States, there is a paucity of studies examining the ways in which members of South Asian diaspora consume mediated information to meet their settlement need; in particular, their usage of transnational media has not been fully explored.

The increase of migrants around the world has been met with increased availability and consumption of transnational media (Croucher, Oommen, & Steele, 2009), including "communication, information or entertainment that crosses international borders without the regulatory constrains normally associated with electronic media" (Gher & Bharthapudi, 2004, p. 2). Hence, there is a growing body of literature on transnational media and immigrant identity construction (Lee, 2004; Lee & Cho, 1990, Moon & Park, 2007), and yet, research on transnational media consumption to maintain family ties is limited.

Since the late 20th century, Korean media products, including K-films (e.g., *Shiri, My Sassy Girl, A Tale of Two Sisters*) and K-dramas (e.g., *What is Love All About? Stars in My Heart, Winter Sonata*) have enjoyed a remarkable popularity in neighboring East, South, and Southeast Asian countries, a cultural phenomenon called the *Korean Wave* ("Hallyu" in Korean) (Kim & Kim, 2011; Jin, 2018; Ju, 2020; Ju & Lee, 2015; Shim, 2006). Furthermore, over the past two decades, Korean popular (K-pop) culture products, such as K-pop songs, television dramas, movies, online games, fashion, cosmetics, and so on, have witnessed rising global popularity among consumers (Ju, 2020; Han & Lee, 2008; Lee & Jin, 2019; Leem, 2017; Shim, 2006), mainly disseminated by social media and giving rise to the Hallyu 2.0 or new Korean Wave (Jin, 2018; Jin & Yoon, 2016). For example, as of December 2019, there are 1,799 Hallyu fan clubs with a total of 99.32 million fans, 72 million in Asia and Oceania, 15 million in Europe, and 12 million in the U.S. (Kim, 2020). In particular, K-dramas have had a significant cultural presence in recent years, expanding transnationally and encompassing transnational communities across Asia, North America, Latin America, Europe, and Middle East (Park & Lee, 2019; Park et al., 2020). For example, as of 2018, more than 18 million Americans are K-drama fans, with greater than 35% representing women between the ages of 16-25 (Orsini, 2018).

In sum, with the proliferation of transnational media, K-pop culture and especially K-drama play a significant role in the day-to-day lives of diasporic communities around the world (Jin, 2018; Ju & Lee, 2015; Park & Lee, 2019). Accordingly, this chapter explores the role of K-drama in nurturing South Asian family ties in the United States, mediating especially a mother-daughter relationship. Krijnen and Van Bauwel (2015) argued, "transnational media can be used to negotiate identities or to renegotiate cultural values" (p. 154). For South Asian diasporic women, mother-daughter relationship is central to creating "ethnic cultures and identities" (Thompson, 2002, p. 415; see also Kurien, 1999). Furthermore, "interviews with South Asian mothers and their daughters about their media use and leisure activities" revealed "joint viewing of ethnic films and television was extremely important in the construction and reaffirmation of their shared cultural identity" (Thompson, 2002, p. 415). In this chapter, employing a critical lens, we locate *My ID is Gangnam Beauty* as a site for South Asian mother-daughter communication about everyday life experiences surrounding interpersonal relationships and social issues.

Methodological and Theoretical Frameworks

Methodologically, our study is rooted in the traditions of autoethnography. Ellis and Bochner (2000) defined autoethnography as an "autobiographical genre of writing and research that displays multiple layers of consciousness, connecting the personal to the cultural" (p. 739).

Using an intergenerational communication approach, which involves interactions that occur between individuals from different generations (Lin, 2017), we engage in mother-daughter communication about our shared experiences as consumers of K-drama within a South Asian diasporic family context. Specifically, we focus on the K-drama *My ID is Gangnam Beauty* as a site for mother-daughter conversation and reflection located in a space that is shaped by our relationship, age, and culture (Ellis, Adams, & Bochner, 2011; Lin, 2017; Trommsdorff & Kornadt, 2003). Potter argues that "Autoethnography engages in life stories as a technique of producing some theoretical understanding of highly personal events" (Potter, 2015, p. 1435).

Theoretically, we locate our study within the notion of "thirdspace" that migrants form as "alternative social spaces located between the two poles of 'here' and 'there' to "often engage in transnational activities that create new spheres of interaction" (Skop, 2013, p. 81). In her study, Skop argues that the Internet is "a 'thirdspace' which unites many Asian Indian migrants in the United States, providing them both a leisure and a shared outlet in which to socialise, network, and collectively reminisce on life back home as well as to imagine life in the future" (p. 81). In this study, we contend that K-drama serves as a thirdspace for us which we fashion by utilizing Information and Communication Technologies (ICTs). Just as "diverse Internet users invest multiple 'thirdspaces' with varied meanings" (Skop, 2013, p. 81), K-drama as a thirdspace transcends temporal and geographic separation between us, creating a cross-cultural communicative space (which refers "to thoughtful interaction and communication, in which experiences are encouraged to be mutually shared, acknowledged and considered, as well as explored, reflected on and negotiated" (Aspfors & Valle, 2017, p. 2)) for mother and daughter to maintain a sense of togetherness "in two (or more) disparate places" (Skop, 2013, p. 98).

In the following, we present our shared experiences consuming K-dramas in the form of an intergenerational discourse, as well as our critical reflections on the K-drama *My ID is Gangnam Beauty* and thereby "describe and systematically analyze [our] personal experience[s] in order to understand [our] cultural experience[s]" (Ellis, Adams, & Bocher, 2011, p. 273). Throughout our conversation and reflection, we "thread together isolated events and milestones to create a coherent and compelling narrative which maintains context throughout" (Elias, 2017, p. 591). We conclude this chapter by underscoring the role of Korean popular culture in nurturing diasporic and transnational family linkages across time and space.

Cross-Cultural Mother-Daughter Communication about K-Dramas

Being fans of the South Korean boy band BTS (an acronym standing for "Bangtan Sonyeondan" in Korean and "Beyond the Scene" in English) influenced us in taking an interest in K-dramas. Watching K-dramas brings us together as we bond over our discussions and provides us with an outlet to unwind from the day-to-day hustle of life and relax. We are always struck by how Koreans use K-dramas as a platform to raise awareness about social issues, values, and educate the public about certain topics. In the following, we engage in a dialogue about our journey into the world of K-dramas.

Intergenerational Discourse

Zerin: How did you start taking an interest in Korean pop culture?

Rukhsana: While in Bangladesh, I remember growing up in a household where my parents exposed us to a lot of different cultures. As a family, we watched cultural programs on TV, attended cultural functions, and savored ethnic cuisines, including Korean. I had Korean friends while in grad school in the U.S., and these intercultural friendships deepened my enthusiasm for Korean culture and entertainment. Through these friendships, I learned more about Korean fashion, beauty products, K-pop, and food.

Zerin: Yes! I never had a problem with watching foreign films, since you exposed me to different cultural programs from a young age, including Korean movies like a *Tale of Two Sisters* and *Mother* while living in the U.S. and in Canada.

Rukhsana: How did you first start taking an interest in K-dramas?

Zerin: It started with BTS while I was doing my undergrad studies in Canada! I used to enjoy watching videos made by a YouTube comedian star called Superwoman (real name Lilly Singh). One day during the spring of 2017, I was watching one of her videos when I noticed that her comment section was flooded with similar requests. Since Superwoman suggests to her fans to comment what type of video she should make next, I read that nearly all of her comments comprised people requesting her to make a reaction video to BTS Blood, Sweat, and Tears. I was curious about BTS, but as soon as I typed in their name into YouTube's search engine and saw the videos were in Hangul (the Korean alphabet), I was not interested in watching it anymore. I didn't bothering clicking the videos to see what they were about, since I felt Korean music videos were not really for me. My second encounter with BTS was a few months later during the summer. We had tuned in to watch the Billboard Music Awards, and BTS had just won the award for Top Social Artist. While they were coming to give their speech on stage, their music for Blood, Sweat, and Tears kept playing in the background. I remember you turning to me and saying how you really liked the song and that you really wanted to listen to it more.

Rukhsana: Yes, I became nostalgic. I remembered watching and discussing K-pop songs with my Korean grad school friend. I became curious about the song and the group and yearned to learn more about how K-pop had evolved since I last looked into it a decade ago.

Zerin: That night, I looked up their song Blood, Sweat, and Tears, saw the music video, showed it to you, and we've been hooked ever since!

Rukhsana: So how was BTS influential in piquing your interest in K-dramas?

Zerin: Yes, regarding K-drama, Kim Taehyung (BTS's V) had acted in the K-drama *Hwarang: The Poet Warrior Youth*. We had one day watched a compilation video with some of his scenes in the drama from YouTube, were really fascinated, and took an interest in some day watching the drama in its entirety. Although watching *Hwarang* was on our wish list, we were unable to watch it due to restraints in our time. I was busy preparing my grad school applications to U.S. schools, studying for the GRE, and finishing up my last year of undergrad studies.

Rukhsana: Yes, I remember that hectic period in our lives all too well! I was also busy with my new job applications to U.S. universities. I was drawn by *Hwarang's* premise about the flower boy elite warriors of the Silla Kingdom. I loved watching Asian historical movies when I was young, and I was looking forward to watching and discussing this historical drama with you while also spending quality mother-daughter time together.

Zerin: Fast forward to August 2018 when it was my first month of being away from home and living on my own while in graduate school. It was a Friday night at the beginning of the fall semester, and I was craving watching *Hwarang*, however, I didn't want to watch it without you. I therefore decided to check out a different popular K-drama. Based on recommendations from people on the internet and online reviews, I selected *Boys Over Flowers* and decided to check it out to see what K-dramas were like. I only intended to watch the first ten minutes of the drama, but I got so hooked that I ended up binge watching 6 episodes (6 hours) that whole night, to the point where Jun Pyo, Jan Di, Ji Hoo, and Ga Eul went to vacation at Jeju Island.

Rukhsana: I very well remember how you got me hooked on the last night before I had to leave while I was visiting you in Blacksburg. You were pestering me to watch at least the first episode, and I caved in during the last night and got hooked immediately. After returning to Albany, I binge watched and surpassed your record by staying up late at night and watching 10 episodes in a row. So, why do you enjoy watching K-dramas? What aspects draw you in?

Zerin: It's my favorite form of relaxing and taking my mind off of school and lab work. It's a great distraction, and I always get immersed in the characters, storylines, setting, and the culture. Before starting grad school, I used to love reading novels during my spare time. However, after starting my PhD, I prefer watching television when taking a break. Since I already have to read so many papers for my classes and research, my urge to read books has dwindled slightly, and I now prefer to watch movies and shows more often than reading. Because K-dramas are so addicting, I have a difficult time watching only a few episodes at a time. Normally, when I watch K-dramas on my own in Blacksburg, I reserve one or two days during the weekend and binge watch the show. It is honestly difficult to carve out time to watch 16-20 hours of a K-drama due to school work and research. During the school semester, I have continuous deadlines, making it difficult for me to find time to relax even during the weekend. However, there are normally a few days during the semester where my schedule permits me to take a little bit of a break for a day. When I'm in the midst of a particularly strenuous and busy schedule, I think about which K-drama I will watch when my deadlines are finished and can afford to take a day or two to watch the show. I find that looking forward to a K-drama after continuously working for several weeks with little sleep and no break helps me keep my sanity and gives me the energy to work well, knowing that I can take a nice break soon.

Rukhsana: I also like K-dramas for their entertainment value to help me unwind and escape from the day-to-day exigencies of life, especially workplace stress. With today's technology, I like the freedom and ability to pace watching K-dramas. I like how K-dramas strike a balance between entertainment and education. K-dramas serve as a platform to address stereotypes in societies, make audiences aware of social issues, humanize their characters by portraying relationships realistically, and promote family values. For instance, *My ID is Gangnam Beauty* exemplifies these aspects of K-dramas which we appreciate.

Critical Reflections on My ID Is Gangnam Beauty

Synopsis. *My ID is Gangnam Beauty* is a 16 episode Korean drama which was aired by JTBC in 2018 and is based on the webtoon published by Naver in 2016. The show focuses on Kang Mi Rae, a freshman college student majoring in chemistry. Since Mi Rae was an outcast for being bullied as a child for her looks, she undergoes plastic surgery to become pretty before starting college, where she hopes to start fresh with her new face and leave her past behind. Complications arise when her handsome former middle school classmate, Do Kyung Seok, turns up. The show highlights Mi Rae's daily struggles and her attempts to navigate the world of college rivalry, gossip, interpersonal relationships, and classes, as well as the obsession and discrimination due to beauty standards in society. Although at first, Mi Rae is able to integrate well with her peers and tries to learn to adjust to the attention that comes with having a beautiful face, her past threatens to resurface when her classmates learn she underwent plastic surgery. She then begins to be bullied for her "Gangnam-style beauty" (Leem, 2017, p. 658), a term used to describe someone who has undergone so many plastic surgeries, that he/she looks fake, artificial, and like a plastic monster. The show follows Mae Ri as, with the support of her friends and family, she learns to love herself and regain her confidence. The drama explores, through its overarching plot as well as subplots, themes about beauty and appearance and their impact on interpersonal relationships, work, and society in a university setting.

We were to drawn *Gangnam Beauty*, because of the manner in which the mother-daughter relationship and bond were represented and further enjoyed the K-drama due to the university setting, as we could relate to the academic setting being a professor and a grad student. In the following, we critically reflect on *My ID is Gangnam Beauty* by focusing on the concept of beauty and its place in society and how it becomes a defining characteristic of people to influence their everyday relationships. Specifically, we locate this K-drama as a site for South Asian mother-daughter communication about everyday life experiences surrounding interpersonal relationships and social issues.

Interpersonal Relationships

Familial relationships. We witness in the drama how interactions between characters depicting familial relationships revolve around the notion of beauty. We see the intricacies of mother-daughter relationships (Eun Sim and Mi Rae), father-daughter relationships (Tae Sik and Mi Rae), and the family dynamics among parents and child influenced by the beauty standards in modern South Korean society. For example, although Mi Rae and her mother internalized society's perception of beauty and appearance, it was heartwarming to see the strong bond Mi Rae and her mother shared still did not wither in the face of the trials and tribulations they went through. If anything, the mother-daughter duo banded together over Mi Rae's experience with bullying to the extent where Mi Rae's mother arranged plastic surgery for Mi Rae without the knowledge of her father. Her mother wanted Mi Rae to feel pretty and have a chance at a normal life with a new and beautiful face as she begins university. Although Mi Rae's father was protective of Mi Rae for being bullied and rejected by people surrounding her, he was always against Mi Rae receiving plastic surgery, as he thought Mi Rae was beautiful just the way she was. Hence, Mi Rae's newfound beauty stood in the way of the close bond she shared with her father. After finding out about Mi Rae's plastic surgery, we see Mi Rae's father being at odds with Mi Rae's idealized appearance, which resulted in a brief period of estrangement between the two of them. Gradually, her father salvaged the close connection and special bond he shared with Mi Rae after witnessing how Mi Rae was experiencing normal things in her life because of her new attractive face. This also resulted in repairing the tumultuous family dynamics and regaining the special bond, demonstrating the extent to which parents will go to provide a better life for their children.

Friendship. Mi Rae and her friend Hyun Jung share a unique and strong friendship, spanning since childhood. While Mi Rae is timid, Hyun Jung is feisty, sassy, and very protective of her best friend, as she is quick to understand when anyone mistreats Mi Rae and is not afraid to stand up for her. The drama demonstrates how Mi Rae is also very protective of her friend. Mi Rae's entire middle school experience was very isolating, especially since she was ridiculed for her looks and bullied by others. Although Hyun Jung attended the same middle school, Mi Rae explains during one episode that she and Hyun Jung were never together during normal school hours and instead hung out together after school ended. In most cases, people would automatically think that Hyun Jung may not have wanted to be with Mi Rae publicly due to her unpopularity. However, it was rather Mi Rae who did not allow her friend to be seen with her at school, in an effort to protect Hyun Jung from being bullied by the same people who bullied Mi Rae. We see through this example how their friendship was not tested by the notion of beauty, but rather it grew stronger with time. We even see that although those around Mi Rae treat her differently after she undergoes plastic surgery, Hyun Jung still continues to treat her friend the same way she always had since childhood. The two women continue to live together as roommates while they are in university, creating a strong support system for each other as they tackle the trials and tribulations of their first year in college.

Sunbae-Hoobae. The notion of beauty is also explored through the Korean culture of age hierarchy in a college setting. In particular, the sunbae (senior) and hoobae (junior) relationships in the chemistry department are quite prominent throughout the drama. Chan Woo, an older student, uses his seniority and experience to aggressively pursue Mi Rae by utilizing power dynamics, when he at first likes her for her beauty. However, when it soon becomes clear that she does not reciprocate his feelings, Chan Woo is quick to turn on Mi Rae and bully her, referring to her as a "plastic monster". Simultaneously, a graduate student and teaching assistant in the department, Woo Young, who teaches Mi Rae's lab course, also develops feelings for her when he is at first attracted by her physical beauty. Although Woo Young does not abuse the power dynamic in an effort to win Mi Rae's heart, he is open about his affection for her and pursues her as well.

Social Issues

Plastic Monster. Ironically, after going through plastic surgery, Mi Rae's newfound beauty had not been met with admiration and fascination by everyone involved in her life. If anything, Mi Rae was criticized, belittled, and ridiculed for changing her face to become pretty. She became too pretty to the point of being called out for fixing her face and earning titles such *plastic monster* and *Gangnam beauty* (someone who is attractive, but owes the attribution to multiple plastic surgeries). The years of very painful childhood experiences of being bullied by her peers for her looks drove Mi Rae to go under the knife with the support and help of her mother. Even though the result had been her apparent metamorphosis from an ugly girl into a pretty young lady, Mi Rae failed to stomp out bullying. We witness how the pretty Mi Rae struggles through the newfound beauty that gave her a fleeting confidence boost. To her utter dismay, shock, and grief, this time Mi Rae finds herself being ridiculed and mocked for being a "Gangnam plastic surgery monster." Mi Rae's resulting decline of self-esteem and social confidence raises the question about the value society places on appearance and beauty and how this value shifts and impacts body image, self-esteem, and happiness.

Face Genius. The notion of beauty is not just illustrated through the female characters in the drama. Male beauty is consistently highlighted through the character of Do Kyung Seok. Kyung Seok is considered to be the most handsome male student on the college campus and is nicknamed "Face Genius," a term used by others to describe his absurdly handsome and inhumanly beautiful face. While other male students envy his good looks, female students particularly fawn over his attractive face. However, Kyung Seok is completely indifferent to the special treatment and shies away from this attention, preferring to keep to himself. He does not particularly care about physical beauty, which is clearly evident by his treatment of Mi Rae. He is the only person, besides Mi Rae's best friend, who had known her and seen her face before she had plastic surgery. It is later revealed that he liked Mi

Rae in middle school, and what is particularly heartwarming is that he continues to like her for her personality, even after she changes her face with plastic surgery. Just like Mi Rae's friend Hyun Jung, Kyung Seok's treatment of Mi Rae is not impacted by beauty. During one episode, he mentions (about Mi Rae): "She is not pretty, but she's not ugly, either. She's just her."

Bullying. The drama poignantly underscores society's beauty standards and appearance concerns that result in bullying. Growing up, we see Mi Rae was bullied at school for her body size and face. She was called a pig, because she loved to eat, and kids in her school would throw food at her and insult her when she ate. Although gradually, Mi Rae lost weight by diet and exercise, her face was still considered unattractive and thus she was socially excluded. The acts of bullying became worse when Mi Rae confessed her growing liking for a boy in school. This boy scorned Mi Rae and demanded she keep her crush on him a secret. The constant experience of bullying engulfed Mi Rae into developing anxiety and depression to the extent that she attempted to commit suicide. Although a stranger helped prevent Mi Rae from taking her own life, she started to develop a very low self-esteem and internalized the belief that she could never love or be loved.

Discussion

In this study, we explored the role of K-drama in nurturing South Asian family ties in the United States. Our autoethnographic intergenerational dialogue and critical reflections reveal that K-dramas afford a cross-cultural communicative space for transcending temporal and geographic separation between mother and daughter within a diasporic family context. Our study findings provide insights into the diffusion and popularity of K-dramas among South Asian immigrant diasporic families and how such transnational media contribute to preserving, recreating, and celebrating diasporic family ties, thereby enhancing the quality of life in transnational spaces. In the following, we highlight two important aspects we locate in our study findings.

First, K-dramas form an important part of immigrant diasporic family settlement experiences. Through the dialogical and reflexive recounting of our shared experiences, it is evident that K-dramas bring us closer together all the while we resettle in the United States and get accustomed to our separate yet connected lives within a South Asian diasporic family context. We bond over watching K-dramas together when we visit each other; K-dramas provide us with a thirdspace to negotiate our diasporic family ties—our being apart and together across time and space. Even long after we finish watching a K-drama, we continue to make references to it and exchange inside jokes when we are reminded of something similar, either while together or when apart. We thus discursively engage in and consume television dramas by actively sharing our experiences of K-drama consumption and discussing story plot and characters. We also tend to talk over phone and exchange messages over social media sites when we want to further discuss a point portrayed in a particular K-drama episode and thereby "[actualize] participatory culture in the Korean Wave context" (Jin, 2018, p. 418).

Park and Lee (2019) underscores how aside from "being enthralled with characters and storylines, fans find themselves listening to soundtracks and following their favorite actors to other K-dramas" (p. 1). After watching K-dramas, we also enjoy listening to the soundtrack. For instance, we buy the album and share the songs with each other, fostering our mutual love for music and bolstering our appreciation of the particular K-drama. We also enjoy reminiscing about the K-drama when we listen to particular songs which remind us of specific scenes or characters and our interactions and conversations around them. In this way, we attach a symbolic meaning to K-drama as a thirdspace upon which we reproduce our South Asian diasporic family ties and reconcile our mother-daughter bond. Scholars have referred to diasporas as 'imagined communities' (Anderson, 1983, as cited in Karim, 2003, p. 2) to underscore "the diasporic connections facilitated by various media and the simultaneous consumption of the same content by members of a transnational group" (Karim, 2003, p. 2).

Second, K-dramas create an intergenerational communicative space for immigrant diasporic families. It is evident from our critical reflection on *My ID is Gangnam Beauty* that K-dramas provide a forum to open discussions among audiences on socially important issues (Papa & Singhal, 2009). Communication scholars have utilized entertainment education strategy to deliberately design and implement "media message to both entertain and educate, in order to increase audience knowledge about an educational issue, create favorable attitudes, and change overt behavior" (Singhal & Rogers, 1999, p. xii) to bring about social change. The entertainment education value of *My ID is Gangnam Beauty* serves as an avenue to explore the social implications of the notion of beauty. One of the most evident examples pertains to bullying. The K-drama demonstrates how bullying can impact the self-esteem of its victims and carry over well into adulthood, thus affecting people's interpersonal relationships. The manner in which the drama puts a spotlight on this issue can serve as a teaching moment to caution people that how we choose to behave with others can leave lasting consequences. *My ID is Gangnam Beauty* juxtaposes the issue of bullying with the concept of Face Genius and male beauty standards. Through the character of Kyung Seok, the show reminds us that while there are people who bully others for how they look, not every beautiful person is concerned with superficial beauty standards. Like Kyung Seok, there are people who truly do see and appreciate others' personality before their face. Therefore, this K-drama serves as a platform to encourage dialogue and reflection on these issues and can help foster intergenerational communication through a medium that not only entertains, but also educates.

Recently, scholarly efforts have been made to examine the use of K-drama as an intervention to address knowledge, attitude, and behavior about school bullying and mental health (Park et al., 2020). Park and colleagues argued that K-dramas can be used "as an innovative social marketing tool to educate communities about mental health and school bullying" (p. 13). At the interpersonal level, when watching K-dramas together, we unpack the nuances of life's important lessons represented either in a historical, romantic, comedy, melodrama, action, or thriller drama. In this way, for us, K-dramas are a source of entertainment education that facilitates, fosters, and nurtures meaningful mother-daughter relationship.

Existing research has underscored the importance of cultural proximity in the appeal of entertainment media across geographical boundaries (Berg, 2017; Burch, 2002; Ksiazek & Webster, 2008). Kim (2013) attributed the popularity of K-dramas to their "emotionally powerful and self-reflexive" forms that "touch the sensibilities of disparate audiences" (p. 7). While we recognize K-dramas have met their fair share of criticism, for example, by Chilean fans "for their unrealistic portrayal of love and relationships" (Min, Jin, & Han, 2019, p. 609) partly due to cultural difference, considering that the consumption of culture "is embedded within the consumers' personal histories and memories" (Kim, 2019, p. 162), we find K-dramas portray realistic relationships, in particular they focus on family relationships as opposed to the friendships portrayed in many Western shows. The side characters in K-dramas are well-developed and memorable, while certain scenes also focus on food and how it brings people together. As a thirdspace, K-dramas "provide a sense of togetherness, engagement in [Korean] cultural traditions" (Skop, 2013, p. 83), allowing us to be both entertained as well as educated (Papa & Singhal, 2009). Watching K-dramas together creates a platform in which we exchange experiences, values, and expectations about important everyday life issues. As such, we argue that K-drama offers us—members of diasporic families—an important way to maintain and recreate transnational linkages across space and time. As demonstrated above, the K-drama *My ID is Gangnam Beauty* presented an interesting case for us to engage in a critical reflection as South Asian diasporic consumers of Korean pop culture. Meeting in this thirdspace affords us "both a material and a symbolic homeplace" (Skop, 2013, p. 82).

What is noteworthy about K-dramas is that their story plots narrate the events of everyday life. Since most K-dramas are short, spanning over two months with two episodes airing per week (Park et al., 2019), and are also typically only one season long with a total of 16-20 episodes, they can easily be binge watched, requiring less commitment on the part of the viewers. With this flexibility comes the opportunity to sample a variety of K-dramas. For example, Game of Thrones was an eight season TV series which spanned from 2011-2019. Similarly, Vampire Diaries was an eight season TV series which spanned from 2009-2017 and spawned two other spinoff series. Whereas, in about less than two years, we have watched 10 K-dramas together when visiting each other while living apart, ranging in genres from romantic comedy to romance, melodrama, action, thriller, and historical.

To summarize, K-dramas play an integral part of our diasporic family life, giving us the space to navigate and negotiate our mother-daughter communication about everyday life experiences. K-dramas offer a thirdspace for us to experience other cultures, learn about historical events, and discuss important interpersonal relationships and critical global social issues in a dramatic format. Watching K-dramas together provides us with a cross-cultural communicative space to share intergenerational family values, including "Confucian values such as responsibility and respect" (Park et al., 2019, p. 3; see also Yi, Chang, & Chang, 2004). While "Korean television dramas [mirror] traditional Confucian values and romantic love stories" (Jin, 2018, p. 412) that we appreciate, "the [hybridity and] impurity embedded in Hallyu 2.0 has become a brand that [we] can identify with" (Jin, 2018, p. 418).

Implications

Mishra (2019) posited, "Media products that are easily available and omnipresent find it easier to transcend cultures" (Mishra, 2019, p. 22). The diffusion of today's digital technology propelled the global reach of Hallyu, including K-dramas, beyond Asian countries to also include western countries, including those in North America (Park et al., 2019; Park et al., 2020). For example, with much ease we found ourselves digesting foreign language programs like K-drama with the help of subtitles and, beyond that, learning the Korean language with the aid of Internet lessons. Not to mention, online streaming services, including Netflix's investment into and expansion of the genre (Ju, 2020; Park et al., 2020), have made K-dramas "much more accessible, often with minimal fees, and sometimes with English translations available within hours of the first broadcast in their home country" (Coker, 2020, p. 146).

The accessibility of K-dramas worldwide can make it a meeting space for immigrant diasporic families to overcome "separation at intra- and international scales" (Skop, 2013, p. 82) by sharing mundane, everyday experiences and thus "construct particular senses of family relatedness over distance" (Long, 2014, p. 246). Immigrant diasporic families can rely on the medium of K-drama in order to nurture and maintain transnational kinship. Likewise, immigrant-serving organizations can utilize K-dramas when designing and communicating settlement related messages and information to immigrant communities.

Conclusion

As a South Asian mother-daughter pair living in the United States, in this chapter we engaged in a conversation with each other about our shared experiences consuming K-dramas and then shared our critical reflections as a practice of intersubjective meaning-making (Garfinkel, 1967; Goodwin & Heritage, 1990). Through this discursive, dialogical approach, we fashioned a communicative space, representing views of non-Korean diaspora on K-pop culture, specifically, South Asian family views on the K-drama *My ID is Gangnam Beauty*. Kim (2019) argued, "Cultural consumption becomes part of the consumers' lived history" (p. 162). Accordingly, an autoethnographic approach allowed us to frame our values, which are reflected in the K-pop cultural product under investigation, and that are negotiated through our active engagement with the narrative. We acknowledge that an autoethnographic approach involves "retrospectively and selectively [writing] about experiences that have their basis in, or are made possible by, being part of a culture and/or owning a specific cultural identity" (Pitard, 2019, p. 1829). We also recognize that we have exploited our "own experiences to tell stories about culture" and that we have done "this by employing [our] senses, [our] feelings and [our] reactions in order to critically analyse and reflect upon the experiences [we] have and reporting [our] observations and interpretations of what we see (Ellias, 2017, p. 590). Notwithstanding these limitations, our study findings illuminate views of South Asian diaspora on the diffusion and popularity of K-pop culture in order to make sense of mundane cross-cultural experiences and thereby enhance life in transnational spaces.

We hope the findings stimulate further discussion on the role of K-pop culture in South Asian diasporic families and beyond, including those "living transnational or diasporic lives" (Long, 2014, p. 244). Our cross-cultural mother-daughter communication about K-dramas is an invitation to those who are "*do*[ing] family in the context of migration; that is, the various ways in which people operate as, experience, conceive of, and mobilize family in a diasporic context and all of the tensions and contradictions that go with that" (Long, 2014, p. 244). We argue that K-pop culture offers a transnational mediated space for families "with members living some or most of the time separated from each other" (Bryceson, 2019, p. 3043) in diaspora, to create and maintain a sense of belonging and familial bond "through the long- or short-term migration and settlement of some family members" (McCarthy & Edwards, 2011, p. 188).

Recommended Readings

Adams, T. (2012). The joys of autoethnography: Possibilities for communication research. *Qualitative Communication Research, 1*(2), 181-194. doi:10.1525/qcr.2012.1.2.181

Fingerman, K. L. (2000). We had a nice little chat: Age and generational differences in mothers' and daughters' descriptions of enjoyable visits. *The Journals of Gerontology: Series B*, 55(2), 95-106. doi:10.1093/geronb/55.2.p95

Ponzanesi, S. (2020). Digital diasporas: Postcoloniality, media and affect. *Intervention. International Journals of Postcolonial Studies.* Online first: February 5, 2020.

Skrbiš, Z. (2008). Transnational families: Theorising migration, emotions and belonging. *Journal of Intercultural Studies, 29*(3), 231-246, doi: 10.1080/07256860802169188

Yoon, K., & Jin, D. Y. (2016). The Korean wave phenomenon in Asian diasporas in Canada. *Journal of Intercultural Studies, 37*(1), 69-83.

Additional Sources

Drama Beans. http://www.dramabeans.com/

KDRAMAPAL. https://www.kdramapal.com/highest-rated-korean-dramas-cable-all-time/

Soompi. https://www.soompi.com/article/1201595wpp/id-gangnam-beauty-comic-artist-reacts-casting-astros-cha-eun-woo-im-soo-hyang

References

Ahmed, R., & Veronis, L. (2017). Multicultural media use and immigrant settlement: A comparative study of four communities in Ottawa, Canada. *Journal of International Migration and Integration, 18*(2), 587-612.

Ahmed, R., & Veronis, L. (2019). Digital technology for community building: An examination of ethnic media consumption across four ethnocultural and immigrant groups in Ottawa, Canada. In S. S. Yu & M. D. Matsaganis (Eds.), *Ethnic media in the digital age* (pp. 97-110). New York, NY: Routledge.

Anderson, B. (1983). *Imagined communities: Reflections on the origins and spread of nationalism.* London, UK: Verso.

Appadurai, A. (1996). *Modernity at large: Cultural dimensions of globalization.* Minneapolis, MN: University of Minnesota Press.

Aspfors. J., & Valle, A. M. (2017). Designing communicative spaces-innovative perspectives on teacher education. *Education Inquiry, 8*(1), 1-16.

Ayyub, R. (2000). Domestic violence in the South Asian Muslim immigrant population in the United States. *Journal of Social Distress and the Homeless, 9*(3), 237-248.

Berg, M. (2017). The importance of cultural proximity in the success of Turkish dramas in Qatar. *International Journal of Communication*, *11*, 3415-3430.

Bryceson, D. F. (2019). Transnational families negotiating migration and care life cycles across nation-state borders. *Journal of Ethnic and Migration Studies*, *45*(16), 3042-3064.

Burch, E. (2002). Media literacy, cultural proximity and TV aesthetics: Why Indian soap operas work in Nepal and the Hindu diaspora. *Media, Culture & Society*, *24*(4), 571-579.

Chadda, R. K., & Deb, K. S. (2013). Indian family systems, collectivistic society and psychotherapy. *Indian Journal of Psychiatry*, *55*(Suppl 2), S299-S309.

Coker, C. (2020). From Sunnydale to Seoul: The vampire "Fan" in Korean dramas. In C. Coker (Ed.), *The global vampire: Essay on the undead popular culture around the world*. Jefferson, NC: McFarland & Company.

Croucher, S. M., Oommen, D., & Steele, E. L. (2009). An examination of media usage among French-Muslims. *Journal of Intercultural Communication Research*, *38*(1), 41-57.

Durham, M. G. (2004). Constructing the "New Ethnicities": Media, sexuality, and diaspora identity in the lives of South Asian immigrant girls. *Critical Studies in Media Communication*, *21*(2), 140-161.

Elias, P. B. (2017). Opening up about birth: An autoethnographic account of prolonged labour. *The Qualitative Report*, *22*(2), 589-600. Retrieved from http://nsuworks.nova.edu/tqr/vol22/iss2/14

Ellis, C., & Bochner, A. P. (2000). Autoethnography, personal narrative, reflexivity: Researcher as subject. In N. K. Denzin & Y. S. Lincoln (Eds.), *The Sage handbook of qualitative research* (2nd ed., pp. 733-768). Thousand Oaks, CA: Sage.

Ellis, C., Adams, T. E., & Bochner, A. P. (2011). Autoethnography: An overview. *Forum: Qualitative Social Research*, *12*(1), 10.

Garfinkel, H. (1967). *Studies in ethnomethodology*. Englewood Cliffs, NJ: Prentice Hall.

Georgiou, M. (2006). *Diaspora, Identity and the media: Diasporic transnationalism and mediated spatialities*. Cresskill, NJ: Hampton Press.

Gher, L., & Bharthapudi, K. (2004). The impact of globalization and transnational media in Eastern Europe at the end of the 20th century: An attitudinal study of five newly independent states. *Global Media Journal*, *3*(4).

Goodwin, C., & Heritage, J. (1990). Conversation analysis. *Annual Review of Anthropology*, *19*, 283-307.

Han, H. J., & Lee, J. S. (2008). A study on the KBS TV drama Winter Sonata and its impact on Korea's Hallyutourism development. *Journal of Travel & Tourism Marketing*, *24*(2-3), 115-126.

Haniffa, A. (2019, May 17). South Asian population in the U.S. grew by 2 million in 7 years: Survey. *India Abroad*. Retrieved from https://www.indiaabroad.com/indian-americans/south-asian-population-in-the-u-s-grew-by-2-million-in-7-years-survey/article_4a93e71c-78fb-11e9-b827-67ee9f6c3ec4.html

Ibrahim, F., Ohnishi, H., & Sandhu, D. S. (1997). Asian American identity development: A culture specific model for South Asian Americans. *Journal of Multicultural Counseling and Development*, *25*(1), 34-50.

Jeong, J.-H. (2012). Ethnoscapes, mediascapes, and ideoscapes: Socio-cultural relations between South Korea and China. *Journal of international and Area Studies*, *19*(2), 77-95.

Jin, D. Y. (2018). An analysis of the Korean wave as transnational popular culture: North American youth engage through social media as TV becomes obsolete.

International Journal of Communication, 12, 404-422.

Jin, D. Y., & Yoon, K. (2016). The social mediascape of transnational Korean pop culture: Hallyu 2.0 as spreadable media practice. *New Media & Society, 18*(7), 1277-1292.

Ju, H. (2020). Korean TV drama viewership on Netflix: Transcultural affection, romance, and identities. *Journal of International and Intercultural Communication, 13*(1), 32-48.

Ju, H., & Lee, S. (2015). The Korean wave and Asian Americans: The ethnic meanings of transnational Korean pop culture in the USA. *Continuum, 29*(3), 323-338.

Karim, K. H. (1998). *From ethnic media to global media: Transnational communication networks among diasporic communities* (No. WPTC-99-02). International Comparative Research Group, Strategic Research and Analysis, Canadian Heritage. Canada. Retrieved from http://www.transcomm.ox.ac.uk/working%20papers/karim.pdf

Karim, K. H. (Ed.). (2003). *The media of diaspora*. London, UK: Routledge.

Karim, K. H. (2007). Nation and diaspora: Rethinking multiculturalism in a transnational context. *International Journal of Media & Cultural Politics, 2*(3), 267-282.

Karim, K. H., & Al-Rawi, A. (2018). *Diaspora and media in Europe: migration, identity and integration*. Switzerland: Palgrave Macmillan.

Kern-Stone, R., & Mishra, S. (2019). Introduction. In S. Mishra & R. Kern-Stone (Eds.), *Transnational media: Concepts and cases* (pp. 1-9). Medford, MA: Wiley Blackwell.

Khanna, A., Mcdowell, T., Perumbilly, S., & Titus, G. (2009). Working with Asian Indian American families: A Delphi study. *Journal of Systemic Therapies, 28*, 52-71.

Kim, J.-S. (2020, January 15). K-pop, hallyu continue global rise. *The Korea Times*. Retrieved from http://www.koreatimes.co.kr/www/news/nation/2020/01/356_281957.html

Kim, S. D. (2019). *The Korean wave. Why it swept the world*. In Y. Kim (Ed.), *The Korean wave: Korean media go global* (pp. 155-163). London; New York: Routledge.

Kim, Y. (2013). *The Korean wave: Korean media go global*. London; New York: Routledge.

Kim, D. K., & Kim, M.-S. (2011). *Hallyu: Influence of Korean popular culture in Asia and beyond*. Seoul, Korea: Seoul National University Press.

Krijnen, T., & Van Bauwel, S. (2015). *Gender and media: Representing, producing, consuming*. New York, NY: Routledge.

Ksiazek, T. B., & Webster, J. G. (2008). Cultural proximity and audience behavior: The role of language in patterns of polarization and multicultural fluency. *Journal of Broadcasting & Electronic Media, 52*(3), 485-503.

Kurien, P. (1999). Gendered ethnicity: Creating a Hindu Indian identity in the United States. *American Behavioral Scientist, 42*(4), 648-670.

Lee, C. (2004). Korean immigrants' viewing patterns of Korean satellite television and its role in their lives. *Asian Journal of Communication, 14*(1), 68-80.

Lee, H. J., & Jin, D. Y. (2019). *K-pop idols: Popular culture and the emergence of the Korean industry*. Lanham, MD: Rowman & Littlefield.

Lee, M., & Cho, C. H. (1990). Women watching together: An ethnographic study of Korean soap opera fans in the US. *Cultural Studies, 4*(1), 30-44.

Leem, S. Y. (2017). Gangnam-style plastic surgery: The science of westernized beauty in South Korea, *Medical Anthropology, 36*(7), 657-671.

Leonard, K. I. (1997). *The South Asian Americans*. Westport, CT: Greenwood Press.

Lin, M.-C. (2017). Intergenerational communication. In M. Allen (Ed.), *The Sage encyclopedia of communication research methods* (pp. 762-766). Thousand Oaks, CA: Sage.

Long, J. C. (2014). Diasporic families: Cultures of relatedness in migration. *Annals of the Association of American Geographers, 104*(2), 243-252.

Matsaganis, M., Katz, V. S., & Ball-Rokeach, S. J. (2011). *Understanding ethnic media: Producers, consumers, and societies*. Thousand Oaks, CA: Sage.

McCarthy, J. R., & Edwards, R. (2011). *Key concepts in family studies*. Thousand Oaks, CA: Sage.

Min, W., Jin, D. Y., & Han, B. (2019). Transcultural fandom of the Korean wave in Latin America: Through the lens of cultural intimacy and affinity space. *Media, Culture & Society, 41*(5), 604-619.

Mishra, S. (2019). Transnational media: Key concepts and theories. In S. Mishra & R. Kern-Stone (Eds.), *Transnational media: Concepts and cases* (pp. 13-25). Medford, MA: Wiley Blackwell.

Moon, S., & Park, C. Y. (2007). Media effects on acculturation and biculturalism: A case study of Korean immigrants in Los Angeles' Koreatown. *Mass Communication & Society, 10*(3), 319-343.

Oh, D. C. (2013). Mediating diasporas and fandom: Second-generation Korean American adolescent diasporas, identification, and transnational popular culture. *The Communication Review, 16*(4), 230-250.

Oh, D. C. (2015). *Second-generation Korean Americans and transnational media: Diasporic identifications*. Landham, MD: Lexington Books.

Orsini, L. (2018, January 8). Korean media hits the big time in North America. *Forbes*. Retrieved from https://www.forbes.com/sites/laurenorsini/2018/01/08/korean-media-hits-the-big-time-in-north-america/#20054dd56be2

Papa, M. J., & Singhal, A. (2009). How entertainment-education programmes promote dialogue in support of social change. *Journal of Creative Communications, 4*(3), 185-208.

Park, J. Y, & Lee, A.-G. (Eds.). (2019). *The rise of K-dramas: Essays on Korean television and its global consumption*. Jefferson, NC: McFarland & Company, Inc.

Park, V. M. T., Olaisen, R. H., Vuong, Q., Rosas, L. G., & Cho, M. K. (2019). Using Korean dramas as a precision mental health education tool for Asian Americans: A pilot study. *International Journal of Environmental Research and Public Health, 16*(12), 2151.

Park, V. M. T., Diwata, J. S., Win, N., Ton, V., Nam, B., Rajabally, W., & Jones, V. C. (2020). Promising results from the use of a Korean drama to address knowledge, attitudes, and behaviors on school bullying and mental health among Asian American college-aged students. *International Journal of Environmental Research and Public Health, 17*(5), 1637.

Pitard J. (2019). Autoethnography as a phenomenological tool: Connecting the personal to the cultural. In P. Liamputtong (Ed.), *Handbook of research methods in health social sciences* (pp. 1829-1845). Singapore: Springer.

Potter, J. E. (2015). The whiteness of silence: A critical autoethnographic tale of a strategic rhetoric. *The Qualitative Report, 20*(9), 1434-1447. Retrieved from https://nsuworks.nova.edu/tqr/vol20/iss9/7

Shim, D. (2006). Hybridity and the rise of Korean popular culture in Asia. *Media,*

Culture & Society, 28(1), 25-44.

Singhal, A., & Rogers, E. M. (1999). *Entertainment-education: A communication strategy for social change.* Mahwah, NJ: Erlbaum.

Skop, E. (2013). Thirdspace as transnational space. In H. de Kruijf & A. Sahoo (Eds.), *Indian transnationalism online: Ethnographic explorations* (pp. 81-102). Aldershot, UK: Ashgate Publishing.

Thompson, K. (2002). Border crossings and diasporic identities: Media use and leisure practices of an ethnic minority. *Qualitative Sociology, 25*(3), 409-418.

Triandis, H. C. (1995). *Individualism & collectivism.* Boulder, CO: Westview Press.

Trommsdorff, G., & Kornadt, H. J. (2003). Parent-child relations in cross-cultural perspective. In L. Kuczynski (Ed.), *Handbook of dynamics in parent-child relations* (pp. 271-306). Thousand Oaks, CA: Sage Publications, Inc.

Tummala-Narra, P., & Deshpande, A. (2018). Mental health conditions among South Asians in the United States. In M. J. Perera & E. C. Chang (Eds.), *Biopsychosocial approaches to understanding health in South Asian Americans* (pp. 171-192). Cham, Switzerland: Springer.

Tzanelli, R. (2011). Cultural flows. In D. Southerton (Ed.), *Encyclopedia of consumer culture* (pp. 384-386). Thousand Oaks, CA: Sage.

Yi, C.-C., Chang, C.-F., & Chang, Y.-H. (2004). The intergenerational transmission of family values: A comparison between teenagers and parents in Taiwan. *Journal of Comparative Family Studies, 35*(4), 523-545.

Zaidi, A. Z., Couture-Carron, A., & Maticka-Tyndale, E. (2016). 'Should I or Should I Not'?: An exploration of South Asian youth's *resistance* to cultural deviancy. *International Journal of Adolescence and Youth, 21*(2), 232-251.

CHAPTER 10

Streaming *Okja*: Netflix and *Hallyu* on the Shores of North America

Ali Na, Queen's University

Korean media exports have surged in recent years in North America. The first video on YouTube to reach 1 billion views, and the most viewed video in YouTube history for five years after its debut, is Psy's 2012 "Gangnam Style," which found traction in embodied transnational connections facilitated by both the critical content of the song and the digital platform (Na, 2017). While not representative of most of *Hallyu*, Psy was for many in North America, their first exposure to Korean culture. The year after "Gangnam Style" was dethroned on YouTube, a more traditional form of K-pop emerged in North America. BTS had three singles top the 2018 Billboard music charts, with their 2019 Love Yourself World Tour selling out every North American site. In 2020, Bong Joon Ho's *Parasite* (2019) took home the best picture Oscar at the Academy Awards. Between what could be described as an unexpected viral hit in "Gangnam Style" and the current meteoric rise of Korean film and pop music was a vital transition period of the Korean Wave's North American prominence: the Netflix Original Film from Bong Joon Ho, *Okja* (2017).

In *Okja*, as *The New York Times* explains, "a girl and her pig take on the food industrial complex" (Scott, 2017). Mija, the girl, and Okja, the pig, have grown up together in the mountains of Korea. But, Okja is no ordinary pig. She is a super pig, genetically modified to feed the masses by the US company, Mirando. When Mirando comes to take Okja, it turns out Mija, played by Ahn Seo Hyun, is no ordinary girl. In a series of action-packed collisions, Mija takes on the Mirando company.

The film has primarily been understood as about environmentalism and animal rights. Even a group of researchers at the University of Minnesota Twin Cities and Texas Tech University based a study around how to address the inaccuracies of genetically modified agriculture found in *Okja* (Steede et al., 2018). The researchers starting point of *Okja* as changing consumptive habits is echoed in the organization People for the Ethical Treatment of Animals (PETA). Pointing to data collected from the first two months of the film's streaming premier, PETA has touted, *Okja* is responsible for a 65% increase in Google searches for the term "vegan". However, Bong has combatted that the film is vegan propaganda, stating "I didn't make this film to oppose meat" but to draw attention to the mass production of meat and "the state of capitalism today" (BBC, 2017). *Okja* demonstrates the consolidation of *Hallyu* in North America through content and medium. This chapter argues *Okja* is the Korean wave as it has washed up on the shores of the West. In other words, *Okja's* North American appeal is found in the shallow waters of *Hallyu*, rather than a complete immersive experience of it. The popularity of the film in North America can be traced to two major factors: (1) *Okja's* production and distribution through Netflix and (2) Bong Joon Ho's appeal to three types of North American audiences: mainstream, alternative, and diasporic.

Netflix: Remapping Transnational Media Terrains

Netflix, the distributor and producer of *Okja*, created a foundation in North America. It is now a globally-present company. Netflix is everywhere—everywhere except "China ('where we [Netflix] hope to also be in the future'), North Korea, Syria, and Crimea (the latter three being countries where Netflix could not legally do business because of U.S. trade sanctions)" (Lobato, 2019, p. 130). While there is not a comprehensive list of all the countries in which *Okja* is available to stream, the film was available widely across the globe, from Kuwait to Poland, and in most Asian countries, including Bangladesh, Hong Kong, and Malaysia.

As an American company, Netflix is culturally wrapped up in US viewing practices. As it has spread globally, it has stayed true to its American audience. It does not meet a global presence with global content. Instead, there is a strong dominance of US content throughout the platform. In the case of Canada, viewership is highly similar to US experiences. Canada is the first place Netflix expanded to outside the US, and the company has been a part of Canadian culture since 2010. This coupled with shared North American filmic industries warrants an approach to thinking through not only *Okja* within the US but also in Canada, as a highly resonant context. Therefore, this chapter takes up North America more broadly in relation to streaming and content viewership. Only about 3% of content available on Netflix is Canadian, with most content coming from the US (Lobato, 2019, pp. 137-140).

In order to think through *Okja* and its technical rise to ubiquity, it is necessary to address the major shifts in traditional mass media towards digital platforms. Netflix, originally a US distributor of DVD rentals by mail, was established in 1997 and shifted towards digital streaming in 2007. The company first expanded outside the US to Canada in 2010 and began producing original content in 2012. Blake Halinan and Ted Striphas argue that this conversion from mass media to digital streaming also shifted the conception of audience, in which traditional distribution sought to appeal to the "'lowest common denominator' in the size and specificity of the intended audience" and digital streaming provided a move "away from an undifferentiated mass toward an aggregation of highly differentiated micro-audiences" (Halinan and Striphas, 2016, p. 128). Digital streaming has meant that content no longer needs to initially have a mass appeal to be popular. Instead, micro-audiences become worthwhile in investing production resources. Thus, the popularity of a film such as *Okja* is enabled by digital streaming, when such an investment would have been considered unprofitable when catering to a US audience.

Okja is the only Korean Netflix Original film (linguistically the film has two primary languages—English and Korean). It is likely that Bong's appeal to Netflix was not only his filmic genius but also his notability in US cinephile circles beginning with the critical attention of *Memories of Murder* (2003). Furthermore, with the massive expenditures of *Snowpiercer* (2013), Bong proved that he could both deliver a multinational cast and a blockbuster quality film (with *The Host* (2006) lending credence to the latter issue).

Moreover, the very identity of Netflix bears an influence on critical reception, as well illustrated with the example of *Okja* at the 70th

Cannes Film Festival. The emergence of Netflix original film content has sparked a controversy over where cinema has to come from.[1] More than a question of whether or not streaming content ever gets a theatrical release, these debates focus on the infrastructure of what gets to be called cinematic art. *Okja* catalyzes this bifurcated arc as it arguably led to digital exclusion at the Cannes Film Festival after controversially competing for the *Palme d'Or*. Before the festival in 2017, Netflix CEO Reed Hastings spent weeks arguing with the festival board and the French film industry's governing body to enable *Okja* to compete for the *Palme d'Or* (Tiffany, 2017). The crux of this debate was about French theater release as a prerequisite to competing at Cannes. While Okja was allowed to compete, it would be a flashpoint of streaming content, which would now be excluded by the new rules put in place after *Okja's* showing.

Okja is a vital turning point in digital streaming and its reframing of the terrain of media consumption and reception. Debates over cinema as infrastructure and film as art were palpable in the festival reception. According to various accounts from the festival, when the Netflix logo came up at the film's screening, it was raucously booed. While *Okja* would go on to lose the competition, it provided an opportunity for Korean film to be highlighted in debates about what art looks like in the Western world of film. Further, it would only be two years before Bong would take home the prize for *Parasite* (2019).

From Netflix to Western Relationality

Okja's popularity in North America combines the ease of digital streaming with the quality of streaming as shallow waters. Streaming is quite realistically about technical shifts in Western viewership; concurrently, streaming functions as a productive metaphor alongside that of *Hallyu*. The Korean Wave as metaphor is about the power and force of Korean culture travelling across the globe. Streaming is the

1 Of course, the issue of streaming content availability is salient in thinking through theatrical infrastructures of distribution, as well noted in the massive boycott of *Okja* by Korean movie theaters.

wave as it washes up on the shores of North America, as shallow waters. That is, *Okja*, catalyzes the ways in which the wave was able to stream into culture little by little, rather than as a crashing wave. Starting as shallow waters, pushing the metaphor, streaming is active and ongoing, continuing to build depth at an almost imperceptible rate of constant increase. So how then should scholarship in North America approach the shallow waters of *Hallyu*?

One approach is to see the shallowness of streaming as a predominantly Western product. In analyzing *Memories of Murder* (2003) and *The Host* (2006), which are markedly different from *Okja*, Christina Klein argues that American Studies should reconceptualize the influence of Korean cinema in the United States. In doing so, Klein astutely rethinks the logic of globalization. As Woongjae Ryoo argues, the renaissance of the Korean film industry is a reworking of the idea of globalization as empire, complicating the idea of cultural imperialism by providing a counterexample of cultural spread (Ryoo, 2008).

However, this chapter ultimately diverges from Klein's argument. She, perhaps unintentionally, subsumes Korean cinema into Hollywood:

> *...having grown up immersed in U.S. popular culture, often claim it as their own and use it in ways that make sense to them in their own unique contexts. Doing so means making international reception and individual acts of creative reworking central to our understanding of U.S. popular culture. It also complicates our notions of national cinemas, and national cultures more generally, by forcing us to recognize the transnational dimension inherent in both contemporary and older cinema. Bong's films, given their thematic concerns, mode of production, and market performance, can rightfully be understood as works of Korean national cinema. But they are also inescapably works of transnational cinema, products of a complex textual engagement and negotiation with Hollywood* (Klein, 2008, p. 895).

Klein wants to claim Korean cinema as part of American Studies; it is vital to temper her language. While US cultural exports have been palpably present Korea, as with many other countries, Klein overplays the significance of American influence and American identity as translated through those cultural exports. *Okja* more so than the films Klein analyzes does some of this work, but not to the end that she proposes.[2]

Klein's call to see Korean cinema's engagement with Hollywood begins from the misguided presumption of intention. In other words, her descriptions of *Memories of Murder* and *The Host* as U.S. interlocutors is unconvincing. Not all forms of engagement are equivocal to dialogue. By overreading the genre structures of such films, Korean cultural elements are easily obscured. In arguing that *Okja* represents the shallow waters of the Korean Wave, this chapter maintains that the film holds great depths in its shallow waters, crafting multilayered narratives and modes of meaning for at least three audiences: mainstream, alternative, and diasporic.

Unlike Klein, this chapter conceives of Korean film as apart from Hollywood, not subordinate to it. As Jinhee Choi contends, "The opening up of the Korean film market, brought about by the world film industry's globalization process, creates demand for commercially viable film; and with conglomerates' and venture capitalists' money pouring into the South Korean film industry, a majority of 386 Generation directors persued cinema with entertainment value, comparable—even superior—to that produced in Hollywood" (Choi, 2010, p. 5). As Choi notes, Bong's films, as highlighted in *Memories of Murder*, balance the commercially successful with artistic vision (p. 13; 144-146). This is perhaps most palpably catalyzed in the international success of *Parasite*. The shallow waters of *Okja* served as a primer for this readiness to accept Korean culture as, in Choi's words, "even superior" to US productions of medial culture.

Shallow Waters: Non-Diasporic North American Viewership

Okja's popularity in North America owes to its ease of consumption by multiple audiences. Within its non-diasporic viewership, the film appeals to both mainstream and alternative North American audiences

2 There are of course nods to Hollywood films in *Okja*. For instance, the character Frank Dawson, a member of the Mirando Corporation played by Giancarlo Esposito, is seen looking at the bottom of his cup, seemingly for Kobayashi, a reference to *The Usual Suspects* (1995). These moments, however, should not come to stand in for an overriding understanding of the film.

by combining Western star power with Western critique. This is perhaps reflected in the cultural touchstones used in the making of the film, from the Colorado slaughterhouse research to filming in British Columbia.

Bong crafts *Okja* as (deceptively) shallow to make it easier for North Americans to wade into *Hallyu*. In this way, the film symbolically foretells and enacts the contemporary struggles of the Korean Wave's success in the West. In dealing with American's aversions to foreign actors and foreign languages, the film proposes a bilingual entry with a cast of well-known Western actors. But, perhaps unlike *Snowpiercer*, *Okja* features a Korean protagonist, Mija.[3] The film has repeatedly been written up in North American news outlets as starring Tilda Swinton and Jake Gyllenhaal. North American media coverage rarely mentions Ahn Seo Hyun by name.[4] The film is instead able to billed as American, and by extension in many ways North American.

However, even for a mainstream audience, the film's success hinged on its outsider status to leverage an easy critique against the US. Using Western critique as a thread throughout the film, Bong creates pockets of depth that undercut *Okja* as simple Hollywood fodder. In part, this involves creating cultural resonance in North America. After the Mirando Corporation takes Okja away, Mija fearlessly heads to Seoul with the grit and determination to reunite with her beloved super pig. She gets some unexpected help from the Animal Liberation Front, who want Okja for their own activist agenda. This culminates in a wild chase through the city and a heap of bad press for the Mirando Corporation. In response, we see the corporate leaders gathered in a conference room watching the TV footage. The scene is filmed as an exact replica of the wide-spread image of the US situation room where attendees watched the live video of the capture and killing of Osama Bin Laden. In it, President Barack Obama sits intently, leaning forward, with a somewhat inscrutable look on his face. Secretary of State Hillary Clinton, on the other hand, seems to give away more of her emotional response with

[3] There is a compelling argument to be had that the film actually pivots on the character of Yona, played by Go Ah Sung. However, on face, the film is led by Curtis, played by Chris Evans.

[4] A similar phenomenon has happened with *Parasite*. In spite of having an all Korean cast, they are rarely mentioned in North American press by name.

her hand covering her mouth, pulling down on her face. Lucy Mirando, the corporate CEO, played by Swinton, stands in for Clinton, while Esposito's character Frank, sits in for Obama. In a way, the image gives a hint to how the power in the room lies with Frank and not Lucy, but it also reframes the narrative of the original photo. Largely covered as a triumph for the Obama administration, the photo represents the "good" of democracy in action. Bong's recasting dislodges the significance of the room to focus on the collateral damage of the war room's battle with their terrorist nemeses.

The film is of course about capitalism across cultures but focuses on the Mirando Corporation as the source of American domination and deception. This is well illustrated in the Mirando twins, both played by Swinton, who represent two faces of capitalism that are, at their core, of the same DNA. CEO Lucy, who tries to appease progressive values through press manipulation and heartwarming stories, is ultimately usurped by her twin Nancy, who represents naked and cold calculations of profits. Bong's story shows us that Nancy is always the threat of Lucy, but also that Nancy's fascistic form of authoritarian capitalism is more honest and transparent than Lucy's disguised exploitation.

There are additional critiques of Western dominance throughout the film, which contribute to the ways in which *Okja* is made agreeable to North American audiences while not losing a critical edge. To cover over the bad press, Mirando hatches a plan to bring Mija to New York for the Super Pig Competition. Lucy's assistant, Jennifer, played by Shirley Henderson, is in charge of pulling together the details. She decides to play it as a "love story" reuniting Mija and Okja, and describes it to her staff, pointing to a tablet with Mija's image on it. "Look at her, so sweet. Cute. Totally gorgeous. Totally sexy. Hot, tiny, perfect."

They objectify Mija in a fashion consistent with Western fantasies about Asian women's sexuality, and then they coopt Korean traditional clothing, marking it as Western. Lucy demands to wear a hanbok for the opening ceremony. Swinton wears one that she had seen on the runway years before that Chanel agreed to make custom for her in the film (Petrarca, 2017). Done in the traditional method of bojagi, the dress stands in for a form of sought-after authenticity on the part of Westerners, while Mija's outfit is a reference to Lucy's, no longer stemming from Korean origins, instead embroidered with Lucy

Mirando's signature as a form of branding.

Sacred Words, Sacred Actions: On Translation

These shallow waters of mainstream appeal are only successful in merging with the more complicated third audience: the diasporic viewers. While, this chapter focuses on Korean diasporic viewership, it also maintains that these issues appeal to a broad cross-section of the immigrant composition in North America, making the film resonate for many in-between populations. This chapter addresses the Korean American and Korean Canadian contexts together under the moniker of Korean North American, given the high similarities between immigration practices in the countries and more generally shared Asian North American histories (Day, 2016). For the Korean North American audience, the message of *Okja* is one of tense ambivalence. This storyline is centered on issues of translation and the character K, played by Korean American actor Steven Yuen.

We first meet the Animal Liberation Front (ALF) as they pull up next to the truck transporting Okja out of Seoul. K pulls up next to Mundo Park, played by Yoon Je Moon, a Mirando employee Mija refers to as Mundo Samchon. Mundo is in the driver seat of the truck; the driver is Wooshik Kim, played by Choi Woo Shik. Donning a black balaclava, K formally says hello in Korean over the amplified radio. Continuing in Korean, he smilingly explains that they are not terrorists. Mundo can't hear him. K overly politely tries to tell them, with some difficulty, to pull over, but looking at the confused face of Mundo, K breaks and says in English, "just cooperate, guy." This scene is meant to introduce us to K's frustrated place as translator. Bong wrote the piece with Yuen in mind, and Yuen has stated on multiple occasions that he made his accent and fluidity worse for *Okja*.

The character of K demonstrates a relatable trend of second-generation Korean speakers in the diaspora to struggle with fluency, which some scholars have attributed to a perception that one does not need to put forth effort to maintain or develop heritage language (Lee 2002, 130). Likewise, some native language speakers of Korean have struggled to understand second-generation speakers' seeming lack of desire to participate in what might be the most effective means of maintaining and improving their Korean (Jeon, 2007). However, K's character is better understood through a mode of negotiated struggle, inflected by pressures from forces of authority. In Jo Hye-Young's research on second-generation Korean Americans in university-level Korean courses, Jo argues "Korean-American students' language expressions reveal hybridity, displacement, and rupture—which are the characteristics of diasporic cultural identities" (Jo, 2001, p. 26). In the classroom setting "their informal versions of language are reminded, contested, and negotiated against the 'standard' Korean language as the institutionalised and superposed register of superiority" (p. 26).

K does not have a detailed backstory from which to draw; however, his struggles seem to be more about formal engagement than comfort with the language. As such, Jo's emphasis on negotiation of diasporic lived life and identity through resistance to structural formations are apt. As Jo continues, "students' language disposition is often bounded to personal, family, or regional dialects that their parents have used at home," which means that corrections of their language are sometimes corrections of their family's use of Korean (p. 34). This presents an issue because students' sense of language is connected to their families, even when their families may not speak standard Korean, and "under the 'superior hegemony' associated with the standard, students might feel that their own utterances are less successful in terms of 'Koreanness'" (p. 39). That is Korean North American second-generation speakers are more likely to have a lived experience that is not simply translatable to standard Korean or English. "Although this can mean a dual 'marginalisation' from both 'native' authorities, they have at the same time potentials to take forms and expressions from both and construct 'new' expressions, crossing the boundaries between different categories of language" (p. 39).

After the ALF have secured Okja and are riding in the back of the semi-truck with Mija aboard, Jay, the leader of the ALF played by Paul Dano, asks K, "will you translate?" For many parts of the scene, the English subtitles are left blank when K speaks. At first, K translates the ideas Jay speaks in English, letting Mija know they free animals, which is why they freed Okja. Then, Jay launches into the history of ALF "For forty years..." K translates, "we do it a lot." Jay asks, "is that it?" K responds "yeah." But before going on, Jay stresses that it is important that Mija get every word he is saying. Jay explains that they want to let Okja go so that they can gain footage to expose the atrocities of Mirando from inside a laboratory where experiments will be run on Okja before revealing her as the star super pig for the public. The ALF say they won't do it without her permission, and K asks her, "Where do you want to go?" Mija states, "I want to go to the mountains with Okja." Importantly, K immediately translates, "she agrees to the mission." As they are jumping out of the truck, leaving Okja and Mija to the police in pursuit, K stops and says "Mija! Also, my name is Goo Soon Bum." However, the translation on screen reads, "Mija, try learning English, it opens new doors" This mistranslation is meant to be only understood by viewers who speak both Korean and English, complicating the character of K, and his relationship to Korean and English. For Bong, the name "Goo Soon Bum" was meant to be humorous, but I'd also like to consider it as old fashioned and hence aligned with both Okja and Mija as more old-fashioned names. Taken together, they might represent a transnational connection to more traditional Korean practices, as K is himself outside of contemporary Korean culture as a diasporic subject.

Later as the ALF is watching Okja's video feed from inside the Mirando laboratory, they become increasingly upset by the torture and rape Okja is undergoing for reproduction and research. Jay attempts to keep them on message, stating "The little girl trusted us with Okja. We have to respect her bravery." K, feeling guilty and disgusted, confesses, "She never agreed to send Okja." He explains what Mija said in the truck and that he lied to keep the mission on track. At first Jay seems to be understanding, telling K "it's okay," but then he proceeds to slam K's head against the table, knocking him to the floor. Kicking him and punching him repeatedly, Jay lectures him on the legacy of the ALF and then says, "Never mistranslate. Translation is sacred."

In mistranslating, K follows Bong's lead in mistranslating for the audience. Further, he demonstrates the problematic need Jay has for a translator that can't be trusted. K, when considered alongside Vincente L Rafael's argument on US military use of translators as weapons, offers a perspective on *Okja*'s diasporic appeal in North America. Since the US invasions of Afghanistan and Iraq "the presence of interpreters is" "a source of great unease among the troops. They are seen by soldiers as Janus-faced: indispensable aides as much as they are potential spies" (Rafael, 2012, p. 9). K embodies this dualism in his so-called betrayal of Jay.

After the New York unveiling ceremony, a hectic and violent clash ensues between the Black Chalk private security forces and the ALF. Black Chalk's numbers, training, and violence prevail. Mija and Jay only escape with the unexpected aid of K. When Jay breathlessly asks him what he's doing, K reveals a newly etched tattoo that reads: Translations are Sacred. A small victory perhaps, K shifts Jay's language of "translation is sacred," implying the act of translation, to "translations are sacred," referencing translations as object.

In *Okja*, Bong Joon Ho has taken on translation across cultures with great verve and enough mystery to leave it a work in progress. As the ALF launches their plan to rescue Okja from the stage, the events escalate until Okja clamps down on Mija's arm, swinging her down to the ground. Jay tries to save Mija from Okja, yelling and swinging a mic stand at Okja, but Mija stops it from hitting Okja, holding it with her free hand. With the disorder of Black Chalk apprehending ALF members around them, Mija whispers something into Okja's ear. Okja opens her mouth releasing Mija and licks her. For Jay, the animal rights activist, violence against Okja is justified in that instance, but for Mija, it isn't about the limits of her politics. She loves Okja and it is that relationship that exists outside of translation, evidenced by the return to the untranslatable in the last scene, when it is Okja who whispers something in Mija's ear.

Conclusion: The Persimmons Aren't Ripe Yet

This chapter outlines the ways in which *Okja* uses both medium and content to find broad appeal in a North American audience. Such an argument begs the question of whether or not the film delivers Korean content at all. If the waters of *Hallyu* are so shallow they appear North American, what part of the Korean Wave is left in *Okja*?

Focusing on the persimmon, this chapter concludes with Bong's Korean message as transmitted through the Netflix Original. *Okja* provides a message that is less about whether people eat meat and more about how to engage in the world. This message is, in particular, the film's Korean message, not because it can only apply to Koreans, but because it presents the message in the Korean context.

When we are first introduced to Mija, she is in a lush green environment standing with *Okja*, opening what appears to be a dried milkweed pod, blowing the seeds into the air. The image provides a sense of wonder and a childlike spirit while also pointing to myriad uses for the plant from a favorite of pollinators to a fiber source for paper and more. After Mija plucks a chestnut bur from Okja's foot, Okja rolls into a persimmon tree. Mija collects the fallen persimmons, remarking that they are not yet ready and feeding one to Okja. She carefully washes the rest in a nearby stream before putting them in her bag to carry home. Given the significance of the persimmon in Korean culture, it is meant to carry the symbolic power of tradition. As the folktale of the Tiger and the Persimmon teaches, there is great strength in the persimmon as symbol.

In another idyllic space, Mija calls to Okja because she would like eat fish stew. The animal bounds over a ledge into the pool of pristine water, splashing out a fish that Mija promptly collects. After adding the fish to her bag, she notices a small one that was splashed out as well. She picks it up and throws it back. Her practices are continually about living sustainably—not as marketing campaign but in traditional practices of everyday life.[5]

The persimmon brings a sense of cultural longevity and tradition that complicates the story of *Okja* as a cautionary tale against genetically modified organisms. To the extent that the film conjures the horrors of genetically modified organisms, the horror is in the system of mass production and consumption, not with the creatures themselves. Afterall, Okja is Mija's best friend. Okja is not the horror. In other words, the film is perhaps too hastily read as against science and technology. Rather, it holds the offspring of science alongside tradition. The film is less a referendum on the super pigs and more on the social modes that move away from traditional Korean life.

Bong's focus on tradition should not be interpreted as conservative. On the contrary, Mija as the strong and unflappable protagonist flies in the face of some traditional values on gender. In one scene, for instance, Hee Bong, Mija's grandfather, played by Byun Hee Bong, takes her into

---

[5] Similarly, when we are then introduced to Mija's grandfather, Hee Bong, played by Byun Hee Bong, who has raised her after the death of her parents, he is laboriously carrying bundles of sticks for the cooking fire on his back, with herbs and plants stuffed in pouches on his front.

the forest and gives Mija a 100% gold pig. When he tells her that they have taken Okja, she shouts at him. Her grandfather is first surprised, then amused at Mija's defiance. He tells her that she is getting too old to play with a pig all day and that maybe she should get a boyfriend. Her anger boils over, and she runs off. She does not represent proper filial obedience. She instead is driven by her own desires and decisions, even as they fly in the face of her grandfather, whom she loves. Her strength is recurrently showcased through long running scenes, in which Mija pushes her body's limits. She is at the center of action scenes, holding onto the back of a moving truck, falling off as it is rammed, and still getting up and running after Okja.

When she finally makes it to Mirando's Seoul location, she is met in the office by a disaffected receptionist. Always representing a break with modern aspirations as packaged by the Mirando Corporation, Mija stands apart. With a running start, Mija attempts to break through the glass front, but bounces off. The glass then shatters, and as she runs in, she tears down a fake tree, grounded by various sparking wires. The false tree has shallow roots, unlike the persimmon tree that was able to withstand Okja's hurling body.

Continuing the role of the persimmon, at the unveiling of Okja in New York, Mija still wears the same fanny pack she has brought from Korea and that the Mirando employees who wanted her to be "so gorgeous" asked her to take off. As the float with Okja approaches the stage, Mija opens the pack and pulls out a persimmon. But, Okja—traumatized and disoriented—knocks the persimmon out of Mija's hand. With everything out of balance, the persimmon is cast out. After rescuing Okja, by way of the gold pig as payment to Nancy Mirando, Mija resumes her life with her grandfather, Okja, and a new piglet saved from the factory farm. The new piglet nuzzles a persimmon and brings it in to where Mija and Hee Bong are eating, laying it down on the ground, offering it back into the family.

Thus, it is important to hold the multiple messages contained in *Okja* at once, in order to examine its popularity as an example of *Hallyu*, appealing to North American audiences. This requires a multifaceted approach to medium, content, and cultural exploration. While these elements do not form a rubric for how to appeal to a North American audience, this chapter has outlined the myriad ways in which Bong Joon Ho has tapped into a distribution of cultural content in order to slowly allow North American viewers to wade into Korean culture. These shallow waters proved an important first step to wider North American acceptance of the Korean Wave.

Recommended Readings

Kyong, Y. & Jin, D. Y. (2016). The Korean wave phenomenon in Asian diasporas in Canada. *Journal of Intercultural Studies*, *37*(1), 69-83.

Lee, S., & Nornes A. M. (Eds.). (2015). *Hallyu 2.0: The Korean wave in the age of social media*. Ann Arbor, MI: University of Michigan Press.

Park, S. Y. (2010). Transnational adoption, hallyu, and the politics of Korean popular culture. *Biography: An Interdisciplinary Quarterly*, *33*(1), 1-16.

Ryoo, W. (2008). The political economy of the global mediascape: The case of the South Korean film industry. *Media, Culture & Society*, *30*(6), 873-889.

Swan, A. L. (2018). Transnational identities and feeling in fandom: Place and embodiment in K-pop fan reaction videos. *Communication, Culture and Critique*, *11*(4), 548-565.

Additional Sources

Jung, E. A. (2017, July 6). Steven Yuen finds life after Glenn. *Vulture*. https://www.vulture.com/2017/07/steven-yeun-interview-okja-walking-dead.html

Mumford, G. (2017, May 19). Cannes apologises after technical problems and booing disrupts Netflix film Okja. *The Guardian*. https://www.theguardian.com/film/2017/may/19/cannes-apologises-after-technical-problems-booing-disrupts-netflix-film-okja

Official SBIFF. (2020, January 24). *SBIFF 2020-Bong Joon Ho Discusses "Okja"*. YouTube. https://www.youtube.com/watch?v=oUTdavcpWro

References

BBC. (2017, June 29). *Okja: A genetic super pig and the environment*. Retrieved November 1, 2019, from https://www.bbc.com/news/world-asia-40337161

Choi, J. (2010). *The South Korean film renaissance: Local hitmakers, global provocateurs*. Middletown, CT: Wesleyan University Press.

Day, I. (2016). *Alien capital: Asian racialization and the logic of settler colonial capitalism*. Durham, NC: Duke University Press.

Halinan, B., & Striphas T. (2016). Recommended for You: The Netflix prize and the production of algorithmic culture. *New Media & Society*, *18*(1), 117-137.

Jeon, M. (2007). Language ideologies and bilingual education: A Korean-American perspective. *Language Awareness*, *16*(2), 114-130.

Jeon, M. (2012). English immersion and educational inequality in South Korea. *Journal of Multilingual and Multicultural Development*, *33*(4), 395-408.

Jo, H. (2001). 'Heritage' language learning and ethnic identity: Korean Americans' struggle with language authorities. *Language Culture and Curriculum*, *14*(1), 26-41.

Kim, E. G. (2011). English educational policies of the U.S. Army Military Government in Korea from 1945 to 1948 and their effects on the development of

English language teaching in Korea. *Language Policy, 10*(193).
Klein, C. (2008). Why American studies needs to think about Korean cinema, or, transnational genres in the films of Bong Joon-ho. *American Quarterly, 60*(4), 871-898.
Lee, H., & Lee, K. (2016). An analysis of the failure(s) of South Korea's national english ability test. *The Asia-Pacific Education Researcher, 25*, 827-834.
Lee, J. S. (2002). The Korean language in America: The role of cultural identity in heritage language learning. *Language Culture and Curriculum, 15*(2), 117-133.
Lobato, R. (2019). *Netflix nations: The geography of digital distribution*. New York, NY: New York University Press.
Na, A. (2017). Gangnam eth(n)ic: The transnational politics of YouTube reperformances. *Liminalities: A Journal of Performance Studies, 13*(3).
Petrarca, E. (2017, June 28). Tilda Swinton's costumes in *Okja* were inspired by everyone from Ivanka Trump to Gwyneth Paltrow. *W Magazine*. Retrieved December 12, 2019, from https://www.wmagazine.com/story/tilda-swinton-okja-costumes
Rafael, V. L. (2012). Translation and the US empire. *The Translator, 18*(1), 1-22.
Ryoo, W. (2008). The political economy of the global mediascape: The case of the South Korean film industry. *Media, Culture & Society, 30*(6), 873-889.
Scott, A. O. (2017, June 27). Review: In 'Okja,' a girl and her pig take on the food industrial complex. *The New York Times*. Retrieved November 15, 2019, from https://www.nytimes.com/2017/06/27/movies/review-okja-bong-joon-ho.html
Steede, G. M., Opat, K., Curren, L. S., & Irlbeck, E. (2018). Genetic modification, factory farms, and ALF: A focus group study of the Netflix original film Okja. *Journal of Applied Communications, 102*(4).
Tiffany, K. (2017, June 26). Okja is the first great Netflix movie—Here's why that matters: A masterpiece that can draw a flame war. *The Verge*. Retrieved October 26, 2019, from https://www.theverge.com/2017/6/26/15747466/netflix-okja-bong-joon-ho-snowpiercer-cannes-hollywood

CHAPTER 11

Media Imports and the One-Inch Barrier: Translation Debates in the Post-*Parasite* Era

Laurena Bernabo, University of Georgia

On February 9th, 2020, the Korean film *Parasite* became the first non-English-language film to win the Oscar for Best Feature Film. In the days that followed, thousands of people weighed in on a debate that had long been restricted to global media scholars and cinephiles: Which is better, dubbing or subtitling? Many who contributed to this newly mainstream debate, be they columnists, bloggers, or simply people with Twitter accounts and opinions, voiced positions that echo decades of scholarship on translation practices. Others, including the U.S. President, went on racist rants (Levenson, 2020). U.S. Americans enjoy considerable privilege in their media consumption practices. The fact that U.S. Americans can avoid hearing another language in the media they consume is a form of media privilege. When watching a dubbed or a subtitled text, viewers are forced to confront the reality that not everything worth consuming is made *for them*. This can be a jarring lesson for people who don't realize that every film is "foreign" to someone. When *Roma* director Alfonso Cuarón won the 2019 Oscar for best Foreign-Language film, he brought this reality to light by discussing *Jaws*, *Citizen Kane*, and other "foreign language films" from which he learned his craft (Fry, 2020).

It can be difficult to get U.S. Americans to be open to international media because they rarely have to choose between a dubbed version and a subtitled version; American producers often simply make local versions, as they did with popular programs like *The Office* (U.K.), *Ugly Betty* (Columbia), *Jane the Virgin* (Venezuela), and *Homeland* (Israel). One of the more contentious publications in the wake of *Parasite*'s wins was a *Vox* piece that suggested "Americans just don't like reading subtitles" (Wilkinson, 2020). In his Golden Globes acceptance speech for Best Foreign Language film, *Parasite*'s director Bong Joon Ho told his audience (through a translator), "once you overcome the one-inch-tall barrier of subtitles, you will be introduced to so many more amazing films." This sentiment gained traction among critics for whom the dubbing/subtitling debate is about individual intelligence, including a *Vox* columnist who wrongly suggests that "a preference for dubbing aligns with closed-mindedness" (Romano, 2020).

Given this context, what does *Parasite*'s success teach us about contemporary translation practices? After all, *Parasite* was the first non-English-language film to win the Oscars' top prize in its 91-year history and was the first South Korean film to be nominated (Adams, 2020). Many (Garcia, 2020; *The Guardian*, 2020; Hong, 2020; Wilkinson, 2020) see *Parasite*'s awards sweep as part of a larger change in U.S. willingness and motivation to consume foreign content, thereby overcoming Ho's famed one-inch barrier. *Parasite*'s box office numbers in the U.S. certainly point in this direction, pulling in more than $45 million, making it the fourth most successful foreign-language import in the U.S. (*The Guardian*, 2020). However, its success is not uniform across America's divided population. Some viewers in New York City, for example, reportedly demanded a refund from a theater after seeing the subtitles (Hong, 2019). This vitriol in the face of non-English media in the U.S. is sad but unsurprising after the outcry that met Coke's 2014 Super Bowl ad in which seven bilingual girls—all U.S. citizens—sang a multilingual "America the Beautiful" (Poniewozik, 2014). Such racist responses are juxtaposed with positions that disparage dubbing based on the poor quality of early dubbing (O'Falt, 2020; Prasad, 2020)

This chapter explored how average U.S. Americans—most of whom are not global media or translation experts—make sense of international media texts. With its critical acclaim and a director who charmingly throws shade at American ethnocentrism, *Parasite* presents a compelling entry point into larger discussions about the place of dubbed and subtitled films in a country that has historically privileged local English-language content.

Korean Media Abroad

The "Korean Wave" refers to the global spread of Korean media that began with Korean dramas in 1997 (Jin, 2018; Jin & Yoon, 2017; Kim & Kim, 2011) and expanded to include Korean films, or "K-movies" (Kim, 2013), like *Parasite, The Host,* and *Snowpiercer.* Though they long competed with Hollywood films in Korea, Korean films gained national prominence early in the 21st century, drawing as much as 64% of the local market share in 2006 (Kim, 2013) and more than 100 million viewers annually in the early 2010s (Kim, 2015). Korean films were popular not just in Korea and its neighboring Asian countries but throughout the world. Korean film exports grew rapidly, from just $427 thousand in 1997 to $11 million in 2001, $31 million in 2003, and $76 million in 2005 (Kim, 2013). One significant reason for the success of K-movies both in Korea and abroad seems to be that they have come to emulate the Hollywood aesthetic (Anderson, 2014; Kim, 2013; Ter Molen, 2014), so much so that many were framed as Korean Blockbuster films (Kim, 2015). From there, Korean films continued to evolve as creative and unique texts that were able to stand as excellent in their own right; as a result, certain directors, such as *Parasite* director Bong Joon Ho, have developed strong national and international fan bases (Kim, 2015). The success of such films in the U.S. is also attributed in part to social media sites and streaming platforms on which fans of Korean films can share these and consume these media texts (Jin, 2017; Jin & Yoon, 2016, 2017; Ju, 2020; Ju & Lee, 2015; Lee, 2018). It is also through social media that the public comments on Korean media and film translation, which was the focus of this study.

Korean movies have flowed into the U.S. despite Hollywood's global dominance, making a strong case for the theory of contra-flow (Kim, 2007; Shim, 2006). Contra-flow (Thussu, 2007) is the phenomenon by which countries other than the top media producers—the U.S., U.K., and Japan—export to those behemoths. With the success of K-movies around the world, South Korea graduates from what Thussu (2007) terms a "third category of geo-cultural media [that] caters to specific cultural-linguist audiences" and joins Bollywood under the heading a "second layer of international media players" that "have a strong regional presence but are also aimed at audiences outside their primary constituency" (p. 13). This theory contrasts with older conceptions of global media flow that take a top-down, West-to-the-rest approach to understanding how media travel. The U.S. has historically enjoyed global media dominance; for example, while K-movies were first making their mark throughout Asia, U.S. films brought in thirty times as much in revenue from exports as it spent on imports (U.S. Government, 2005). Because of its easy availability, affordability, and familiarity, U.S. media has been long regarded as "the nearly universal second choice" (Tunstall, 1994, p. 19). Despite U.S. media dominance, Korean media consumption has increased in the U.S. This is not to say that the U.S. and South Korea have a balanced trade of media content—they assuredly do not. Indeed, six of Korea's top ten 2019 box office hits were from the U.S. while *Parasite* was barely in the top 100 in the U.S. (Kokas, 2020). Similarly, Korea exported $39 million in media to the U.S. in 2014 compared to the $307 million it spent on imports. Still, these numbers reflect a significant 254% increase since 2006 (U.S. Department of Commerce, 2015). Furthermore, Korean media exports increased from $287.5 million in 2000 to more than $4 billion in 2014 (Korea Creative Content Agency, 2015).

Given this continued disparity between media from the U.S. and non-dominant nations, the aforementioned significance of social media for the proliferation of Korean media cannot be understated. This is especially true in North America where social media platforms like YouTube and Facebook offer fans a place to celebrate and share the K-movies that enjoy staggering popularity (Ju & Lee, 2015). Streaming platforms like Hulu and Netflix host a growing library of Korean content; Korean media is thus increasingly available to U.S. viewers who are fascinated by culturally unfamiliar content (Lee, 2018). But while valuable for the insight they offer into why people in the U.S. enjoy Korean media and the role of digital media in increasing said consumption, the above studies do not address translation. Most people in the U.S. do not speak Korean and thus require that Korean films be translated. Lee's (2018) study illustrates how the role of translation is often ignored when evaluating audience K-wave reception; the occasional reference to viewers who learn some Korean by watching Korean content suggests that they use subtitles, yet the role of translation is otherwise ignored. As public debates following *Parasite*'s Oscar win demonstrate, this is a cultural significant element of K-movies that warrants more attention.

Dubbing vs. Subtitling

Dubbing and subtitles are the primary modes of audiovisual linguistic translation. Translation localizes content for those who do not speak or understand the source language, and is therefore a central, albeit overlooked, component in conversations about Korean media in the U.S. Discussions and debates about dubbing and subtitling often address issues of technical constraints, accessibility, and cultural implications. Dubbing and subtitling are subject to different technical constraints and concerns about accessibility. In terms of technical constraints, subtitles require that text fit at the bottom of a screen and is visible long enough to be read, thus requiring simplification, whereas dubbing professionals emphasize lip synchronization (Antonini, 2005; Chiaro, 2009; Chaume Varela, 2004; Kilborn, 1993). Because of these constraints, some genres lend themselves better to one form over another. For example, dramas often use close-ups of faces, making poor lip synchronization more apparent, whereas subtitles distract from action sequences (Kilborn, 1993). Because much translation scholarship is preoccupied with making foreign languages intelligible, it tends to emphasize these technical constraints and overlook issues of accessibility that were quite prominent in Twitter's post-*Parasite* translation debates. In terms of accessibility concerns, the obvious answer might be to make both options available for Korean media imports in the U.S. so that viewers can choose whatever method(s) best serve those watching, but this requires substantial added expense for the media provider. While discussions about technical constraints and accessibility are valuable, so too are the cultural implications of different translation practices.

It is important to critically engage issues surrounding the cultural work done by each mode of translation. As Kilborn (1993) points out, language is not merely a tool for information exchange or a barrier to our understanding across languages; language is an expression of a culture. Issues of class work in complex ways here because dubbing is more expensive, but subtitles require a certain level of literacy (Chiaro, 2009; Kilborn, 1993), which explains why children's content is typically dubbed around the world. There are also historical explanations for national preferences regarding translation methods. Dubbing arguably makes a media text more local because dubbing serves to assert the importing nation's language—albeit unofficial in the U.S.—as supreme within its borders. Subtitles remind viewers of media imports' foreignness, and so dubbing can be understood as the preferred mode of translation in nationalistic systems (Danan, 1991). In this context, subtitles are a weaker defense against the potential cultural threats of media imports and hearing one's own language both confirms its importance and reifies its relevance. Those who get distracted by concerns surrounding the use of dubbing in Nazi propaganda (Romano, 2020) tend to ignore the cultural value of dubbing in other countries where it is used not as propaganda but as a way to defend against an imperialistic U.S. that floods its theaters and television channels with American English-language media.

Offering both a dub and subtitle option is not outside the realm of possibility, and many regions in fact already offer both versions of films with regularity (Romano, 2020). Netflix already makes some media texts like *Love Alarm* and *My First First Love* available in their original Korean while including audio options in English, Spanish, French, and Mandarin, with subtitle options in English, Spanish, and Korean captions. But Netflix is not consistent, and many Korean texts, including hits like *That Winter, the Wind Blows* and *Boys Over Flowers*, are available only with Korean audio and the choice of English, Spanish, or Chinese subtitles along with the Korean captions. It is unclear why Netflix is inconsistent, though the lower costs of subtitles (Romano, 2020) is certainly a factor in why its Korean library offers a host of subtitles and rarely dubs. Still, Netflix (along with other streaming services) is an important factor in current global media flows (Romano, 2020), both from South Korea to U.S and otherwise. Netflix boasts roughly 160 million paying subscribers, only 60 million of whom are in the U.S. (Garcia, 2020; Hong, 2020; Prasad, 2020), meaning Netflix content must be available in any number of languages around the globe.

The presence and popularity of 'foreign' content on Netflix is of great significance for both global media flows and the flourishing of more global citizens. Netflix reports that U.S. users who watch foreign-language content prefer to consume popular foreign shows in their dubbed forms (Prasad, 2020); though this does not perhaps immerse viewers in a new culture through its language as much as subtitles would, it is nevertheless an important opportunity for U.S. Americans who want to move beyond the contemporary resurgence of xenophobia in the U.S. Instead of fear or rage, U.S. fans of Korean media meet these foreign texts with fascination and pleasure (Chung, 2011; Ju, 2020; Lee, 2018); while differences in language and culture make it more difficult to consume Korean media compared to U.S. texts, these differences in fact motivate viewers in their content selection. Studies of U.S. K-wave fandom thus illustrates Jenkins's (2006) theory of pop cosmopolitanism, by which pop culture flows transculturally, inspiring consumers to become more culturally competent. According to Jenkins, such consumers distinguish themselves from others, including older generations, by consuming "foreign" media content and participating in cultural engagement. Such pop cosmopolitanism is valuable, and it is important to recognize that it poses a significant first step by which people become more globally conscious.

It is noteworthy, therefore, that the concerns surrounding the presence of a foreign spoken language in one's media diet have not historically been experienced by most people in the U.S. The United States' status as a dominant media producer on a global scale means most Americans are easily able to avoid media that is not produced in English and/or find media in other languages that they can consume through either subtitling or dubbing. This fact has allowed debates about dubbing and subtitles to remain very much out of mainstream U.S. discourses in the 21st century, until now. This fact, combined with *Parasite*'s Oscar wins and comments made by its director, paved the way for a contentious debate in February of 2020.

Responses to Dubbing and Subtitling on Twitter

Parasite serves as a recent media darling of pop cosmopolitanism in the U.S., though the reasons why it enjoys this status are less clear, as are the implications of its consumption by U.S. audiences. One potential explanation is that diverse representations of and stories about Asian cultures are becoming trendy in the 21st century (Hong, 2020), as evidenced by successful films like *Crazy Rich Asians, Always Be My Maybe*, and *The Farewell*. People's willingness to experience cultures different from their own, if only through media, is of the utmost importance, because "[w]hen xenophobia and intolerance are widely understood to be on the rise, such proof of curiosity between and across cultures are useful reminders that while some minds may be closed, many others are open" (Guardian, 2020). Another explanation for *Parasite*'s popularity is that its narrative offers a universal story, a critique of capitalism that, as Adams (2020) points out, "could have been told in any number of advanced countries." The fact that an international film won Best Feature is a message to U.S. viewers that, as one columnist puts it, "some of the best films require subtitles" (Fly, 2020). Finally, *Parasite*'s success and the subsequent mainstreaming of the dubbing/subtitling debate is perhaps due to the fact that so many people are increasingly comfortable with subtitles (Hong, 2020; Jackson, 2020); for example, the HBO series *Game of Thrones*, although largely in English, often utilized subtitles when representing various cultures within its narrative world, and was wildly popular with U.S. audiences.

Despite the growing presence of subtitles in popular media in the U.S., political blogger Kevin Drum (2020) wrote a divisive piece originally titled "Dubbing is Better than Subtitles." Published the day after the 2020 Oscars, Drum asserted that "No one likes subtitles" and that they're "only common in countries too poor to afford a dubbing industry." Drum's column was almost immediately revised; the title was changed to "It should come as no surprise that most film audiences prefer dubbing to subtitling," and his comment about "poor" countries was changed to say that subtitles are "only common in markets where film revenues aren't high enough for studios to recoup the cost of producing dubbed versions." These revisions were likely in response to the furor brought on by Drum's original post. Media reporter Max Tani saw Drum's article and tweeted a link to it with the caption, "what the fuck." Tani's tweet got more than 52,000 retweets and 202,000 likes and spurred a thread of more than 400 tweets. These tweets offer a glimpse into the average U.S. American's thoughts on the values of dubbing and subtitling in popular media.

Many of the people who tweeted in this thread addressed issues of accessibility. People who are deaf or have auditory processing disorders require subtitles. Subtitles are also beneficial when characters speak with a dialect or hard-to-understand accent; as one person pointed out, "Imagine game of thrones with no subtitles. Or trainspotting!" referring to a popular film in which the characters' heavy Scottish dialects make the dialogue all but unintelligible. On the other hand, people who are blind, dyslexic, or illiterate (due to either age or education) require dubbing; people on Twitter asked "literally what about blind people," and "When will someone make the actual good pro-dubs argument that blind people and dyslexic people and people with other conditions like them exist and that they deserve to watch movies too."

As many others noted on Twitter, for people who do not require a particular form of translation due to accessibility issues, dubbing and subtitling offer trade-offs in what they can do for viewers. Subtitles afford viewers the opportunity to learn another language by hearing the source language and reading the translation. For those who must be respectful of roommates or family members by keeping their televisions' volume low, subtitles help viewers not to miss content. Subtitles are also useful when, as one woman put it, "there are sometimes things in the subtitles that no one could reasonably hear, other than my dog. And he's not good at filling me in on those bits." By contrast, another voiced appreciation that dubbing allows viewers to "actually do other shit without having to pay as much attention to the screen." While rarely demonstrated on Twitter, this perspective was popular in blogs and columns in which people recognized two modern trends in the U.S. First, many people consume media while multitasking and aren't able to keep their eyes on their screens (Hong, 2020; Prasad, 2020); secondly, the small sizes of screens on which many consume media—phones and tablets, for example—are perhaps not as conducive to on-screen text, again putting dubbing at an advantage.

The primary element engaged throughout this Twitter thread was the simple matter of personal preference, though such preferences are arguably entrenched in neoliberal ideology that prioritizes individual actors' labor within a text. One person, for example, pointed out that in a dubbed film "you can't hear the work of the actors who worked on the film.. You hear some other actors talk.. And no only the voice acting can be pretty inferior, but sometimes the soundtrack suffers as a whole." Another argued that "Dubbing kills the emotional expression of the performer." This line of response from audiences illustrates two concerns regarding dubbing. First, it seems to rely on outdated assumptions about the quality of dubbing; martial arts films, for example, have long been mocked for their outrageously incongruous synchronization. This perspective fails to recognize improvements in the dubbing industry and diminishes the professional skills of dubbing actors who are just that—actors, as much as the people who appear on screen. That leads to the second issue, whereby ideologically, the "real" actor is preference over the "voice" actor. Ultimately, the visual embodiment of a character is positioned as more important than the actualized voice of the character. Those who recognized this subtle ideological underpinning surprisingly called out this preference for visual form. For example, one argued that "Voice actors are just as talent as live performers. In fact it takes more effort as they have to convey that emotion while fitting mouth movements and matching the original performance while still trying to make it feel natural." Thus, U.S. Americans in the debate tended to show a strong preference for neoliberal investments in individual performance connected to visual form, despite the smaller subset who acknowledged the labor of voice actors.

Another aspect of the debate that exposed U.S. audiences' framing of the issue as a visal one appeared in several posts attacking subtitling as inferior to dubbing based on the constraint of reading. One respondent lamented that "having your eyes fixated on the subtitles also makes you lose half of the visual space." This position is mistaken in that subtitles do not, in fact, take up half the screen, and furthermore downplays how easy subtitles are to follow. This emphasis on visual space was critiqued by other posts, as when one user responded, "I'm sorry that you have difficulty focusing on the plot while reading subtitles. It must be hard for you;" another user challenged, "we get it your braincells are miniscule no need to force it on anyone else," thus highlighting viewers' belief that both options should be available for individual choice. This perspective, that "'Reading takes effort, so we shouldn't read' is at the core of so many of our problems," echoes that of *Parasite*'s director, as well as the Vox columnist whose interpretation that "Americans just don't like reading subtitles" (Wilkinson, 2020) fueled Drum's (2020) original post and this subsequent translation debate. However, other users took a more forgiving approach to such critiques, pointing out that subtitles cease being distracting over time and that reading skills improve, suggesting that the "one-inch barrier" is a mental one that can easily be overcome with practice and/or patience. In other words, this side focused less on the visual embodiment of the actors as agents and more on consumers of media as agents—emphasizing how their own labor as viewers was increased through the use of subtitles.

Paradoxically, as one user pointed out, many on Twitter responded to Drum's "crappy elitist article by turning around and being elitist themselves about dubs." The vast majority of contributors took a pro-subtitles stance—or, more accurately, an anti-dubbing stance. While people frequently employed rhetoric that characterized fans of dubbing as lazy or illiterate as described above, there was a subset that tied people's preferences to their national background, specifically with regards to class; these Twitter users challenged Drum's assertion that countries only subtitle (or its citizens prefer subtitles) if the country is poor, though one maintained that "Poor people are lucky not to have countries who waste money on dubbing." Various users pointed out that the U.S. and Scandinavia are "rich" enough to afford dubbing, but do not typically do so. In the case of Sweden, for example, a Swedish user stated that the "Only thing dubbed here is children's cartoons and movies rest is subbed," adding that this was how they learned English as a child. Drum's characterizations were further challenged by a self-proclaimed "third-worlder" who claimed, "our dubbing industry is amazing and ppl love it."

Very few participants articulated why, in the U.S. context, the dub versus subtitle debate is so culturally significant. One person asserted that "the world doesn't revolve around english-speaking countries," calling Drum "just lazy" and qualifying his prejudice against subtitles as "a huge testament to the myopic mindset that americans do it better than anyone else." This sentiment was supported by the person who said that "America is so rich, they just make crappy English-language versions of all the great subtitled movies," leading to a tangential debate about what foreign films the U.S. has successfully remade. Though the majority of participants on this Twitter thread devolved into an echo chamber of vitriol, this nuanced minority focused on the U.S. cultural context brought much-needed attention to the privilege experienced by U.S. Americans as media consumers. As one particularly eloquent commenter said, subtitles "allow you to hear a film in the original language. Languages are culture. And a representation of culture is art." This perspective makes perhaps the strongest argument for why, when setting aside issues of accessibility and viewers' tendency to multitask, *Parasite* and other foreign-language films consumed with subtitles are far more likely to offer a culturally immersive experience for U.S.

Americans who are simply not used to regularly hearing languages other than English in media content.

Conclusion

Given the success of Korean media in the U.S., *Parasite*'s success with viewers is not unfounded, but *Parasite* is nevertheless unique. While there is a small but vocal contingent of U.S. Americans that identify as fans of Korean media and sing its praises, *Parasite* is the most popular Korean film to reach a larger swathe of the U.S.—beyond those who already consumed Korean media with regularity. At the crest of the Korean wave, *Parasite* reached a larger audience as it washed ashore in the U.S. than any other individual Korean media text. Part of the larger ideological backlash by media consumers, then, is against the idea that U.S. media and the spoken English language are not inherently the best. Those who denigrated *Parasite*'s subtitles and demanded an English-language dub represent a U.S. American predilection for the visual form, thereby marginalizing the value of hearing or consuming media in languages besides English.

As this chapter has demonstrated, much of the popular post-*Parasite* debate about dubbing and subtitling, as vociferous as its participants are, is not ultimately about the cultural implications of these options for U.S. American media consumers in the current political climate—at least not on the surface. Instead, the debate is about (anti) intellectualism. The transition from Barack Obama to Donald Trump illustrates an anti-intellectual "America first" turn in the U.S., one that is echoed by Drum's claims that nobody likes to read subtitles. The success of a subtitled Korean film and the subsequent championing of subtitles on Twitter, then, indicates a resurgence of U.S. Americans' thirst to consume international content and engage with a diverse range of cultures. On Twitter and in blogs and columns, the discourses surrounding *Parasite*'s translation expose the ways U.S. audiences foster immediate assumptions that content will be produced in English, particularly when it comes to critically acclaimed films. And yet, while an anti-intellectual faction forwards anti-subtitles rhetoric that demands secondary media producers placate them with English-language dubs, *Parasite* and its subtitles provide hope; *Parasite* is the rare film has the potential to motivate people to expand their personal borders, if viewers open their ears, eyes, and minds.

Recommended Readings

Adams, T. (2020, February 3). South Korea's 'Parasite' crashes the subtitles barrier. *Variety*. https://variety.com/2020/film/awards/south-koreas-parasite-crashes-the-subtitles-barrier-1203488979/

Chiaro, D. (2009). Issues in audiovisual translation. In J. Munday (Ed.), *The Routledge companion to translation studies* (pp. 141-165). London; New York: Routledge.

Ju, H. (2020). Korean TV drama viewership on Netflix: Transcultural affection, romance, and identities. *Journal of International & Intercultural Communication, 13*(1), 32-48. https://doi.org/10.1080/17513057.2019.1606269

Kim, D. K., & Kim, M. S. (Eds.). (2011). *Hallyu: Influence of Korean popular culture in Asia and beyond*. Seoul, Korea: Seoul National University Press.

O'Falt, C. (2020, February 25). Subtitles vs. dubbing: The big business of translating foreign films in a post-'Parasite' world. *IndieWire*. https://www.indiewire.com/2020/02/subtitles-vs-dubbing-what-you-need-to-know-1202212800/

Additional Sources

France, L. R. (2020, April 10). Hulu is not here for your 'Parasite' subtitle complaints. *CNN*. https://www.cnn.com/2020/04/10/entertainment/hulu-parasite-subtitles-trnd/index.html

Garcia, S. E. (2020, February 17). After 'Parasite,' are subtitles still a one-inch barrier for Americans? *The New York Times*. https://www.nytimes.com/2020/02/12/movies/movies-subtitles-parasite.html

Kokas, A. (2020, February 11). 'Parasite' was a triumph for a film industry trapped between the U.S. and China. *The Washington Post*. https://www.washingtonpost.com/outlook/2020/02/11/parasite-was-triumph-film-industry-trapped-between-us-china/

References

Adams, T. (2020, February 3). South Korea's 'Parasite' crashes the subtitles barrier. *Variety*. Retrieved from https://variety.com/2020/film/awards/south-koreas-parasite-crashes-the-subtitles-barrier-1203488979/

Anderson, C. S. (2014). HallyU. SA. In V. Marinescu (Ed.), *The global impact of South Korean popular culture: Hallyu unbound* (pp. 123-134). Lanham, MD: Lexington Books.

Antonini, R. (2005). The perception of subtitled humour in Italy: An empirical study. *Humor International Journal of Humor Research, 18*(2), 209-225.

Chaume Varela, F. (2004). Synchronization in dubbing: A translational approach. In P. Orero (Ed.), *Topics in audiovisual translation* (pp. 35-52). Amsterdam; Philadelphia: John Benjamins Publishing Company.

Chiaro, D. (2009). Issues in audiovisual translation. In J. Munday (Ed.), *The Routledge companion to translation studies* (pp. 141-165). London; New York:

Routledge.

Chung, H. S. (2011). Medium hot, Korean cool: Hallyu envy and reverse mimicry in contemporary U.S. pop culture. In D. K. Kim & M. S. Kim (Eds.), *Hallyu: Influence of Korean popular culture in Asia and beyond* (pp. 63-90). Seoul, Korea: Seoul National University Press.

Danan, M. (1991). Dubbing as an expression of nationalism. *Meta: Translators' Journal, 36*(4), 606-614.

Drum, K. (2020, February 10). It should come as no surprise that most film audiences prefer dubbing to subtitles. *Mother Jones*. Retrieved from https://www.motherjones.com/kevin-drum/2020/02/subtitles-really-do-suck-you-know/

Fry, M. (2020, January 7). Who's afraid of subtitles? *Washington Examiner*. Retrieved from https://www.washingtonexaminer.com/opinion/whos-afraid-of-subtitles

Garcia, S. E. (2020, February 17). After 'Parasite,' are subtitles still a one-inch barrier for Americans? *The New York Times*. https://www.nytimes.com/2020/02/12/movies/movies-subtitles-parasite.html

Guardian. (2020, February 19). The Guardian view on foreign-language cinema: Great escapes. Retrieved from https://www.theguardian.com/commentisfree/2020/feb/19/the-guardian-view-on-foreign-language-cinema-great-escapes

Hong, E. (2020, February 12). 'Parasite's win is an awesome test of the one-inch barrier. *CNN*. Retrieved from https://www.cnn.com/2020/02/10/opinions/subtitle-barrier-parasite-hong/index.html

Jackson, L. M. (2020, February 13). You should watch everything with subtitles on. *The Washington Post*. Retrieved from https://www.washingtonpost.com/outlook/2020/02/13/you-should-watch-everything-with-subtitles/

Jenkins, H. (2006). *Convergence culture: Where old and new media collide*. New York, NY: New York University Press.

Jin, D. Y. (2017). Digital platform as a double-edged sword: How to interpret cultural flows in the platform era. *International Journal of Communication, 11*, 3880-3898. Retrieved from https://ijoc.org/index.php/ijoc/article/view/6201/2146

Jin, D. Y. (2018). An analysis of the Korean wave as transnational popular culture: North American youth engage through social media as TV becomes obsolete. *International Journal of Communication, 12*, 404-422. Retrieved from https://ijoc.org/index.php/ijoc/article/view/7973

Jin, D. Y., & Yoon, K. (2016). The social mediascape of transnational Korean pop culture: *Hallyu 2.0* as spreadable media practice. *New Media & Society, 18*(7), 1277-1292.

Jin, D. Y., & Yoon, T. J. (2017). The Korean wave: Retrospect and prospect. *International Journal of Communication, 11*, 2241-2249. Retrieved from https://ijoc.org/index.php/ijoc/article/view/6296

Ju, H. (2020). Korean TV drama viewership on Netflix: Transcultural affection, romance, and identities. *Journal of International & Intercultural Communication, 13*(1), 32-48.

Ju, H., & Lee, S. (2015). The Korean wave and Asian Americans: The ethnic meanings of transnational Korean pop culture in the USA. *Journal of Media & Cultural Studies, 29*(3), 323-338.

Kilborn, R. (1993). 'Speak my language': Current attitudes to television subtitling and dubbing. *Media, Culture & Society, 15*(4), 641-660.

Kim, D. K., & Kim, S. J. (2011). *Hallyu* from its origin to present: A historical overview. In D. K. Kim & M. S. Kim (Eds.), *Hallyu: Influence of Korean popular culture in Asia and beyond* (pp. 13-34). Seoul, Korea: Seoul National University Press.

Kim, K. (2015). *K-movie: The world's spotlight on Korean film*. Korean Culture & Information Service.

Kim, Y. (2007). The rising East Asian 'wave'. In D. K. Thussu (Ed.), *Media on the move: Global flow and contra-flow* (pp. 131-152). London; New York: Routledge.

Kim, Y. (2013). Korean media in a digital cosmopolitan world. In Y. Kim (Ed.), *The Korean wave: Korean media go global* (pp. 1-27). London; New York: Routledge.

Kokas, A. (2020, February 11). 'Parasite' was a triumph for a film industry trapped between the U.S. and China. *The Washington Post*. https://www.washingtonpost.com/outlook/2020/02/11/parasite-was-triumph-film-industry-trapped-between-us-china/

Korea Creative Content Agency. (2015). *2015 content white paper*.

Lee, H. (2018). A 'real' fantasy: Hybridity, Korean drama, and pop cosmopolitans. *Media, Culture & Society*, *40*(3), 365-380.

Levenson, M. (2020, February 22). Trump denounces Oscar winner 'Parasite.' *The New York Times*. Retrieved from https://0-search-proquest-com.read.cnu.edu/docview/2359886831?accountid=10100

O'Falt, C. (2020, February 25). Subtitles vs. dubbing: The big business of translating foreign films in a post-'Parasite' world. *IndieWire*. Retrieved from https://www.indiewire.com/2020/02/subtitles-vs-dubbing-what-you-need-to-know-1202212800/

Poniewozik, J. (2014, February 2). Coca-Cola's 'It's Beautiful' Super Bowl ad brings out some ugly Americans. *TIME*. Retrieved from https://time.com/3773/coca-colas-its-beautiful-super-bowl-ad-brings-out-some-ugly-americans/

Prasad, R. (2020, February 23). Dubs or subs? Parasite renews debate on how to watch foreign films. *BBC News*. Retrieved from https://www.bbc.com/news/world-us-canada-51567425

Romano, A. (2020, February 20). The debate over subtitles, explained. *Vox*. Retrieved from https://www.vox.com/2020/2/20/21134355/subtitles-or-dubs-which-is-better-parasite-debate-history-anime

Shim, D. (2006). Hybridity and the rise of Korean popular culture in Asia. *Media, Culture & Society*, *18*(1), 25-44.

Ter Molen, S. L. (2014). Hallyu for hire. In V. Marinescu (Ed.), *The global impact of South Korean popular culture: Hallyu unbound* (pp. 107-122). Lanham, MD: Lexington Books.

Thussu, D. K. (2007). Mapping global media flow and contra-flow. In D. K. Thussu (Ed.), *Media on the move: Global flow and contra-flow* (pp. 11-29). London; New York: Routledge.

Tunstall, J. (1994). *The media are American*. Constable.

U.S. Department of Commerce. (2015). *U.S. trade in services*. Retrieved from http://bea.gov/iTable/iTable.cfm?reqid=62&step=1&isuri=1#reqid=62&step=6&isuri=1&6210=4&6200=160&6211=168

U.S. Government. (2005). *U.S. international services: Cross-border trade in 2004 and sales through affiliates in 2003*. Retrieved from https://apps.bea.gov/scb/pdf/2005/10October/1005_xborder.pdf

Wilkinson, A. (2020, February 10). Parasite absolutely deserved to win best picture. I didn't think it could. *Vox*. Retrieved from https://www.vox.com/culture/2020/2/10/21131004/parasite-best-picture-oscars-2020

CHAPTER 12

A Critical Rhetorical Analysis of the International Reception of Bong Joon Ho's *Parasite*

Marouf Arif Hasian, Jr., University of Utah

Within a very short period of time Bong Joon Ho's film, *Parasite* (2019), has become a movie classic, a film that tells the dystopic tale of the difficulties that are faced by many classes of South Koreans who are living in one of the world's most powerful global cityscapes. This is a cinematic production that uses a variety of communicative strategies and diverse genres to critique some of the darker aspects of capitalism, and there are evident reasons why *Parasite* won the Palme d'Or at the Cannes film festival and dozens of other accolades (Kermode, 2020; Lodge, 2019).

National and international film critics have already started to unpack the aesthetic, technical, architectural (Hess, 2020) and affective features of this fascinating movie, and *Parasite* made cinematic history when it became the first foreign-language film to win Best Picture at the Oscars. The varied communicative features of the film—that combines several tragic, comedic, and other genres—has clearly contributed to the film's popularity, creating moviegoing situations where audiences become active participants and societal critics at the same time that they passively enjoy trying to unpack the layers of symbolic meanings that can be found in *Parasite*.

For those communication scholars who are interested in studying the critical or ideological features of rhetorical artefacts (McGee, 1980; McKerrow, 1991) Joon Ho's film can be productively critiqued as an ideological fragment, a form of political satire and biting societal critique that uses film as a rhetorical weapon in the arsenal of those who wish to comment on economic and social structures in order to help better our world. Bong Joon Ho, along with the actors and supporters of the film who share his worldviews, should be viewed as interventionists in debates about class struggle who are creating messages that resonate with many others who identify with the difficulties that are faced by many of the characters in *Parasite*.

The evocative power of ideologies conveyed through film varies in efficacy, depending on the presentist needs of viewing audiences as well as the artistry involved in the production of cinematic representations. There were those who recognized that the ambiguities, the twists and turns, and surprises in *Parasite* fascinated global observers. This "tale of the rich Park family and the poor Kim family," opined Ulaby (2019), "is an international sensation—partly because of universal themes like the conflict between haves and have nots" (para. 1). Goldberg (2020), a writer for the *New York Times*, argued after the Oscars that there was "something resonant" about Joon Ho's cinematic projection, perhaps because of this "radical parable of inequality" that was producing a "bleak social vision" that movie-goers could relate to (paras. 1-2).

While some critics who watched *Parasite* tried to downplay the ideological features of this film, others traced some of the genealogical features of Bong Joon Ho's other works and argued that common radical democratic, socialist or Marxist motifs could be found in many of his cinematic productions. For Goldberg (2020), this was a South Korean movie that was very different from anything coming out of America's Hollywood, and "its reception" was evidence "of the same crisis of faith in capitalism" that was making Bernie Sanders into one of the front-runners for the U.S. democratic nomination in February of 2020 (para. 2).

Throughout late 2019 and early 2020 national and international commentators on the film could not help seeing parallels between what was happening in the movie *Parasite* and the economic, social, and political struggles that were taking place outside of movie theatres. Many movie goers who go to their local theatres or cineplex in New Zealand or Singapore or Canada can identify with characters who search for a "plan" that might help them overcome poverty, class discrimination, ethnic prejudice, and other societal issues.

From a critical rhetorical vantage point, is it possible that by the end of the second decade of the 21st century the world was ready to go to their local movie theatres so that they could see a film about the urban poverty, the capitalist exploitation, and the access to resources or "opportunity" (Pike, 2019, para. 1) that contributed to class alienation. Did moviegoers identify with *Parasite's* suggestions that large economic and societal forces prevented the upward mobility of South Korean classes who dreamed of a better life?

Blurring the lines that existed between traditional genres *Parasite* was described by a writer for the United Kingdom's *Guardian* as a "melancholic ghost story, albeit one disguised beneath umpteen layers of superbly designed" generic materials (Kermode, 2020, para. 8). An American writer for the *New Yorker* described *Parasite* as a "satirically comedic thriller about poverty, about the contrast between the rich and poor, and about the injustice of inequality, that avoids the conventions and habits of realistic social dramas" (Brody, 2019, para. 2). In India, Sharma (2020) averred that this was a movie with "world class content," and he complained that while film industries in China, Japan, and South Korea were producing excellent work, the Indian film industries should be ashamed because no Indian film had won any major awards at Cannes or the Golden Bear at Berlin.

While there is no question that many observers have mentioned in passing that Bong Jon-ho's movie has everything to do with depictions of class wars and the challenges of surviving in emerging Asian capitalistic markets there have been very few detailed, systemic studies of the communicative features of *Parasite*. Here, I argue that many international communities in places like the United Kingdom, Japan, Canada, Australia, and South Africa identify with the characters or subplots in *Parasite* because of the polysemic (multiple meanings) and polyvalent (multiple values) that swirl around Bong Joon Ho's award winning film.

In this chapter I use critical rhetorical methods of analysis to help explain the ideological and materialist features of *Parasite* that resonate with so many global audiences. I argue that part of the massive appeal of Joon Ho's masterpiece has everything to do with filmic plotlines and characterological development that turns the movie into a weaponized critique of the varied facets of capitalism. In spite of the director's public remarks regarding the apolitical nature of *Parasite*, a critical rhetorical analysis of this movie illustrates how the preferred readings of this film are conveyed and appreciated by audiences who also begin to see themselves—regardless of class rank—as mere cogs in the machinery of modern global capitalism.

With this in mind, I argue in this essay that a study of both Bong Joon Ho's communicative strategies and tactics in some of his prior films, as well as a decoding of *Parasite*, reveals that global audiences seem to be drawn to three key dimensions of this film: 1) the use of deceptive strategies by the impoverished; 2) the visualization of the destructive nature of the co-dependence of proletariat and bourgeois classes; and 3) the visualized depictions of situations where the poor who are oppressed end up fighting each other. This chapter provides readers with an interpretation and understanding of how Bong Joon Ho was able to use filmic techniques and ideological content in *Parasite* to show the limits of even the best familial "plans" of the lower classes when they encounter the hegemonic power of capitalist *dingpolitiks* (Latour, 2004).

Class Warfare in Bong's Movies before *Parasite*

As often happens, when a famous director gains stardom for a blockbuster film there a tendency to go back and use genealogical studies to see if global audiences would also be interested in studying his own life, or in seeing some of Bong Joon Ho's other filmic productions. In this particular case, Joon Ho, who studied sociology at South Korea's Yonsei University, gained a reputation during the last several decades of the 20th century for producing a series of movies that critiqued everything from the repressive military rule of some national governments to corporate abuses (*Agency France-Press* Staff, 2020). For example, some commentators trace Joon Ho's fame back to 2003 when he produced *Memories of Murder*—a film that was based, in part, on some real live events that scared thousands in South Korea during the 1980s. Three years later Joon Ho came out with a very popular movie entitled *The Host* (see Lee, 2018), that showed state organizations scrambling to deal with a national disaster. The very titles of this movie, and *Parasite*, invited observers to think of societal diseases and autoimmunity responses to those diseases.

More than a few international movie goers in Europe have compared some of the social criticism in *Parasite* with Bong Joon Ho's 2013 movie, *Snowpiercer*, a film about class warfare on a train where humans who survived global warming devastation now battled for scarce resources. *Snowpiercer* was a movie that allowed moviegoers to see what happened when remnants of humanity after a massive global warming catastrophe are forced to live on a constantly-moving train. Described as Joon Ho's "most Marxist-seeming film" (Goldberg, 2020) most of the action in *Snowpiercer* focuses on how members of classes may betray each other as they battle others in vicious societal warfare.

In 2017 Joon Ho and his backers came out with an adventure tale called *Kola*, a movie about how a country girl is doing her best to try and save a genetically engineered animal from exploitation by a "greedy international firm" (*Agency France-Press* Staff, 2020, para. 11). Critical rhetoricians studying these thematic strands of Bong Joon Ho's work would note the common biopolitical (politics of life) as well as thanatopolitical (politics of death) motifs in these visualities.

By 2018 observers who unpacked the ideological features of Bong Joon Ho's films could argue that his unique blending of comedic and tragic genres was being used in interventionist ways to critique South Korea's—and the world's—responses to various natural and humanly produced disasters. It was no coincidence that he also used filmic mediums to critique capitalism's biotechnological advances, exploitation of animals and humans, and destruction of societies' social fabric. Joon Ho's films oftentimes underscored the point that worshipers of capitalist solutions to environmental and societal problems were deceiving themselves and others.

Avoiding the "Crossing of Lines": The First Allusions to Parasites and the Visual Representations of the Kim and Park Familial Relations

Although *Parasite* is an interventionist study of the interrelationships between *three* families, most of the early action in this film centers on the character development and activities of the Kim and Park families. The wealthy Parks and the impoverished Kims become co-dependent when the Kim family, living a life of urban poverty in South Korea, tries to infiltrate the "host" home of the rich Park family. While the Kim family needs the pay or potential upward mobility from the Parks, the Park family, in turn, needs the Kim family around in order to maintain their lifestyle as well as their status.

As noted above, part of the allure for international moviegoers is the ambiguity that moves between characterological life on the screen and the quotidian demands of the everyday life of those who live in capitalistic societies filled with promise and perils. Many observers who have commented on *Parasite* have noted how verticality and horizontal drawing of architectural building lines are used in the film to convey class differences and class expectations. Characters' movement upstairs, or toward higher elevations, conveys a sense of success, growth, financial independence, and goodness, while downward movement toward places like lower sub-apartments or basements symbolizes desperation, failure, poverty, and evil.

These rhetorical vertical and horizontal lines were not created *ex nihilo*. A real estate agent recently explained to readers that wealth, in Seoul, is sometimes measured by using metrics that are based on looking at how high a member of a class lives. The Kim family, argues Coury (2020) seems to represent in *Parasite* the "*banjiha*, living at ground-level, or just below," who "live in constant fear that if prices increase" and if "wealth inequality becomes even greater" they may be "swallowed into the ground" (para. 3).

Throughout *Parasite*, Bong Joon Ho uses the contrasting subterranean life of the Kims and the hilltop living of the Parks to highlight class differences and capitalistic rankings of communities living in South Korea. For example, during some of the early segments of this film moviegoers are invited to view the Kim family members as potential parasites who, rising from below, one by one, start to move out of their lowly dwelling and perform key roles to help the Park family, including taking on the roles of an English tutor to a young adolescent girl (Ki-woo, played by Woo-sik Choi), an art therapist to a young Park son (Ki-jung, played by So-dam Park), a chauffer (Ki-taek, played by Kang-ho Song), and a knowledgeable housekeeper (Chung-sook). The gullible Parks are configured as guileless, well-intentioned members of South Korean upper classes who don't realize that their home on the hill has been invaded.

Bong Joon Ho uses all sorts of figurative devices to communicate the idea that social classes can become parasitic in capitalist societies through infestation, social dehumanization, economic dislocation, or environmental degradation. For example, the theme of class warfare that is linked to biological warfare is conveyed when a fruit allergy is used deceptively to convince the Parks that they must protect their children by getting rid of a housekeeper who spent many years working for the Parks. The Kim family works together to convince the Parks that the housekeeper—who suffered from an allergy—actually has tuberculosis, and members of the Kim family are not above using fake IDs, forged documents, and other deceptive practices to ingratiate themselves with various members of the Park household.

During the first half of the movie it is not hard for global movie-goers to identify with the pragmatic—if devious—members of the Kim family who carry out various ruses. The Kims, individually and collectively, seem to be bright and crafty members of down-on-their luck lower classes who are cheery and supportive of each other.

If the Kim family members are the first metaphoric sources of infestation in *Parasite*, they are affable ones. Bong Joon Ho uses everything from scenes of smashed bugs on the table in the Kim family's sub-apartment to family discussions of smell or filth to convey the sense that the members of the Kim family seem, at times, to have resigned themselves to living in decayed surroundings. The Kim family is portrayed as moving from host to host as they look for their next job. In order to survive the Kims continually come up with their next beguiling or subversive "plan" that might help them survive a capitalistic system that is filled with fumigations, floods, rising costs of living, and other thanatopolitical experiences.

It is the street smarts of the Kim family—their willingness to fold pizza boxes, look for part time jobs, leave behind small business failures, firings, etc.—that helps them stay together in a cramped South Korean urban dwelling that has tiny rooms. In Foucauldian terms, this is their everyday, mundane, biopolitical, heterotopic world, and the second half of the film complicates matters when the Kim family seems to catch a break in life that might help them move into the middle class. This occurs when the Kims' familial son, Ki-woo, has a friend who has to go overseas, and the friend wants Ki-woo to pose as a tutor for one of the Park children.

When Ki-woo first tries to visit the Parks and becomes a tutor we, as movie goers, are allowed to see the geopolitical and spatial positionality of the Parks. The Parks are well-dressed and well-mannered, and even the objects in their home are used by the director to highlight class disparities. The Park mansion is filled with burnished wood, crystal glass, and labyrinthine rooms and staircases, and these eventually become objects to display the *dingpolitiks* (the politics of things) and the *realpolitik* (the politics of realistic deliberation) (Latour, 2004) of Kim-Park familial and class relationships.

Bong Joon Ho allows the Kim family to dream about upward class mobility, but their reach exceeds their grasp. This does not dissuade them from the idea that they can pool their talents and perhaps escape their subterranean abode by working for the Parks. The Kim family members hide their true identities from the Parks when they interview for positions, and eventually the Kims begin to feel secure enough about their positions that they begin dreaming of eventually living in a place like the Park's household. Were the Kims willing to cross real, seemingly invisible, class lines, and leave their poverty behind? Were they forgetting about distinctions that could be made between parasites and hosts? This is one of the reasons why a British critic has called *Parasite* a "home invasion-thriller" (Lodge, 2019).

Grammatologies as well as vertical and horizontal movements in the Park home are used to convey social status, and Bong Joon Ho uses all types of experiential and technical cinematic techniques to get across the idea that in spite of the Kims' abilities and their salaries perceptual and real chasms separate the Parks and the Kims. At one point in the film, Mr. Park indicates that he likes to be tolerate of his employees and that he treats them well—as long as they do not "cross the line."

By the end of the film transcontinental moviegoers have a textured sense of where that mythic class line might be, and what might happen if a person crosses that line. Talking openly about the boundaries of these class and social lines has portentous consequences, and in many portions of *Parasite* both the Kims and the Parks seem to go out of their way to try and avoid accusing each other of crossing those class lines. The Kims don't want to mention exploitation, and the Parks avoid openly critiquing the Kim family's shortcomings.

As the movie progresses some of these line-drawing taboos break down, and global audiences begin to realize that the Kims may not be the only metaphorical parasites in this movie. We see the wealthy Parks displaying their wealth, shopping for groceries, buying silly materials like U.S.-made Indian teepees, and having pets that wear glittery clothes. Scenes in the movie contrast this flaunting of wealth by the Parks with the daily trials and tribulations of the Kims. A diluvial rain turns into a massive eco-disaster for those living in South Korean sub-apartments who, like the Kims, see their homes flooded after massive rains.

Bong Joon Ho uses spatial and temporal cinematic techniques so that global audiences can see how environmental rain—that is just an inconvenience for the Park family on a camping outing—creates dangerous situations for the Kim family who are trying to move up while they avoid giving offense. The members of this poorer family are threatened by the actual "risk of infection by water-borne parasites" when Ki-jung is shown "seated precariously atop a toilet spewing fecal sludge, smoking her cigarette and clutching her phone" (Pike, 2019, para. 2). Meanwhile, the Parks simply worry about packing their-rain soaked objects and driving back to their safe abode. By this point in the movie, crossing lines now seems to signal risk, hazards, and catastrophe, and the Kims begin to sense that their higher salaries may not immunize them from the precarious nature of their sub-apartment living.

More than a few movie goers have noted that it may be plausible that the wealthy Parks are also some of the metaphoric parasites in the film, who end up rendering visible class lines and social hierarchies when they feel disrespected or threatened by their supposed inferiors. Critical communication scholars would note here that Joon Ho may simply be using choreographic scenes and cinematic techniques to allow viewers to debate amongst themselves and others about the symbolic meanings of the rain scenes. The *dingpolitik* aspects of rain and floods remind viewers that the formation of class lines may involve more than just improved salaries, and the polysemic (multiple meanings) and polyvalent (multiple values) aspects of the movie's title are now becoming more evident. The more that the Parks ignore the plight of the Kims the more that global filmgoers start to debate about whether it is the Park family, the urban environment, the rising South Korean economy, or even capitalism in general that might be the true parasites. Do capitalist class lines prevent the Parks from seeing the devastating nature of floods in Seoul?

For global citizens who identify with Marxist, socialist, or radical democrat ideologies the contrasting portrayals of the Kims, Parks and those members of a 3rd family living below the Park household allows movie goers to think about their own social status and their own personal relationship to economic systems. Has the capitalist nature of so many international societies complicated the ways we all think about chance or necessity, merit or power, or some other factors that may have aided or hindered class mobility in South Korean society?

In Bong Joon Ho's films it is not always easy to tell who are the antagonists and who are the protagonists in his class-oriented visualities, and a pivotal moment in *Parasite* arrives when we see the Kim family discussing their future after the Parks leave for their ill-fated camping trip. The departure of the Parks leaves the Kim family "servants" alone in the massive Park home, and the Kim family members drink and party and laugh at how comfortable and how natural some of them feel in this architectural wonder of a home.

Have these "parasites" now become "hosts," and have they surmounted some of the obstacles placed in their paths by real or mythic societal "lines"? At this point in the movie the Kims seem to be winning some of the early skirmishes in this protracted class warfare, and the Kim family patriarch, Ki-taek, implies that their recent good fortune and their nice salaries are going to help them move out of their flooded sub-apartment basement. He exclaims: "Money is an iron. It smooths out all the creases" (Kennedy, 2019, para. 3).

This conceptualization of money turns out to be an illusory way of thinking about class mobility and social status, and the Kims quickly find that monetary gains cannot iron out all creases. At this point in the action, near the conclusion of the first half of the film, global audiences are left wondering: Is this just another movie that shows how the poor get the better of the rich, where the tables are turned and those who are naturally meritorious and hard-working are going to win out over exploitive upper classes?

In spite of Ki-taek's hopes for his family this becomes an ominous part of the film where audiences have a foreboding sense that something dramatic and unexpected is about to happen. Bong Joon Ho's films are always filled with all sorts of twists and turns, and as Kennedy (2019) observed, "Bong can also take us deeper down" and there's "always an extra flood somewhere in this masterpiece" (para. 2).

In intriguing ways the metaphoric usages of floods and other natural catastrophes help sharpen class lines that cannot be easily crossed, and conceptual analytics associated with smell and other senses are used by Bong Joon Ho to underscore how different classes in capitalistic systems include or exclude those of a different social status. The director and characters of this film illustrate how motifs, metaphors, and allegories about infestation and class warfare can become entangled in conversations about smell and perceptual otherness in *Parasite*. When the Parks' son, Da-song, comments on how the Park employees seem to smell the same, this threatens to unmask the Kims. The pictorial representations of the Kims trying to get rid of this familial smell provides international audiences with yet another sympathetic reading of class warfare that they can readily understand.

Allusions to smell are used in this film to communicate class difference, societal prejudices, and rich obsessions with cleanliness. When viewers start to see more and more of the character development of the Parks the levity that entertained so many is gradually replaced with more brooding and dark features of the film. Global audiences get the impression that regardless of how hard the Kims struggle they may always "remain in the same dirty, verminous basement flat" (Goldberg, 2020, para. 7) that appears in the first frames of the film.

No doubt the tensions, as well as the co-dependent relationships, that exist between the rich Park family and the impoverished Kim family provide metaphors, allegories, and allusions for South Korean observers who are knowledgeable about class divisions within South Korean economic and cultural communities. That said, it would be a mistake to overlook how many other foreign movie goers also appreciate Bong Joon Ho's abilities to critique more cosmopolitan capitalist issues that confront countless others. For example, Goldberg (2020) averred that although American moviegoers might get the impression that South Korea is an extremely stratified society, "it's by some measures less unequal than our own" (para. 3). The threat of poverty is a pervasive and global condition that possesses existential dangers to hundreds of millions, and those class lines are pervasive characteristics of all capitalistic societies.

For U.S. citizens who get to see massive differences in societal treatments of the rich and poor in American venues *Parasite's* "fatalism about social mobility, so foreign to traditional American sensibilities," is "particularly bracing" (Goldberg, 2020, para. 3). What right, supporters of capitalistic systems might ask, do producers who benefit from entrepreneurial opportunities, have when it comes to critiquing the very system that helps circulate these types of movies?

More than a few global citizens who believe that capitalism breaks down class barriers, instead of putting them up, are bothered by the rhetorical figurations found in *Parasite*. Some U.S. observers who are quick to defend capitalism have sought to find international detractors of the film who resent Joon Ho's way of visualizing class warfare. Note, for example, how White (2019), a contributor to America's popular conservative outlet, *National Review*, contextualized Bong Joon Ho's masterpiece:

> ...Bong is an unfunny extremist. In *Parasite*, he annihilates the concept of the nuclear family by setting a brood of lower-class con artists against an upper-class family unit. The slum-dwelling Kim family runs scams from their filthy, but-infested hovel.... The film's hidden subject follows the economic inequality rants by leftists. Bong extends this enmity into a murderous, blood, meant-to-be hilarious climax, then maudlin finale. Bong himself becomes a political con artist (paras. 2-4).

Obviously Joon Ho's supporters were not the only audiences who understood some of the preferred messages about social inequities that swirled around *Parasite*.

Global audiences who are interested in studying the origins of class lines—or in siding with the nurture side of the nature-nurture debates associated with stratification—might argue that Bong Joon Ho is trying to show that the wealthy Parks are delusional and unfairly obsessed with maintaining otherness or class difference through smell. Perhaps Joon Ho is using smell and other thanatopolitical devices to show how the Parks misunderstand how they themselves gained their wealth in South Korea. Eugenical subtexts in *Parasite* add even more layers of possible critiques of the wealthy, who, in spite of their asserted superiority, are gradually seen as losing control of their surroundings.

The easy route that the director chooses not to take would have been to end the film on a "feel good" note that would allow movie goers to conclude that changing material circumstances or environmental conditions or educational opportunities would help the Kims traverse class lines and escape their poverty. However, Bong Joon Ho does not go in that direction, and he—and those who support his views—seem to be critiquing not only capitalist structures but also the nature of those who exude too much optimism or utopianism.

The Cinematic Portrayal of Moon-gwang, Guen-sae, and Kim-Park Family Conflicts

Critical rhetoricians and other materialist researchers in international communication studies often comment on the importance of studying both presences and absences in influential filmic productions, and it could be argued that it is telling that moviegoers don't "see much of the middle class in *Parasite*" because most of the action in this film "toggles from a gleaming modernist mansion floating in the hills above Seoul to a squalid basement apartment" (Ulaby, 2019, para. 3).

There must be a reason for this absence of any middle classes in *Parasite*, and I argue that that is because Bong Joon Ho wanted to include the character development of Moon-gwang (Lee Jung Eun) and Guen-sae (Park Myeong-hoon), members of a third family portrayed in this film. The director introduces these characters in order to prominently display the violence that takes place in capitalist situations that pit not only the rich against the poor, but also the poorer classes against each other. If moviegoers are only focusing on the class struggles that exist between the Parks and Kims they are missing some of the most horrific dimensions of capitalist class warfare—the heated, often violent fights that take place between different lower classes who compete for the right to work for societies' wealthier classes.

During earlier parts of *Parasite* viewers might get the impression that the massive, fortress-like home of the Parks-that used to belong to a famous architect—would be a place of refuge, warmth, and well-being—but the directors and producers of Joon Ho's masterpiece foreshadow how the vertical stairs, basements, and yards in the Park home are about to be turned into spaces of horror and places of destruction.

The action in the second part of this film runs from "comedy into thriller when the ex-maid [Moon-gwang] returns" to the Park residence (Rhee, 2020, para. 8). Moon-gwang—who lost her job because the

Parks believed she had TB—is now allowed into the Park house by the puzzled Kim family. The ex-maid tells the Kims that she has simply returned to retrieve something that was left in the basement, but what she doesn't tell them is that her husband is living underneath the Park home.

Moviegoers quickly learn that Moon-gwang's husband, Guen-sae, heavily in debt, has been living in the Park basement for about four years. When the Kim matriarch, Chung-sook, learns about the presence of Guen-sae, Moon-gwang begs Chung-sook to watch over and take care of Guen-sae. Bong Joon Ho could have allowed this moment to be turned into an example of class solidarity, but instead we see Chung-sook make fun of Moon-gwang and Guen-sae. In an incredibly ironic twist, Chung-sook seems to be implying that Moon-gwang and Guen-sae are the real parasites in the film, sponging off of the Parks. As far as Chung-sook is concerned, her own family has nothing in common with this third family (Goldberg, 2020).

By the time viewers get to the last quarter of this movie they see the Social Darwinian competition that takes place between the Kims and Moon-gwang and her husband. For a time, after Moon-gwang learns that the Park employees are all members of the Kim family, she and Guen-sae take pictures and threaten the Kims with exposure. Moon-gwang, armed with a cellphone with pictures of the Kim family, breaks out into an impersonation of a famous North Korean news anchor, and both families soon start hurling insults at each other (Rhee, 2020, para. 9).

At this point movie-goers might fully expect that the Parks are going to return home at any moment, and that Moon-gwang will show them the pictures. The handing over of those revelatory images would have meant that the Kims would be forced to go back to their sub-apartment in shame, but that is not what happens. Instead, the Kims are able to get hold of the cellphone, and they tie up Moon-gwang and Geun-sae and put them in the Park basement. During one scene, Moon-gwang manages to try and run up out of the basement, only to be kicked down the stairs by Chung-sook

Smell once again becomes a major vehicle for Bong Joon Ho to convey class differentiation when the Parks return home and three of the four Kims find themselves hiding under a living room table. The tired Park parents decide to sleep on a couch, and Mr. Park begins a conversation with his wife about how their employees usually never break societal rules, but that the smell that emanates from the Kim patriarch, Ki-taek, "crosses the line." Rhee (2020) has insightfully argued that as "Mr. Kim begins to understand his smell, and how his employer smells him," Mr. Kim gains "class consciousness," and resentment builds (para 2).

Now the violence in *Parasite* quickly escalates, and the contradictions and exploitative aspects of capitalism are now highlighted. When the exhausted Kims, having returned to their flooded sub-apartment, are asked to come back to the Park home for a planned party, global audiences begin to see some of the contradictions and absurdities that take place when members of different classes are indifferent, or are unaware, of the difficulties that confront those who are simply trying to survive in hierarchal, capitalist societies.

In order to help prepare a garden party for the Park son's birthday it dawns on the Kims that regardless of their fine salaries and their hard work they are still going to be viewed as inferior beings. They are at the beck and call of the clueless Parks who plan on hosting an extravagant garden party while Seoul's poor are still recovering from the flood in lower parts of the city.

In a wild and bloody scene Guen-sae discovers that his wife is dead. He bashes Ki-woo with the academic's rock that was once given to the Kim family. Guen-sae leaves the Park basement, picks up a knife in the Park kitchen, and then proceeds to rush across the outside lawn and stab Ki-jung, the Kim daughter. When the Park's youngest child faints from watching all of this horror, Mr. Park orders Mr. Kim to get the chauffer keys and drive the Parks to the hospital. The Kim patriarch—who is still traumatized after watching his daughter die from her wounds—becomes even more enraged when Mr. Park holds his nose when he gets near Guen-sae, and it is at this point in the movie that Mr. Kim attacks Mr. Park. As Kennedy (2019) insightfully observes, those who watch these scenes might fairly conclude that here there are no villains and no heroes, only families, rich and poor, who are "chafing against each other" in a movie that conveys "a bleak message" about class warfare (para. 10).

For many international movie-goers these twists and turns in *Parasite* have complicated matters and helped turn a warm, biopolitical home into a place of thanatopolitical class warfare and revolutionary change. Global audiences begin to realize that the basement that served as the home for Guen-sae only provides one more graphic venue for observing how agony and depravation can be located within a "rich and frivolous family's lavish, well-protected, spacious, comfortable," and "aesthetically pleasing villa" (Brody, 2019, para. 3). Perhaps even the perceived beneficiaries of capitalistic exploitations suffer in their own ways.

The denouement in *Parasite*'s final scenes focuses on the dismantling of the lives of the surviving members of the Kim family. Chung-sook and her son face Seoul judicial authorities who eventually allow them to go free, and the Kim mother and son are paroled. They search for the Kim patriarch, and after the passage of time they learn that Mr. Kim is living in the very same basement of the old Park home that is now owned by a German family.

Once again, by the time that moviegoers are about to exit their movie theatres, Bong Joon Ho is inviting his viewers to mull over this now complicated question: Who are the real "parasites" in the film? The director's implied answer to that question is polarizing. For example, conservatives around the world fumed when they got the sense that Bong was purposely implying that the rich used and abused their workers and kept them in states of servile employment and in demeaning and dehumanizing conditions. It was more than a little ironic that the American president, Donald Trump, praising a very racist American movie from the 1930s—*Gone from the Wind*—at the same time that he indicated that he was not a "*Parasite* fan" (*Associated Press* Staff, 2020). Arguing that the U.S. had "enough problems with South Korea on trade" he asked reporters why this foreign movie from a competitor was winning Oscar awards (paras. 1-2)?

What Trump—with his sense of American exceptionalism—failed to mention was that *Gone with the Wind* was an old nostalgic 1939 movie about the preservation of antebellum racism and slavery that tried to configure post-Civil emancipation and the Reconstruction years (1865-1877) as if they were Unionist events that had victimized Southern whites and destroyed the lives of carrying slave owners. Trump was focusing on the nationalistic origins of *Parasite* and not on the symbolism or heuristic value of this cinematic vehicle. Clearly foreign viewers might have agreed about the symbolic messages that were conveyed in *Parasite* having to do with class differences, but they could have polyvalent ways of responding to Bong Joon Ho's anti-capitalist critiques.

Conclusion

This chapter, extending the work of critical rhetorical scholars interested in the symbolic and materialist aspects of communication (McGee, 1980; McKerrow, 1991), has demonstrated how a critical decoding of *Parasite* illustrates why both South Korean and international audiences would be attracted to the ideological messages displayed in Bong Joon Ho's cinematic masterpiece. By putting on display the Kim family's deceptions and desires global moviegoers are invited to see the comedic and tragic nature of capitalistic ventures that divide so many classes. This is a film that uses infestation metaphors, architectural designs, allegories about proletariat and bourgeois class habits, and the *dingpolitiks* of everything from floods to references to tuberculosis to violent birthday party scenes to get across one key universalist message—all of us are potential victims of unfettered capitalism and the drawing of class lines.

Bong Joon Ho uses his artistic talents to show us not only the class warfare that takes place between the rich and poor classes, but the antagonism and desperation that comes from lower classes who battle each other in attempts to climb real and mythic social ladders.

I argue that by critically evaluating the film's usage of strategic ambiguity—and paying attention to international responses to Joon Ho's critiques of modern capitalism—communication scholars and others may gain an appreciation of how both filmmakers as well as critics can become interventionists in key societal debates. The melancholic portrayals of class struggle in *Parasite* are not simply being used for purposes of artistic creativity, aesthetic production, or the winning of awards. A brief genealogical study of Joon Ho's prior works shows that both his supporters and detractors have had a difficult time avoiding commentary on the ideological messages found in his films. There are reasons why Joon Ho's movies can be viewed as more "weapons of the weak" (Scott, 1985) by those who applaud his efforts, and why he infuriates many international conservatives who object to his leftist symbol making behavior.

Those who think that *Paradise* may have a short self-life, or those who might believe that it may only be remembered for a short number of years by a few Marxist radicals are sadly mistaken. Granted, this award-winning South Korean film had its own unique local and national inflections that may be coded in ways that may appeal to South Korean audiences, but as noted above, there are other layers of symbolic signification in the film that clearly have more universal and transcendent appeal. The class struggles and the challenges that are experienced by those living within a South Korea that has become the world's 11th largest economy are some of the same class struggles that are experienced by hundreds of millions of global citizens.

While Bong Joon Ho has himself shied away from discussing some of the specific political, cultural, or social features of *Parasite*—arguing that it is "a comedy without clowns, a tragedy without villains" (quoted in Kermode, 2020, para. 2)—other viewers inside and outside of South Korea have not hesitated to view this movie as a rhetorical vehicle that warns audiences of what happens when too many of us ignore the ravages of rampant and unfettered capitalism. Ulaby (2019), for example, characterized this hit movie as a visuality that "puts basement structures in structural inequality" (para. 1). Lodge (2019) similarly described *Parasite* as a film that "taps into a kind of anti-capitalist rage against rigid structures of class and privilege that are being felt everywhere from Korea to America to Brexit Britain" (para. 7).

Is it any wonder, as the arrival of the Coronavirus (COVID-19) brings with it so much economic and social dislocation, some international observers would find parallels between the thanatopolitics of *Parasite* and the fear of contagion that was threatening to outdistance the spread of the disease itself (Murphy, 2020)?

Recommended Readings

Choe, S. (2017). *Sovereign violence: Ethics and South Korean cinema in the new millennium.* Amsterdam, Netherlands: Amsterdam University Press.

Gabilondo, J. (2020). Bong Joon Ho's *Parasite* and post-2008 revolts: From the discourses of the master to the destituent power of the real. *International Journal of Zizek Studies, 14*(1), 1-21.

Han, K. (2019, October 14). Bong Joon-ho on weaving his personal memories into Parasite. *Polygon.* Retrieved from https://www.polygon.com/2019/10/14/20906430/parasite-bong-joon-ho-interview-rock-peach-spoilers

Kim, H. S. (2017, Fall). Film auteurism as a Cold War governmentality: Alternative knowledge and the formation of liberal subjectivity. *Journal of Korean Studies, 22*(2), 317-342.

Kline, C. (2008, December). Why American studies needs to think about Korean cinema, or transnational genres in the films of Bong Joon-Ho. *American Quarterly, 60*(4), 871-898.

Additional Sources

ABC News Staff. (2020, February 9). *Bong Joon Ho accepts the Oscar for directing.* YouTube. Retrieved from https://www.youtube.com/watch?v=ftz-BPqCiZU

Jung, E. A., & Willmore, A. (2020, April 9). A Guide to director Bong Joon-Ho's deeper cuts. *Vulture.* Retrieved from https://www.vulture.com/2020/04/best-bong-joon-ho-movies-parasite-director-must-sees.html

Vanity Fair Staff. (2019, November 12). "Parasite" director Bong Joon-ho breaks down the opening scene. *Vanity Fair.* Retrieved from https://www.youtube.com/watch?v=bP-eqx2X9AY

References

Agence France-Press Staff. (2020, January 6). *Parasite's* Bong Joon-ho: Biting satirist goes to dark places. *AsiaOne.com.* Retrieved from https://www.asiaone.com/entertainment/parasites-bong-joon-ho-biting-satirist-goes-dark-places

Associated Press Staff. (2020, February 21). Trump not a "*Parasite*" fan, praises "*Gone with the Wind.*" *Associated Press.* Retrieved from https://apnews.com/672b7e731ec43e40da06b1ff8c8c57ed

Brody, R. (2019, October 14). How "*Parasite*" *falls short of greatness. The New Yorker.* https://www.newyorker.com/culture/the-front-row/how-parasite-falls-short-of-greatness

Coury, D. (2020, March 4). What you should be watching: *Parasite. CAHSS and Effect.* Retrieved from https://cahsseffect.org/what-you-should-be-watching/what-you-should-be-watching-parasite/

Goldberg, M. (2020, February 10). Class war at the Oscars. *The New York Times.* Retrieved from https://www.nytimes.com/2020/02/10/opinion/parasite-movie-oscar-inequality.html

Hess, A. (2020, February 14). The real star of Bong Joon-ho's Oscar-winner *Parasite*? The house. *The Guardian.* Retrieved from https://www.theguardian.com/film/2020/feb/14/house-real-star-bong-joon-ho-oscar-winner-parasite

Kennedy, M. (2019, October 24). "*Parasite*" is a brilliant depiction of class warfare. *Detroit Free Press.* Retrieved from https://www.freep.com/story/entertainment/movies/2019/10/31/parasite-movie-review-south-korea/40524381/

Kermode, M. (2020, February 20). *Parasite* review-a gasp-inducing masterpiece. *The Guardian,* https://www.theguardian.com/film/2020/feb/09/parasite-review-bong-joon-ho-tragicomic-masterpiece

Latour, B. (2004). From realpolitik to *dingpolitik*, or how to make things public. *Bruno.Latour.fr.* Retrieved from http://www.bruno-latour.fr/sites/default/files/downloads/96-MTP-DING.pdf

Lee. M. (2018). Monstrosity and humanity in Bong Joon-ho's *The Host. Positions, 26*(4), 719-749.

Lodge, G. (2019). *Parasite*: How Bong Joon-ho returned home to make his masterpiece. *The Guardian*, https://www.theguardian.com/film/2019/oct/09/parasite-how-bong-joon-ho-returned-home-to-make-his-masterpiece

McGee, M. C. (1980). The “ideograph”: A link between rhetoric and ideology. *The Quarterly Journal of Speech, 66*, 1-16.

McKerrow, R. E. (1991). Critical rhetoric in a postmodern world. *The Quarterly Journal of Speech, 77*, 75-78.

Murphy, E. (2020, March 27). If you loved “Parasite” these movies by Bong Joon-ho are must-watch. *Showbiz Cheatsheet.* Retrieved from https://www.cheatsheet.com/entertainment/if-you-loved-parasite-these-movies-by-bong-joon-ho-are-a-must-watch.html/

Pike, D. L. (2019, November 27). Of parasites and their hosts: Bong Joon-ho’s *Gisaengchung* (2019). *Bright Lights Film Journal.* Retrieved from https://brightlightsfilm.com/of-parasites-and-their-hosts-bong-joon-hos-gisaengchung-2019/

Rhee, M. (2020). Class as smell: The universality of *Parasite. Entropy.* Retrieved from https://entropymag.org/class-as-smell-the-universality-of-parasite/

Scott, J. C. (1985). *Weapons of the weak: Everyday forms of peasant resistance.* New Haven, CT: Yale University Press.

Sharma, R. (2020, February 17). *Parasite* should embarrass Bollywood: The truth is that India is not making world class movies, and has not for quite some time. *The Times of India.* Retrieved from https://timesofindia.indiatimes.com/blogs/toi-edit-page/parasite-should-embarrass-bollywood-the-truth-is-that-india-is-not-making-world-class-movies-and-has-not-for-some-time/

Ulaby, N. (2019, November 5). The hit movie “*Parasite*” puts basement structures in structural inequality. *National Public Radio.* Retrieved from https://www.npr.org/2019/11/05/776388423/the-hit-movie-parasite-puts-basement-structures-in-structural-inequality

White, A. (2019, October 11). *Parasite*: Antifa comedy for the cancel-culture era. *National Review.* Retrieved from https://www.nationalreview.com/2019/10/movie-review-parasite-laughs-at-family-and-social-ruin/

Yi, Y. D. (2017, June). Locating a transnational film between Korean cinema and American cinema: A case study of *Snowpiercer* (2014). *Plaridel, 14*(1), 17-32.

Index

Contributors

(Preface/Editor)

Do Kyun David Kim (Ph.D.) is Professor and the Richard D'Aquin BORSF Endowed Professor in the Department of Communication at the University of Louisiana at Lafayette. He has served as president of the Louisiana Communication Association and founder/director of the AI Communication Research Consortium. His research and praxis focus on the diffusion of innovations (DOI) and social marketing for social/organizational change and public health promotion. Specifically, he examines how the advancement of communication technology induces individuals' attitude and behavior changes and contributes to public health promotion, how opinion leadership can be harnessed to transform organizations and communities, and how communicative influences affect decision-makings at the individual, organizational, and community levels. He has applied his knowledge and skills to diverse communication projects in many countries including the United States, South Korea, Japan, India, and Botswana. His research has appeared in many scholarly journals and books.

(Chapter 1)

Nancy Wiencek, (Ph.D., APR) is an associate professor and chair of the Department of Communication, Journalism, and Media at Rider University. She has more than 20 years of professional experience in public relations with expertise in campaign planning, special events, fundraising, crisis communication and executive communication, and has been accredited in public relations (APR) for her professionalism in the field. After earning her Ph.D. at Rutgers University, she joined the faculty at Rider University and teaches a variety of courses in the Public Relations major, as well as in the Master of Arts in Business Communication program. Her research interests include public relations and social media, as well as the role that public relations plays in both contemporary business contexts and popular culture.

Aimee Wiencek is an undergraduate student with a double major at Case Western Reserve University in English and Business Management, where she received an Arnaud Gelb Journalism Award from the English Department. She is an Arts & Entertainment writer for the student newspaper, "The Observer," and has written an extensive paper about the music of Malibu titled, "Malibu as Heaven on Earth." Aimee has gained professional experience as an intern for a New York City-based public relations agency and has interned for The White House in Washington, D.C.

(Chapter 2)
Carolyn A. Lin (Ph.D.) is a faculty at the University of Connecticut. Her research and teaching interests focus on digital, marketing, environmental, health, risk, crisis and cross-cultural communication at an individual, community and societal level. As the recipient of a University Distinguished Research Faculty award, she is also the founder of the Communication Technology Division at the Association for Education in Journalism & Mass Communication. She has published over 130 journal articles and book chapters, in addition to 4 books and other publications. Her research has been funded by the NIH and NSF, among others. Currently, she is the editor of *Journal of Broadcasting & Electronic Media.*

Suji Park (Ph.D.) is an instructor at Sungkyunkwan University and Woosong University in South Korea. She conducts research in the areas of interactive media on communication outcomes, emotions and cognition. Specifically, Dr. Park's recent research has focused on the role of personological traits (emotion dysregulation, trait empathy, and attitudes toward violence) in explaining the effects of video games and social media on emotions and health risk behaviors. Dr. Park has also explored the impact of media multitasking on users' enjoyment of the media content. In addition to this, Dr. Park's research embraces popular culture, including the Korean Wave and its impact on cultural identities.

Xiaowen Xu is an assistant professor at the Department of Strategic Communication at Butler University. She is interested in how mass/new media influence intercultural, consumer, health and environmental motivation, attitudes and behaviors. Her recent research focuses on effects of innovative advertising forms such as social media newsfeed advertising and online personalized advertising on consumer flow experience and attitudes.

(Chapter 3)

Hyeri Jung (Ph.D.) earned her doctorate from the Moody College of Communication at the University of Texas at Austin. Her research interests revolve around transnational media culture, digital media culture, and audience reception studies. She has published several articles in peer-reviewed journals and has won several top research paper awards at prestigious conferences around the world. She is currently Assistant Professor in the Communication Studies Department at Eastern University, teaching and researching digital media and global media culture.

(Chapter 4)

Samantha James is a doctoral student in Organizational Communication & Technology at the University of Texas at Austin. A proud Aca-fan (Jenkins, 2013), Sam is excited by the ways technology influences how people organize around the things they love. Her current research surrounds the interplay of affect, culture, and organizing in contemporary society. Sam would like to thank Dr. Jessy Ohl, assistant professor of Communication at the University of Alabama, for his ongoing support and mentorship since this project's conception.

(Chapter 5)

Chen Yang (Ph.D.) is an Assistant Professor of Communication at Robert Morris University. Prior to completing his doctorate study at Bowling Green State University, Dr. Yang has worked in multinational corporations in China and also earned two master's degrees: one in Linguistics and one in Applied Statistics. Dr. Yang's scholarship covers a variety of areas such as social media usage, intercultural communication, media effects, digital news, and more. Dr. Yang has presented his research in multiple academic conferences including National Communication Association (NCA), Broadcast Education Association (BEA), Association for Education in Journalism and Mass Communication (AEJMC), and International Academy for Intercultural Research (IAIR). His research is published in book chapters and peer-reviewed journals such as *Journalism, Electronic News*, and *Journal of Asian Communication.*

(Chapter 6)

Hannah Christine Fassbender is a graduate of the Communication Arts and Sciences program at of Pennsylvania State University, Berks (honors: Lambda Pi Eta). She received the Pennsylvania Communicator of the Year Award in 2019. Her research is focused on global pop culture. She is an avid ARMY member.

Xzavior Rain Sweeny is a graduate of Pennsylvania State University, Berks (honors: Lambda Pi Eta/cum laude). He is a dedicated BTS fan and researcher. He believes in their message and the positive impact they are having on the world in relation to creating positive mental health messages for all.

Cheryl L. Nicholas (Ph.D) is an Associate Professor of Communication Arts & Sciences and Global Studies at Pennsylvania State University, Berks. Her research is based on how symbolic activity constitutes and is constituted by cultural worldviews. Her research has appeared in venues such as *Journal of Popular Music Studies, Communication Quarterly, Storytelling, Self & Society*, and the *Journal of International and Intercultural Communication.* She was also recognized at National Communication Association's 2017 Teacher's on Teaching series, named the 2018-19 Penn State Alumni Teaching Fellow, and received the 2011 Outstanding Undergraduate Teaching Award at Penn State Berks. She has just started listening to K-pop and is looking forward to her first BTS concert.

(Chapter 7)

Hayley Rummel is a graduate student in the Department of Communication at the University of Louisiana at Lafayette. Her concentration is Public Relations. Her area of interest include communication in the entertainment business as she aims to develop her career in the field of entertainment management. She has experience to produce a K-pop radio program at KRVS in Lafayette, Louisiana.

Do Kyun David Kim (Ph.D.)

(Chapter 8)
Aino Rinhaug (Ph.D.) is a Korean-born adoptee to Norway. She received a Ph.D. in European literature from University of Oslo and currently teaches Norwegian at University of California Los Angeles and Berkeley. She conducts research on Korean adoption and culture and is working on a documentary film about Scandinavian adoptee artists and writers.

(Chapter 9)
Rukhsana Ahmed (Ph.D.) is Associate Professor and Chair in the Department of Communication at the University at Albany, State University of New York. Aside from advancing research at the intersection of health, communication, culture, and media, she indulges is consuming popular culture including K-pop and K-drama with her daughter for entertainment as well as educational values.

Zerin Mahzabin Khan is a biomedical engineering Ph.D. student in the Virginia Tech-Wake Forest University School of Biomedical Engineering and Sciences program at the Virginia Tech campus. Her research interests include developing novel biomaterial strategies to treat brain cancer. Outside of her lab work, she can be found reading, writing, painting, keeping up with the latest Korean pop culture, and binge watching K-dramas with her mom.

(Chapter 10)
Ali Na (Ph.D.) is an Assistant Professor of media studies at Queen's University. As a media scholar working at the intersections of race, queer, and feminist studies, her research focuses on how media performances define and defy conceptions of Asian/Asian diasporic bodies. Drawing on transnational cultural histories, she theorizes resistance, complicity, and ambivalence in new border crossings facilitated by digital media. Her scholarship traverses the areas of digital media, performance, popular culture, and media installation. In the digital age, the ideas of media as immaterial, virtual, and transcendent dominate. Her work pushes against this impulse by culturally grounding the body, the material, and the haptic. Dr. Na's research has been published in a number of academic journals. She is currently working on her first book manuscript *Trans Medial Performance: Affirming Asian/American Femininity Otherwise.*

(Chapter 11)

Laurena Bernabo (Ph.D.) is an Assistant Professor at the University of Georgia in the Department of Entertainment & Media Studies, where she teaches courses on global media industries and texts, identity and media representations. She earned her Ph.D. at the University of Iowa's Department of Communication Studies. Dr. Bernabo's doctoral research brought her to Mexico City where she conducted a production ethnography at a dubbing studio that dubs many American films and television programs including *The Fast and the Furious* and *Family Guy*. She is currently expanding this line of inquiry to other Spanish-language dubbing sites in Miami, Florida and Madrid, Spain. Her work on linguistic translation in media has been published in the journals *Critical Studies in Media Communication* and *The Velvet Light Trap* and has earned awards from the International Communication Association and the Organization for the Study of Communication, Language & Gender.

(Chapter 12)

Marouf Arif Hasian, Jr. (Ph.D.) is a Professor in the Department of Communication, and a Distinguished professor at the University of Utah. He is the author of more than 18 books and 140 journal articles and book chapters. His major contributions in the field of communication are in the areas of critical intercultural/international communication, rhetoric and law, critical memory studies, and humanitarian discourses. His work appears in journals such as *Critical Studies in Media Communication, The Quarterly Journal of Speech, Communication Theory*, and the *Western Journal of Communication*. He has written on topics such as critical cultural studies, visual rhetoric, humanitarian rhetorics, Ebola rhetorics, medical witnessing during times of crisis, genocides, Holocaust trials, and indigeneity studies. He is currently working on a book dealing with the spread of white genocide rhetorics.